Reflexivity and Economics

The form of 'reflexivity' – defined by the dictionary as that which is 'directed back upon itself' – that is most relevant to economic methodology is that where observation of the economy leads to ideas that change behavior, which in turn changes (is directed back upon) the economy itself. As George Soros explains: "if investors believe that markets are efficient then that belief will change the way they invest, and that in turn will change the nature of the markets they are observing . . . That is the *principle of reflexivity*".

Although various versions of reflexivity have long been discussed, in recent years George Soros has been particularly effective in bringing ideas about reflexivity to the attention of the economic and financial communities. In a series of writings he has systematically argued that reflexivity is not only an important aspect of economic life, it is an aspect that is neglected in most mainstream theorizing; and in addition, that the neglect of reflexivity has been responsible for the failure of economists to predict, explain, or offer a solution for events such as the recent financial crisis.

Soros' ideas about reflexivity have important methodological significance and his chapter in this book summarizes and clarifies his arguments. His contribution is joined by those of thirteen scholars from a wide range of relevant fields, who provide a commentary on the idea of reflexivity in economics.

This book was originally published as a special issue of the *Journal of Economic Methodology*.

John B. Davis is Professor of Economics at Marquette University, Milwaukee, WI, USA, and Professor of Economics at the University of Amsterdam, The Netherlands. He is the author of *Keynes's Philosophical Development* (1994), *The Theory of the Individual in Economics* (2003), and *Individuals and Identity in Economics* (2011), and co-author of *Economic Methodology: Understanding Economics as a Science* (2010, with Marcel Boumans). He is co-editor of the *Journal of Economic Methodology* and the *Elgar Companion to Recent Economic Methodology* (2011, with Wade Hands).

D. Wade Hands is Distinguished Professor of Economics at the University of Puget Sound, WA, USA. He has written on a wide range of topics in the history of economic thought and economic methodology. He is co-editor of the *Journal of Economic Methodology* and the author of *Reflection Without Rules: Economic Methodology and Contemporary Science Theory* (2001). He is co-editor of *Agreement on Demand: Consumer Choice Theory in the 20th Century* (2006, with Philip Mirowski) and *The Elgar Companion to Recent Economic Methodology* (2011, with John B. Davis).

Reflexivity and Economics

George Soros's theory of reflexivity and
the methodology of economic science

Edited by
John B. Davis and D. Wade Hands

 Routledge
Taylor & Francis Group

LONDON AND NEW YORK

First published 2017
by Routledge
2 Park Square, Milton Park, Abingdon, Oxfordshire OX14 4RN
711 Third Avenue, New York, NY 10017

Routledge is an imprint of the Taylor & Francis Group, an informa business

First issued in paperback 2018

British Library Cataloguing in Publication Data
A catalogue record for this book is available from the British Library

ISBN 13: 978-1-138-20348-8 (hbk)
ISBN 13: 978-0-367-03007-0 (pbk)

Typeset in Times New Roman
by RefineCatch Limited, Bungay, Suffolk

Publisher's Note
The publisher accepts responsibility for any inconsistencies that may have
arisen during the conversion of this book from journal articles to book chapters,
namely the possible inclusion of journal terminology.

Disclaimer
Every effort has been made to contact copyright holders for their permission to
reprint material in this book. The publishers would be grateful to hear from any
copyright holder who is not here acknowledged and will undertake to rectify
any errors or omissions in future editions of this book.

Contents

CONTENTS

Citation Information

The chapters in this book were originally published in the *Journal of Economic Methodology*, volume 20, issue 4 (December 2013). When citing this material, please use the original page numbering for each article, as follows:

Introduction
Introduction to symposium on 'reflexivity and economics: George Soros's theory of reflexivity and the methodology of economic science'
D. Wade Hands
Journal of Economic Methodology, volume 20, issue 4 (December 2013) pp. 303–308

Chapter 1
Fallibility, reflexivity, and the human uncertainty principle
George Soros
Journal of Economic Methodology, volume 20, issue 4 (December 2013) pp. 309–329

Chapter 2
Reflexivity, complexity, and the nature of social science
Eric D. Beinhocker
Journal of Economic Methodology, volume 20, issue 4 (December 2013) pp. 330–342

Chapter 3
Reflexivity unpacked: performativity, uncertainty and analytical monocultures
Richard Bronk
Journal of Economic Methodology, volume 20, issue 4 (December 2013) pp. 343–349

Chapter 4
George Soros: Hayekian?
Bruce Caldwell
Journal of Economic Methodology, volume 20, issue 4 (December 2013) pp. 350–356

Chapter 5
Reflections on Soros: Mach, Quine, Arthur and far-from-equilibrium dynamics
Rod Cross, Harold Hutchinson, Harbir Lamba and Doug Strachan
Journal of Economic Methodology, volume 20, issue 4 (December 2013) pp. 357–367

For any permission-related enquiries please visit:
http://www.tandfonline.com/page/help/permissions

Notes on Contributors

Eric D. Beinhocker is Executive Director of the Institute for New Economic Thinking at the Oxford Martin School, University of Oxford, UK. He is the author of *The Origin of Wealth: The Radical Remaking of Economics and What it Means for Business and Society* (2006).

Richard Bronk is a writer and Visiting Fellow at the European Institute, London School of Economics, UK. His particular expertise lies in the history of ideas, the philosophy of economics, comparative corporate governance, and European political economy.

Bruce Caldwell is a Research Professor in the Department of Economics at Duke University, NC, USA. His research focuses on the history of economic thought, with a specific interest in the life and works of Hayek, on whom he has written an intellectual biography, *Hayek's Challenge* (2004).

Rod Cross is Emeritus Professor in the Department of Economics at the University of Strathclyde, Glasgow, UK. His writing and research both focus on financial economics, macroeconomics, and applied mathematics.

John B. Davis is Professor of Economics at Marquette University, Milwaukee, WI, USA, and Professor of Economics at the University of Amsterdam, The Netherlands. He is the author of *Keynes's Philosophical Development* (1994), *The Theory of the Individual in Economics* (2003), and *Individuals and Identity in Economics* (2011).

J. Doyne Farmer is Director of the Complexity Economics program at the Institute for New Economic Thinking, Oxford Martin School, University of Oxford, UK. His current research is in economics, including agent-based modeling, financial instability, and technological progress.

Roman Frydman is Professor of Economics at New York University, USA. His research on economic models is presented in *Imperfect Knowledge Economics* (2007) and *Beyond Mechanical Markets* (2011), both co-authored with Michael D. Goldberg.

Michael D. Goldberg is Professor of Economics at the University of New Hampshire, USA. He has written extensively in the fields of international finance and macroeconomics, including *Imperfect Knowledge Economics* (2007) and *Beyond Mechanical Markets* (2011), both co-authored with Roman Frydman.

Francesco Guala is a Professor in the Department of Economics, Management and Quantitative Methods at the University of Milan, Italy. He is a philosopher and experimental economist interested primarily in the foundations and the methodology of social science.

D. Wade Hands is Distinguished Professor of Economics at the University of Puget Sound, WA, USA. He has written on a wide range of topics in the history of economic thought and economic methodology. He is co-editor of the *Journal of Economic Methodology* and the author of *Reflection Without Rules: Economic Methodology and Contemporary Science Theory* (2001).

Cars Hommes is Professor in the Faculty of Economics and Business at the University of Amsterdam, The Netherlands, and a Research Fellow at the Tinbergen Institute. His work focuses on complexity economics.

Harold Hutchinson is a Power and Utilities Analyst for Investec Bank, based in London, UK. He conducts research on a set of pan-European power generation companies, alongside issues in the global renewables area.

Harbir Lamba is Associate Professor in the Department of Mathematical Sciences at George Mason University, Fairfax, VA, USA. His current research interests are dynamical systems and mathematical modeling in economics.

Mark Amadeus Notturno is affiliated with the Interactivity Foundation in Washington DC, USA. He has lectured and written on Karl Popper and his philosophy and is the author of *On Popper* (2003) and *Science and the Open Society* (2000).

Alex Rosenberg is Professor of Philosophy at Duke University, NC, USA. His interests focus on problems in metaphysics, the philosophy of social sciences, and most of all, the philosophy of biology, in particular the relationship between molecular, functional, and evolutionary biology.

Anwar Shaikh is Professor of Economics at the New School, New York City, USA. His work in political economy focuses on the economic theory and empirical patterns of developed capitalism. His most recent book is *Capitalism: Competition, Conflict, Crises* (2016).

George Soros is the Chairman of Soros Fund Management and the Open Society Foundations. He is a businessman, investor, philanthropist, and author. His writings focus heavily on the concept of reflexivity, a theory he first explored in *The Alchemy of Finance* (1988).

Doug Strachan is an Honorary Senior Lecturer in the Department of Economics at the University of Strathclyde, Glasgow, UK.

Yi-Cheng Zhang is Professor and Chair of the Department of Physics at the Université de Fribourg, Switzerland.

Introduction: 'Reflexivity and economics: George Soros's theory of reflexivity and the methodology of economic science'

D. Wade Hands

Department of Economics, University of Puget Sound, Tacoma, WA, USA

Nature does not care ... whether we penetrate her secrets and establish successful theories about her workings and apply these theories successfully in predictions. In the social sciences, the matter is more complicated and in the following fact lies one of the fundamental differences between these two types of theories: the kind of economic theory that is *known* to the participant in the economy has an effect on the economy ... There is thus a "backcoupling" or "feedback" between the theory and the object of the theory, an interrelation which is definitely lacking in the natural sciences ... In this area are great methodological problems worthy of careful analysis." (Oskar Morgenstern, 1972, p. 707).

The dictionary definition of 'reflexivity' is that which is 'directed back upon itself' and in this general sense reflexivity can occur in a wide range of human activities from the literature, to art, to science. The reflexivity that is most relevant to economic methodology is where observation of the economy leads to ideas that change behavior which in turn changes (is directed back upon) the economy itself. As George Soros explains in the opening essay to this symposium: 'For example if investors believe that markets are efficient then that belief will change the way they invest, and that in turn will change the nature of the markets they are observing ... That is the *principle of reflexivity*' (Soros, 2013, p. 310). Various philosophers and social scientists have argued that the possibility of 'reflexivity' is the main, or at least one of the main, differences between the social and natural sciences. Despite how one interprets scientific theories (realist, instrumentalist, etc.), the standard ontological presumption is that nature stays as it is while we examine it: or at least it stays as it is to a greater degree than the social world.

1. Reflexivity, social science, and economic methodology

Although various versions of reflexivity have long been discussed within the literature on the philosophy of social science, in recent years Soros has been particularly effective in bringing ideas about reflexivity to the attention of the economic and financial community (both academic and practitioner). In a series of writings (e.g., Soros, 1987, 1998, 2010), he has systematically argued that reflexivity is not only an important aspect of economic life, it is an aspect that is neglected in most mainstream theorizing, and in addition, that the neglect of reflexivity has been responsible for the economics profession's failure to predict, explain, or offer a solution for events such as the recent financial crisis. Although Soros is best known as an investor and philanthropist, his ideas about reflexivity have important methodological significance and thus provide an excellent topic for a symposium in *The Journal of Economic Methodology*. The symposium consists of a Soros paper summarizing and clarifying his arguments about reflexivity and its relationship with economics, along with 13 commentaries by various scholars from a wide range of relevant fields. The authors were instructed to refer to the Soros paper, but they were also free to address Soros's theory of reflexivity and its relationship with economic methodology in whatever way they found appropriate.

There are of course many different interpretations of reflexivity, but I will focus on just three (in addition to Soros's) that do a good job conveying the wide range of ideas that have been called 'reflexivity' over the years. These three are the traditional idea of a reflexive, or 'self-fulfilling,' public prediction; the 'performativity' version of reflexivity from the science studies literature; and the Grunberg–Modigliani–Simon version of a reflexive public prediction which had an impact on rational expectations macroeconomics. All of the symposium papers discuss Soros's theory of reflexivity, but some authors discuss these, and other, versions as well.

An early discussion of reflexivity that still draws quite a bit of attention is the 'self-fulfilling prophesy' originally discussed by the sociologist Robert K. Merton in 1948. For Merton a self-fulfilling prophesy was an empirical prediction that became true because it was publicly predicted. Specifically, a person has a false understanding of a particular social situation, but making a prediction based on that false understanding leads to behavior that ultimately causes the prediction to be true. An example that is particularly relevant to the recent financial crisis (and one that Merton also used) is a run on a bank:

> Imagine you are an economist studying Smith's bank, and you notice after crunching some numbers that your theories predict that Smith's bank will soon collapse. Unbeknownst to you, your theories are garbage, and the bank will be fine if you keep your mouth shut. But you decide to publish your findings, and, upon hearing of your prediction, Smith's concerned customers quickly run to the bank in an attempt to withdraw their savings. Smith's bank collapses ... and therefore your prediction came true. (Kopec, 2011, p. 1249)

Since a case like this – initially false, but becomes true because of a public prediction – seems to be symmetric with the opposite case in which a prediction that was initially true turns out to be false because it was publicly predicted, the philosophical literature generally uses the term 'reflexive predictions' for both self-fulfilling and self-frustrating public predictions (Buck, 1963, p. 359). The prediction is reflexive if and only if it is 'a causal factor relative to the prediction's coming out true or false' (Kopec, 2011, p. 1250; Romanos, 1973, p. 106). As some of the authors in the symposium note, a version of reflexive prediction was discussed by Karl Popper in his writings on the methodology of the social sciences (e.g., Popper, 1957, 1976). Popper explained that it was possible for a prediction to influence the event that is predicted – either to 'bring about' or 'prevent' the event (Popper, 1957, p. 13) – and he called this possibility the 'Oedipus effect.'

Reflexivity has always been a part of the science studies and sociology of scientific knowledge literature. One of the central themes of that literature is that science is a social activity/organization like any other social activity, and that the beliefs of scientists are determined by the same social forces and relations that determine the beliefs of the members of any other society. This is of course potentially quite critical, or a debunking, of the epistemic privilege of science, but it also has a reflexive component. Since the science studies community is also a community of scientists, their own beliefs – like, say, their belief that the beliefs of scientists are determined by social factors – must also be socially determined. For some within the science studies community this is no problem – it is an opportunity to be embraced – because 'otherwise sociology would be a standing refutation of its own theories' (Bloor, 1991, p. 7), but for others it is a troublesome issue. However interesting this type of self-reference-based reflexivity might be, it generally carries us too far away from economics to discuss here[1], but there is one exception. There is a version of reflexivity that originated within science studies that should be noted because it is fundamentally causal (not just self-referential) and has been applied directly to financial economics and financial markets: the performativity literature associated with Donald MacKenzie and his associates (e.g., Callon, 1998; MacKenzie, 2006; MacKenzie, Muniesa, & Siu 2007). Performativity takes many forms but the basic idea is that economics performs – shapes, conditions, formats, etc. – the economy, rather than simply describing it. Economic theory conditions behavior and institutions in ways that have significant effects on the economy itself; in other words, the economy is constructed, at least in part, by economic theorizing. The example that is often used in the performativity literature is the efficient markets hypothesis:

> The efficient-market hypothesis is not simply an analysis of financial markets as "external" things but has become woven into market practices. Most important, it helped inspire the establishment of index-tracking funds. Instead of seeking to "beat the market" (a goal that the hypothesis suggests is unlikely to be achieved except by chance), such funds invest in broad baskets of stocks and attempt to replicate the performance of market indexes such as the S&P 500. Such funds have become major investment vehicles, and their effects on price can be detected when stocks are added or removed from indexes .... (MacKenzie et al., 2007, p. 4)

The third reflexivity literature I would like to note is based on two papers on self-fulfilling public predictions published in 1954: Grunberg and Modigliani (1954) and Simon (1954). The Grunberg and Modigliani paper was primarily concerned with economics (the cobweb model of agricultural markets) and the Simon paper was primarily concerned with political science (predicting election results), but both papers were essentially possibility theorems: attempts to respond to the reflexive prediction literature of Merton and others by showing that a correct public prediction was actually possible. The goal was to show that it was possible to have a correct social theory, make a public prediction based on the theory which changes the expectations and behavior of individuals in the economy, and still have the prediction turn out to be correct. Both papers used a fixed-point argument to demonstrate that such a self-fulfilling public prediction was possible:[2] essentially the correct prediction was a fixed point of the reaction function of the agents influenced by the public prediction. In a sense both of these papers are examples of models which include a type of reflexivity – the public prediction changes the behavior of the relevant agents – and yet they show that it is possible that such reflexivity does not matter to the accuracy of the prediction.

The Grunberg–Modigliani–Simon result generated a small literature within the philosophy of social science (e.g., Grunberg, 1986; Grunberg & Modigliani, 1965; Ofsti & Osterberg, 1982), but more importantly to this symposium, it contributed to John Muth's seminal 1961 paper on rational expectations. The correct public prediction of Grunberg, Modigliani, and Simon is the prediction that one would make if they formed expectations rationally, i.e., expectations based on 'the relevant economic theory' (Muth, 1961, p. 316).[3] The result that Grunberg, Modigliani, and Simon demonstrated was possible thus became the only rational result in the hands of Muth. Given that both Modigliani and Simon had a negative view of rational expectations, and given the way that Soros and many others have (I would say rightly) used reflexivity to critique rational expectations macroeconomics, it seems a bit ironic that Merton's reflexive prediction contributed in some way to rational expectations and thus the rise of New Classical macroeconomics. Of course the history of economic thought is full of such ironies.

It is not really necessary to discuss Soros's theory of reflexivity in detail here since the argument is clearly presented in his essay. But it does seem useful to note a few features of his argument in order to contrast it with the interpretations of reflexivity discussed above. The first aspect of Soros's approach is its Popperian heritage. As Soros explains, he was Karl Popper's student and Popper's philosophical views formed the backdrop for his thinking about scientific knowledge throughout his life. In the domain of natural science, Soros generally followed his teacher, but he deviated from Popper on the methodology of economics and other social sciences. That deviation is based on the relevance of reflexivity to social life and properly recognizing that fact prevents 'the social sciences from parading with borrowed feathers' (Soros, 2013, p. 320). Popper thought that his philosophy of natural science applied equally well to social sciences such as economics,[4] but Soros disagrees. Since economics involves reflexivity, it requires a different approach than the 'slavish imitation of natural science' (Soros, 2013, p. 320). The second point is that Soros has used his theory to explicitly critique mainstream economic practice (at least the practice of the last quarter of the twentieth century: rational expectations, new classical macroeconomics, and the efficient markets hypothesis). His point is not only that reflexivity matters, but that mainstream economic theory does not account for it and thus has serious problems. Third, Soros put his theory of reflexivity to work in his own trading strategy and it was quite successful (i.e., his theory of reflexivity was not falsified). Popper always argued that defenders of a particular scientific theory should stick the theory's neck out by making bold empirical conjectures and exposing them to severe empirical tests. Putting one's personal wealth and professional reputation on the line by employing a reflexivity-based trading strategy seems to be an excellent example of sticking a theory of reflexivity's neck out.

2. Conclusion

Introductions to symposia often briefly summarize the contents of each of the papers in the symposium, but that does not seem necessary since the papers are clear and the topic is sufficiently circumscribed. This final section will just mention a few of the common themes that emerge within the commentaries. Although no single consensus view emerges – other than the general importance of reflexivity – there are a few themes that warrant mentioning. Without pigeonholing the various authors into these various thematic groupings, it is useful to list a few of the approaches that authors took in their commentaries. This list is not exhaustive and is not presented in order of importance (or frequency).

- *On methodological unity*: Several authors argue that the line between social and natural science is not as sharp as Soros seems to suggest. In some cases this argument comes via Popper – arguing that Popper's defense of the methodological unity of the sciences is warranted – and in some cases the argument is made without explicit reference to Popper.
- *Soros and Popper*: At least one author argues that Popper's own approach to social science captures more of what Soros is arguing about social science than Soros seems to recognize.
- *Mainstream reflexivity*: It is argued that mainstream economics is not as problematic with respect to reflexivity as Soros suggests.

- *New developments within economics*: A number of different authors discuss new research programs and new theoretical tools that do allow economists to accommodate various kinds of reflexivity.
- *Soros and Hayek*: Several authors discuss the relationship between Soros's methodological approach and that of Friedrich Hayek.
- *Varieties of reflexivity*: Many argue that reflexivity comes in a variety of different forms and that not all are as potentially disruptive as Soros seems to suggest (some feedback loops are stabilizing not destabilizing).
- *Ontology*: It is argued that the reflexivity critique of contemporary economics can and should be extended to the ontological, not just methodological or epistemological, domain.

These are only a few of the significant themes that emerge within the commentaries, but it gives the reader an idea of what to expect. Soros's theory of reflexivity is an extremely important topic in economic methodology and this symposium gives it the serious attention it deserves within the academic literature.[5]

Notes

1. See Davis and Klaes (2003) and Sandri (2009) for a discussion of this literature and its relationship to economics. Sent (1998, 2001) provide nice examples of how this approach can be applied to particular research programs within economics.
2. It is interesting that these two papers were published the same year as the famous Arrow and Debreu proof of the existence of general equilibrium which also used a fixed point argument (although in a more mathematically sophisticated way).
3. See Hands (1990) for a discussion of the relationship between the Grunberg-Modigliani-Simon results and rational expectations.
4. Although this has been contested (e.g., Caldwell, 1991; Hands, 1985; Koertge, 1975).
5. **Disclosure:** Through the Open Society Foundations George Soros is a major financial supporter of the Institute for New Economic Thinking (INET), a non-profit foundation that provides grants to scholars and institutions engaged in economic research. Mr Soros plays no role in INET's grant-making and INET is governed by an independent board of directors (see <http://www.ineteconomics.org/>). Neither the Journal of Economic Methodology nor any of the contributors to this symposium have received any direct financial support from Mr Soros. However, the following contributors to this symposium are or have been grantees of INET: Eric Beinhocker, Bruce Caldwell, John Davis, J. Doyne Farmer, Roman Frydman, Michael Goldberg, Wade Hands, Cars Hommes and Anwar Shaikh.

References

Arrow, K. J., & Debreu, G. (1954). Existence of equilibrium for a competitive economy. *Econometrica, 27*, 265–290.

Bloor, D. (1991). *Knowledge and social imagery* (2nd ed.). Chicago, IL: University of Chicago Press.

Buck, R. C. (1963). Reflexive predictions. *Philosophy of Science, 30*, 359–369.

Caldwell, B. (1991). Clarifying Popper. *Journal of Economic Literature, 29*, 1–33.

Callon, M. (1998). *The laws of the markets*. London: Blackwell.

Davis, J. B., & Klaes, M. (2003). Reflexivity: Curse or cure? *Journal of Economic Methodology, 10*, 329–352.

Grunberg, E. (1986). Predictability and reflexivity. *American Journal of Economics and Sociology, 45*, 475–488.

Grunberg, E., & Modigliani, F. (1954). The predictability of social events. *Journal of Political Economy, 62*, 465–478.

Grunberg, E., & Modigliani, F. (1965). Discussion: Reflexive prediction. *Philosophy of Science, 32*, 173–174.

Hands, D. W. (1985). Karl Popper and economic methodology: A new look. *Economics and Philosophy*, *1*, 303–335.

Hands, D. W. (1990). Grunberg and Modigliani, public predictions and the new classical macroeconomics. *Research in the History of Economic Thought and Methodology*, *7*, 207–223.

Koertge, N. (1975). Popper's metaphysical research program for the human sciences. *Inquiry*, *19*, 437–462.

Kopec, M. (2011). A more fulfilling (and frustrating) take on reflexive predictions. *Philosophy of Science*, *78*, 1249–1259.

MacKenzie, D. (2006). *An engine, not a camera: How financial models shape markets*. Cambridge, MA: MIT Press.

MacKenzie, D., Muniesa, F., & Siu, L. (Eds.). (2007). *Do economists make markets? On the performativity of economics*. Princeton, NJ: Princeton University Press.

Merton, R. K. (1948). The self-fulfilling prophecy. *Antioch Review*, *8*, 193–210.

Morgenstern, O. (1972). Descriptive, predictive and normative theory. *Kyklos*, *25*, 699–714.

Muth, J. F. (1961). Rational expectations and the theory of price movements. *Econometrica*, *29*, 315–335.

Ofsti, A., & Osterberg, D. (1982). Self-defeating predictions and the fixed-point theorem: A refutation. *Inquiry*, *25*, 331–352.

Popper, K. R. (1957). *The poverty of historicism*. New York, NY: Harper Torchbooks.

Popper, K. R. (1976). *Unended quest: An intellectual autobiography*. LaSalle, IL: Open Court.

Romanos, G. D. (1973). Reflexive predictions. *Philosophy of Science*, *40*, 97–109.

Sandri, S. (2009). *Reflexivity in economics: Experimental examination on the self-referentiality of economic theories*. Heidelberg: Physica-Verlag.

Sent, E. -M. (1998). *The evolving rationality of rational expectations*. Cambridge: Cambridge University Press.

Sent, E. -M. (2001). Sent simulating Simon simulating scientists. *Studies in the History and Philosophy of Science*, *32*, 479–500.

Simon, H. (1954). Bandwagon and underdog effects and the possibility of election predictions. *Public Opinion Quarterly*, *18*, 245–253.

Soros, G. (1987). *The alchemy of finance*. Hoboken, NJ: Wiley & Sons.

Soros, G. (1998). *The crisis of global capitalism*. London: Little Brown.

Soros, G. (2010). *The Soros lectures at the Central European University*. New York, NY: Public Affairs.

Soros, G. (2013). Fallibility, reflexivity and the human uncertainty principle. *Journal of Economic Methodology*, *20*, 309–329.

Fallibility, reflexivity, and the human uncertainty principle

George Soros

Soros Fund Management and the Open Society Foundations, New York, NY, USA

1. Introduction

I am honored that the editors of the *Journal of Economic Methodology* have created this special issue on the subject of reflexivity and have invited me, as well as a distinguished group of scholars, to contribute.

Of course I did not discover reflexivity. Earlier observers recognized it, or at least aspects of it, often under a different name. Knight (1921) explored the difference between risk and uncertainty. Keynes (1936, Chapter 12) compared financial markets to a beauty contest where the participants had to guess who would be the most popular choice. The sociologist Merton (1949) wrote about self-fulfilling prophecies, unintended consequences, and the bandwagon effect. Popper spoke of the 'Oedipus effect' in the *Poverty of Historicism* (1957, Chapter 5).

My own conceptual framework has its origins in my time as a student at the London School of Economics in the late 1950s. I took my final exams one year early, so I had a year to fill before I was qualified to receive my degree. I could choose my tutor, and I chose Popper whose book *The Open Society and Its Enemies* (1945) had made a profound impression on me.

In Popper's other great work *Logik der Forschung* (1935), which was published in English as *The Logic of Scientific Discovery* (1959), he argued that the empirical truth cannot be known with absolute certainty. Even scientific laws cannot be verified beyond a shadow of a doubt: they can only be falsified by testing. One failed test is enough to falsify, but no amount of conforming instances is sufficient to verify. Scientific laws are always hypothetical in character, and their validity remains open to falsification.

While I was reading Popper I was also studying economic theory, and I was struck by the contradiction between Popper's emphasis on imperfect understanding and the theory of perfect competition in economics, which postulated perfect knowledge. This led me to start questioning the assumptions of economic theory. I replaced the postulates of rational expectations and efficient markets with my own principles of fallibility and reflexivity.

After college, I started working in the financial markets where I had not much use for the economic theories I had studied in college. Strangely enough, the conceptual framework I had developed under Popper's influence provided me with much more valuable insights. And while I was engaged in making money I did not lose my interest in philosophy.

I published my first book, *The Alchemy of Finance*, in 1987. In that book, I tried to explain the philosophical underpinnings of my approach to financial markets. The book attracted a certain amount of attention. It has been read by many people in the hedge fund industry, and it is taught in business schools. But the philosophical arguments in that book and subsequent books (Soros, 1998, 2000) did not make much of an impression on the economics departments of universities. My framework was largely dismissed as the conceit of a man who has been successful in business and therefore fancies himself as a philosopher. With my theories largely ignored by academia, I began to regard myself as a failed philosopher – I even gave a lecture entitled 'A Failed Philosopher Tries Again.'

All that changed as a result of the financial crisis of 2008. My understanding of reflexivity enabled me both to anticipate the crisis and to deal with it when it finally struck (Soros, 2008, 2009). When the fallout of the crisis spread from the USA to Europe and around the world it enabled me to explain and predict events better than most others (Soros, 2012). The crisis put in stark relief the failings of orthodox economic theory (Soros, 2010). As people have realized how badly traditional economics has failed, interest in reflexivity has grown.

Thus, this issue of the *Journal of Economic Methodology* is timely. Economics is in a period of intellectual flux and while some economists will cling to ideas of market efficiency and rationality to their final days, many others are eager to pursue alternative approaches.

In this essay, I will articulate my current thinking. In Section 2, I shall explain the concepts of fallibility and reflexivity in general terms. In Section 3, I will discuss the implications of my conceptual framework for the social sciences in general and for economics in particular. In Section 4, I will describe how my conceptual framework applies to the financial markets with special mention of financial bubbles and the ongoing euro crisis. I will then conclude with some thoughts on the need for a new paradigm in social science.

2. Fallibility and reflexivity

I have a peculiar problem in explicating my conceptual framework. The framework deals with the relationship between thinking and reality, but the participants' thinking is part of the reality that they have to think about, which makes the relationship circular. Circles have no beginning or end, so I have to plunge in at an arbitrary point. That makes my ideas less clear when I put them into words than they are in my own mind. I am not the only one affected by this difficulty but I feel obliged to warn the reader that this section will be more convoluted and less elegant than it ought to be; the rest of the paper is not affected.

My conceptual framework is built on two relatively simple propositions. The first is that in situations that have thinking participants, the participants' views of the world never perfectly correspond to the actual state of affairs. People can gain knowledge of individual facts, but when it comes to formulating theories or forming an overall view, their perspective is bound to be either biased or inconsistent or both. That is the *principle of fallibility*.

The second proposition is that these imperfect views can influence the situation to which they relate through the actions of the participants. For example, if investors believe that markets are efficient then that belief will change the way they invest, which in turn will change the nature of the markets in which they are participating (though not necessarily making them more efficient). That is the *principle of reflexivity*.

The two principles are tied together like Siamese twins, but fallibility is the firstborn: without fallibility there would be no reflexivity. Both principles can be observed operating in the real world. So when my critics say that I am merely stating the obvious, they are right – but only up to a point. What makes my propositions interesting is that they contradict some of the basic tenets of economic theory. My conceptual framework deserves attention not because it constitutes a new discovery, but because something as commonsensical as reflexivity has been so studiously ignored by economists. The field of economics has gone to great lengths to eliminate the uncertainty associated with reflexivity in order to formulate universally valid laws similar to Newtonian physics. In doing so, economists set themselves an impossible task. The uncertainty associated with fallibility and reflexivity is inherent in the human condition. To make this point, I lump together the two concepts as the *human uncertainty principle*.

2.1 Fallibility

The complexity of the world in which we live exceeds our capacity to comprehend it. Confronted by a reality of extreme complexity, we are obliged to resort to various methods of simplification: generalizations, dichotomies, metaphors, decision rules, and moral precepts, just to mention a few. These mental constructs take on a (subjective) existence of their own, further complicating the situation.

The structure of the brain is another source of fallibility. Recent advances in brain science have begun to provide some insight into how the brain functions, and they have substantiated David Hume's insight that reason is the slave of passion. The idea of a disembodied intellect or reason is a figment of our imagination. The brain is bombarded by millions of sensory impulses, but consciousness can process only seven or eight subjects concurrently. The impulses need to be condensed, ordered, and interpreted under immense time pressure; mistakes and distortions cannot be avoided. Brain science adds many new insights to my contention that our understanding of the world in which we live is inherently imperfect.

Fallibility pervades our attempts to understand both natural and social phenomena, but it is not fallibility that distinguishes the social from the physical sciences. Rather, as will be discussed further in Section 3, the distinction comes from the fact that in social systems fallible human beings are not merely scientific observers but also active participants in the system themselves. That is what makes social systems reflexive.

2.2 Reflexivity

The concept of reflexivity needs some further explication. It applies exclusively to situations that have thinking participants. The participants' thinking serves two functions. One is to understand the world in which we live; I call this the *cognitive function*. The other is to make an impact on the world and to advance the participants' interests; I call this the *manipulative function*. I use the term 'manipulative' to emphasize intentionality.

The two functions connect the participants' thinking (subjective reality) and the actual state of affairs (objective reality) in opposite directions. In the cognitive function, the participant is cast in the role of a passive observer: the direction of causation is from the world to the mind. In the manipulative function, the participants play an active role: the direction of causation is from the mind to the world. Both functions are subject to fallibility.

When both the cognitive and manipulative functions operate at the same time they may interfere with each other. How? By depriving each function of the independent variable that would be needed to determine the value of the dependent variable. The independent variable of one function is the dependent variable of the other, thus neither function has a *genuinely independent variable* – the relationship is circular or recursive. It is like a partnership where each partner's view of the other influences their behavior and vice-versa.

2.3 Lack of an independent criterion of truth

If the cognitive function operated in isolation, without any interference from the manipulative function, it could produce knowledge. Knowledge is represented by true statements. A statement is true if it corresponds to the facts – that is what the correspondence theory of truth tells us. But if there is interference from the manipulative function, the facts no longer serve as an independent criterion because the statement may be the product of the manipulative function.

Consider the statement 'It is raining.' That statement is true or false depending on whether it is, in fact, raining. And whether people believe it is raining or not cannot change the facts. The agent can assess the statement without any interference from the manipulative function and thus gain knowledge.

Now consider the statement 'I love you.' The statement is reflexive. It will have an effect on the object of the affections of the person making the statement and the recipient's response may then affect the feelings of the person making the statement, changing the truth value of his or her original statement.

2.4 Self-reference

Reflexivity has some affinity with the Liar's Paradox, which is a self-referential statement. 'This sentence is false' is paradoxical. If the sentence is true, it means it is false, but if it is false, it means it is true. Bertrand Russell resolved the paradox by putting self-referential statements into a separate category and declaring them to be meaningless.

Following Russell, an important school of philosophy, logical positivism, banned self-referential statements. Ludwig Wittgenstein carried this program to its logical conclusion in his *Tractatus Logico-Philosophicus* and in the end he concluded that he had embarked on an impossible task. In practice, it is impossible to avoid either self-referential or reflexive statements. Consequently, the cognitive function cannot produce all the knowledge agents need to make decisions; they have to act on the basis of imperfect understanding. While the manipulative function can make an impact on the world, outcomes are unlikely to correspond to expectations. There is bound to be some slippage between intentions and actions, and further slippage between actions and outcomes. Since agents base their decisions on inadequate knowledge, their actions are liable to have unintended consequences. This means that reflexivity introduces an element of uncertainty both into the agents' view of the world and into the world in which they participate.

While self-reference has been extensively analyzed by the Vienna school with which Popper was associated, reflexivity has received much less attention. This is strange because reflexivity has an impact on the real world, while self-reference is confined to the universe of statements. In the real world, the participants' thinking finds expression not only in statements but also, of course, in various forms of action and behavior. That makes reflexivity a much broader phenomenon than self-reference: it connects the universe of thoughts with the universe of events. Bertrand Russell analyzed the Liar's Paradox in a timeless fashion. But reflexive systems are dynamic and unfold over time as the cognitive and manipulative functions perpetually chase each other. Once time is introduced, reflexivity creates indeterminacy and uncertainty rather than paradox.

Reflexive feedback loops between the cognitive and manipulative functions connect the realms of beliefs and events. The participants' views influence but do not determine the course of events, and the course of events influences but does not determine the participants' views. The influence is continuous and circular; that is what turns it into a feedback loop. As both the cognitive and manipulative functions are subject to fallibility, uncertainty is introduced into both the realms of beliefs and events. The process may be initiated from either direction, from a change in views, or from a change in circumstances.

2.5 Objective and subjective aspects of reality

Reflexive feedback loops have *not* been rigorously analyzed and when I originally encountered them and tried to study them, I ran into various difficulties. The main source of the trouble was that thinking is part of reality and the relationship of a part to the whole is very difficult to describe. The fact that thinking is not directly observable adds further complications; consequently, the definition of reflexivity will be much more complicated than the concept itself. The idea is that there is a two-way feedback loop connecting thinking and reality. The main feedback is between the participants' views and the actual course of events. But what about a direct two-way interaction between the various participants' views? And what about a solitary individual asking herself who she is and what she stands for and changing her behavior as a result of her own internal reflections?

To resolve these difficulties, I propose distinguishing between the *objective* and *subjective* aspects of reality. Thinking constitutes the subjective aspect. It takes place in the privacy of the participants' minds and is not directly observable; only its material manifestations are. The objective aspect consists of observable events. In other words, the subjective aspect covers the participants' thinking and the objective aspect denotes all observable facts, whether in the outside world or inside the brain.

2.6 Free will versus determinism

There is only one objective reality, but there are as many different subjective views as there are thinking participants. The views can be divided into different groups such as doubters and believers, trend followers and contrarians, Cartesians and empiricists – but these are simplifications and the categories are not fixed. Agents may hold views that are not easily categorized; moreover, they are free to choose between categories and they are free to switch. This is what is usually meant by free will but I consider free will a misnomer. People's views are greatly influenced but not determined by external factors such as the views of others, heredity, upbringing, and prior experiences. So, reality is halfway between free will and determinism.

Reflexivity can connect any two or more aspects of reality, setting up two-way feedback loops between them. We may then distinguish between two kinds of reflexivity: reflexive *relations*, like marriage or politics, which connect the subjective aspects of reality, and reflexive *events*, like the fiscal cliff or the euro crisis, which connect the subjective and objective aspects. In exceptional cases, reflexivity may even occur within a single subjective aspect of reality, as in the case of a solitary individual reflecting on his own identity. This may be described as *self-reflexivity*.

When reality has no subjective aspect, there can be no reflexivity. In other words, the presence or absence of reflexivity serves as a criterion of demarcation between social and natural phenomena – a point I will discuss in detail in the next section.

Let me illustrate the difficulties in analyzing the relationship between thinking and reality with the help of a diagram. Figure 1 describes the roles of the cognitive and manipulative functions, fallibility, and intentionality. Together this might be thought of as a *reflexive system*.

I have indicated the presence of multiple participants, and therefore multiple subjective realities. Nevertheless, the diagram is inadequate because it would require three

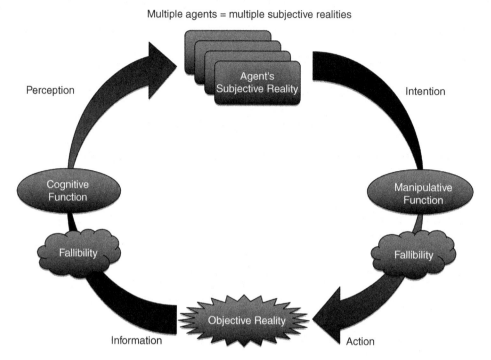

Figure 1. A reflexive system.

dimensions to show the multiple participants interacting with each other as well as with the objective aspect of reality.

2.7 The human uncertainty principle

Knight (1921) introduced an important distinction between risk and uncertainty. Risk is when there are multiple possible future states and the probabilities of those different future states occurring are known. Risk is well described by the laws of probability and statistics. Knightian uncertainty occurs when the probabilities of future states, or even the nature of possible future states is not known.

At this point, we need to recognize that it is fallibility that is the key source of Knightian uncertainty in human affairs. Yes, reflexivity does introduce an element of uncertainty into both the participants' views and the actual course of events, and there are also other forms of fallibility that have the same effect. For instance, different participants have different goals, some of which may be in conflict with each other. Moreover, as Isaiah Berlin pointed out, each participant may be guided by a multiplicity of values that may not be self-consistent. The uncertainties created by these factors are more extensive than those specifically associated with reflexivity.

We must also remember that not all forms of fallibility create Knightian uncertainty. Some forms are subject to statistical analysis – human errors leading to road accidents for example, or the many biases and errors discovered by behavioral economists. Other aspects of fallibility qualify as Knightian uncertainty – for example, probability analysis is not much help in understanding the misconceptions at the heart of the euro crisis.

Humans face quantifiable risks as well as Knightian uncertainty. There are many activities that are predictable or at least their probabilities can be calculated. Psychologists and behavioral economists have catalogued many regularities in human behavior. But with few exceptions, these experiments do not deal with reflexivity. Most behavioral experiments assess people's perception of objective reality (e.g. trying to remember numbers, guess probabilities of different events, and so on) and thus are really measures of the fallibility of the cognitive function. The manipulative function is rarely studied. Thus, there is both uncertainty and regularity in human affairs. Reflexivity is only one source of uncertainty, albeit a powerful one.

Earlier, I referred to the combination of reflexivity and fallibility as the *human uncertainty principle*. That makes it a broader concept than reflexivity. The human uncertainty principle is much more specific and stringent than the subjective skepticism that pervades Cartesian philosophy. It gives us objective reasons to believe that the theories held by the participants, as distinct from statements of specific facts, are liable to be biased, incomplete, or both.

3. Philosophy of social science

The idea that the sciences should be unified goes back to the pre-Socratic Greeks and has been a subject of debate in philosophy ever since. Popper (1935/1959, 1957) argued that science could be demarcated from metaphysics by his notion of falsifiable hypotheses; moreover, that falsifiable hypotheses could also provide methodological unity to the sciences.

While I have drawn much inspiration from Popper, this is an important point where I differ from my mentor. I believe that reflexivity provides a strong challenge to the idea that natural and social science can be unified. I believe that social science can still be a valuable human endeavor, but in order for it to be so, we must recognize its fundamental differences from natural science.

3.1 Popper's theory of scientific method

I base my argument on Popper's (1935/1959) theory of scientific method. Let me start by summarizing his beautifully simple and elegant scheme. It consists of three elements and three operations. The three elements are scientific laws of universal and timeless validity and two sets of singular conditions that Popper calls the cause and the effect. The three operations are prediction, explanation, and testing. When a scientific law is combined with the cause it provides predictions. When a scientific law is combined with the effect it provides explanations. In this sense, predictions and explanations are symmetrical and reversible through the logic of deduction. That leaves testing.

On this last point Popper had a key insight. According to Popper, scientific laws are hypothetical in character; they cannot be verified, but they can be falsified by empirical testing. The key to the success of scientific method is that it can test generalizations of universal validity with the help of singular observations. One failed test is sufficient to falsify a theory, but no amount of confirming instances is sufficient to verify it. Generalizations that cannot be tested do not qualify as scientific.

This is a brilliant construct that makes science both empirical and rational. According to Popper, it is empirical because we *test* our theories by observing whether the predictions we derive from them are true, and it is rational because we use deductive logic in doing so. Popper dispenses with inductive logic, which he considers invalid and gives testing a central role instead. He also makes a strong case for critical thinking by asserting that scientific laws are only provisionally valid and remain open to re-examination. The three salient features of Popper's scheme are the symmetry between prediction and explanation, the asymmetry between verification and falsification, and the central role of testing. These three features allow science to grow, improve, and innovate.

3.2   Problems of social science

Popper's scheme has worked extraordinarily well for the study of natural phenomena, but the human uncertainty principle throws a monkey wrench into the supreme simplicity and elegance of Popper's scheme. The symmetry between prediction and explanation is destroyed because the future is genuinely uncertain, and therefore cannot be predicted with the same degree of certainty as it can be explained in retrospect. One might object that uncertainty exists in all realms of science. But while Werner Heisenberg's uncertainty principle in quantum mechanics is subject to the laws of probability and statistics, the deep Knightian uncertainties of human affairs associated with the human uncertainty principle are not.

Even more importantly, the central role of testing is endangered. Should the initial and final conditions include or exclude the participant's thinking? The question is important because testing requires replicating those conditions. If the participants' thinking is included, it is difficult to determine what the initial and final conditions are because the participants' views can only be inferred from their statements or actions. If the participants' thinking is excluded, the initial and final conditions do not constitute singular observations because the same objective conditions may be associated with very different subjective views. In either case, testing cannot meet the requirements of Popper's scheme. This limitation does not preclude social sciences from producing worthwhile generalizations, but they are unlikely to match the predictive power of the laws of physics. Empirical testing ought to play a central role in social science as well but it should not be expected to produce universal and timeless generalizations with symmetrical and reversible explanatory and predictive powers. This point will be elaborated at the end of Section 4.

3.3   The structure of events

I contend that situations that have thinking participants have a different structure from natural phenomena. The difference lies in the role thinking plays. In natural phenomena, thinking plays no *causal* role. Events unfold irrespective of the views held by the observers. The structure of natural events can be described as a chain of cause and effect generating a steam of objective facts, without any interference from the subjective aspects of reality (see Figure 2).

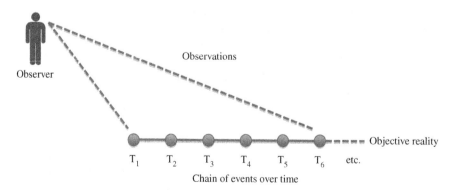

Figure 2.   Natural phenomena.

In natural science, the outside observer is engaged only in the cognitive function, and the facts provide a reliable criterion by which the truth of the observers' theories can be judged. So the outside observer can obtain knowledge about the natural phenomena she is observing. Based on that knowledge, nature can be successfully manipulated. That manipulation may change the state of the physical world, but it does not change the laws that govern that world. We can use our understanding of the physical world to create airplanes, but the invention of the airplane did not change the laws of aerodynamics.

By contrast, in human affairs, thinking is *part of* the subject matter The course of events leads not only from facts to facts but also from facts to the participants' perceptions (the cognitive function) and from the participants' decisions to facts (the manipulative function).

Figure 3 is a simplified presentation of the structure of social events. It illustrates that there is only one objective aspect but as many subjective aspects of reality as there are thinking participants. The reflexive feedback loops between the objective and subjective aspects of reality create a lace-like pattern, which is superimposed on the direct line leading from one set of facts to the next and deflects it from what it would be if there were no feedback loops. The feedback sometimes brings the subjective and objective aspects closer together and sometimes drives them further apart. The two aspects are aligned, but only loosely – the human uncertainty principle implies that a perfect alignment is the exception rather than the rule.

3.4 *Physics envy*

Popper's scheme would require social scientists to produce generalizations of universal and timeless validity that determine the alignment of the objective and subjective aspects of reality. If the human uncertainty principle is valid, that is an impossible task. Yet, the achievements of natural science, exemplified by Newtonian physics, were so alluring that economists and other social scientists have tried incredibly hard to establish such generalizations. They suffered from what I like to call 'physics envy.' In order to achieve the impossible, they invented or postulated some kind of fixed relationship between the participants' thinking and the actual course of events. Karl Marx asserted that the material

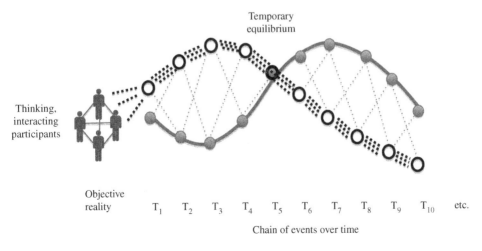

Figure 3. Social phenomena.

15

conditions of production determined the ideological superstructure; Freud maintained that people's behavior was determined by the unconscious. Both claimed scientific status for their theories but Popper rightly argued that their theories could not be falsified by testing.

However, Popper did not go far enough. The same argument applies to the mainstream economic theory currently taught in universities. It is an axiomatic system based on deductive logic, not on empirical evidence. If the axioms are true, so are the mathematical deductions. In this regard, economic theory resembles Euclidian geometry. But Euclid's postulates are modeled on conditions prevailing in the real world while at least some of the postulates of economics, notably rational choice and rational expectations, are dictated by the desire to imitate Newtonian physics rather than real-world evidence.

This ill-fated attempt by economists to slavishly imitate physics has a long history. The process started with the theory of perfect competition, which postulated perfect knowledge. That postulate was later modified to universally available perfect information. When that postulate proved inadequate Lionel Robbins, who was my professor at the London School of Economics, defined the task of economics as the allocation of limited means to unlimited alternative ends (Robbins, 1932). He specifically excluded the study of the means and the ends themselves. By taking the prevailing values and methods of production as given he eliminated reflexivity as a possible subject of study for economics. Subsequently, this approach reached its apex with the rational expectations and efficient market hypotheses in the 1960s and 1970s.

To be sure, physics envy is not unjustified. The achievements of natural science stand as convincing testimony to man's ability to use reason. Unfortunately, these achievements do not ensure that human behavior is always governed by reason.

3.5 *Human uncertainty as an impediment to scientific method*

The human uncertainty principle not only prevents the social sciences from producing results comparable to physics; it interferes with scientific method in other ways as well. I shall mention only one of them.

As we have seen, natural phenomena provide a genuinely independent criterion for judging the validity of generalizations but the facts produced by social processes do not do so because they are influenced by theories held by participants. This makes social theories themselves subject to reflexivity. In other words, they serve not only a cognitive but also a manipulative function.

To be sure, the generalizations and observations of natural scientists are also theory laden, and they influence the selection of facts but they do not influence the facts themselves. Heisenberg's uncertainty principle showed that the act of observation impacts a quantum system. But the discovery of the uncertainty principle itself did not alter the behavior of quantum particles one iota. The principle applied before Heisenberg discovered it and will continue to apply long after human observers are gone. But social theories – whether Marxism, market fundamentalism, or the theory of reflexivity – can affect the subject matter to which they refer.

Scientific method is supposed to be devoted to the pursuit of truth. But why should social science confine itself to passively studying social phenomena when it can be used to actively change the state of affairs? The temptation to use social theories to change reality rather than to understand it is much greater than in natural science. Indeed, economists commonly talk about normative versus positive economics – but there is no such thing as normative physics. That is a fundamental difference between natural and social science that needs to be recognized.

3.6 A spectrum between physical and social sciences

In my argument, I have drawn a sharp distinction between the social and natural sciences. But such dichotomies are usually not found in reality; rather we introduce them in our efforts to make some sense out of an otherwise confusing reality. Indeed, while the dichotomy between physics and social sciences seems clear cut, there are other sciences, such as biology and the study of animal societies, that occupy intermediate positions.

The distinction I have drawn between natural and social science consists of the presence or absence of thinking participants' who have a will of their own. That begs the question of what constitutes a 'thinking participant.' One might reasonably ask whether a chimpanzee, a dolphin, or a computerized stock-trading program is a thinking participant. In some fields, superior data crunching capacity may trump the human imagination, as the chess contest between Big Blue and Gary Kasparov has shown. And automatic trading systems appear to be currently outperforming hedge funds run by humans. However, I would note that humans have some unique characteristics, notably language, emotions, and culture. Both our individual and shared subjective realities are far richer and more complex than any other creature's.

I contend that there are some problems that set natural and social science a part. I have focused on reflexivity as one such fundamental problem area. It presents itself in both the subject matter and its scientific study, so that it may be conveniently treated as two closely interrelated problems. Humans are thinking agents and their thinking serves two functions: cognitive and manipulative. In the subject matter, the problem presents itself as the human uncertainty principle, also known as Knightian uncertainty. That has no equivalent in natural science. For scientific method, the problem is more complicated because scientists are also human beings and their thinking also serves two functions. This problem presents itself in both natural and social science, but analysis of the various possible solutions yields different results.

Science is a discipline that seeks to perfect the cognitive function by artificially isolating itself from the manipulative function. It does so by submitting itself to a number of conventions such as insisting on empirical tests that can be replicated and/or observed by others. Popper's scheme shows what natural science can achieve by obeying those rules and conventions. As I have shown, the human uncertainty principle prevents social science from matching these achievements. But there is also a flip side to be considered: what happens when those rules and conventions are not observed? Remember that my criterion of demarcation between natural and social science is that the latter is reflexive, the former is not. In other words, social science can change objective reality by influencing the participants' views, but natural science cannot because its subject matter has no thinking participants. That is what I meant when I remarked in *The Alchemy of Finance*, that the alchemists made a mistake in trying to change the nature of base metals by incantation. Instead, they should have focused their attention on the financial markets, where they could have succeeded. Now I need to take my analysis further.

Natural science can work wonders as long as it follows Popper's scheme because it has a purely objective criterion, namely the facts, by which the truth or validity of its laws can be judged, but it cannot produce anything worthwhile by cheating on the testing process. Cars that do not obey the laws of physics will not move; airplanes will not fly.

How about social science? We have seen that Popper's scheme cannot be expected to produce comparable results. On the other hand, social theories also serve a manipulative function and their influence on objective reality may prove quite satisfactory from the point of view of their proponents – at least for a while, until objective reality reasserts itself and the outcome fails to correspond to expectations. There are many statements that fit this pattern. President Obama managed to make the post 2008 recession shorter and shallower by asserting that the economy was fundamentally sound and promising a speedy recovery, but he paid a heavy political price when reality failed to live up to his promises. Fed chairman Alan Greenspan operated much the same way, but his Delphic utterances were more difficult to prove wrong. Both Freud and Marx sought to gain acceptance for their theories by claiming scientific status. One of the most interesting cases is the efficient market hypothesis and its political companion, market fundamentalism. We shall see that the mechanism that provides some degree of justification for the claim that markets are always right is reflexivity, not rational expectations. Yet, a false explanation can be subjectively more appealing than what I consider to be the true one. The efficient market hypothesis allows economic theory to lay claim to the status of a hard science like physics. And market fundamentalism allows the financially successful to claim that they are serving the public interest by pursing their self-interest. That is a powerful combination that dominated the field until it caused a lot of damage in the financial crisis of 2007/2008. Surprisingly it survived that debacle: the conservative wing of the Republican party managed to pin the blame for the financial crisis on the government rather than on the private sector. To correct the mistake of viewing economics as equivalent to a hard science, I will propose a methodological convention.

3.7 A methodological convention

I propose renouncing Popper's doctrine of the unity of science and recognizing a fundamental difference between natural and social phenomena – not as an empirical truth but as a methodological convention. The convention asserts that social science cannot be expected to produce results comparable with physics by using the same methods; however, it sets no limits on what social science may be able to accomplish by employing different methods. The convention will protect scientific method by preventing the social sciences from parading with borrowed feathers. It should not be taken, however, as a demotion or devaluation of social science. On the contrary, it should open up new vistas by liberating social science from the slavish imitation of natural science and by protecting it from being judged by the wrong standards.

3.8 The limits and promise of social science

Interestingly, both Karl Popper and Friedrich Hayek recognized in their famous exchange in the pages of *Economica* (Popper, 1944) that the social sciences cannot produce results comparable with physics. Hayek inveighed against the mechanical and uncritical application of the quantitative methods of natural science. He called it 'scientism.' and Popper wrote *The Poverty of Historicism* (1957) in which he argued that history is not determined by universally valid scientific laws. Nevertheless, Popper proclaimed what he called the 'doctrine of the unity of method,' by which he meant that both natural and social sciences should use the same methods and be judged by the same criteria.

By proclaiming the doctrine, Popper sought to distinguish pseudo-scientific theories like those of Marx and Freud from mainstream economics. As mentioned earlier, Popper did not go far enough: rational choice theory and the efficient market hypothesis are just as pseudo-scientific as Marxist and Freudian theories.

As I see it, the implication of the human uncertainty principle is that the subject matter of the natural and social sciences is fundamentally different; therefore, they need to develop different methods and should be held to different standards. Economic theory should not be expected to meet the standards established by Newtonian physics. In fact, if it did produce universally valid laws, as Knight (1921, p. 28) pointed out, economic profit itself would be impossible:

> if all changes were to take place in accordance with invariable and universally known laws, [so that] they could be foreseen for an indefinite period in advance of their occurrence, ... profit or loss would not arise.

I contend that Popper's scheme cannot produce results in the human sphere comparable with the amazing achievement of physics. The slavish imitation of natural science can easily produce misleading results, sometimes with disastrous consequences.

A methodological convention that merely asserts that social sciences should not be confined to the same methods and be judged by the same criteria as the natural sciences may not seem like an adequate remedy for the ills I have identified. But look at the straightjacket Lionel Robbins imposed on economics: it prevented economists from recognizing reflexivity and encouraged the development of synthetic financial instruments and risk management techniques that ignore Knightian uncertainty with disastrous consequences from which we have not yet found an escape.

I admit that the proposed methodological convention is only a starting point and it begs the question of what social scientists *should* do, what methods they should use, and by what criteria they should be judged. Others writing in this journal may have specific answers; I have only a partial one. Any valid methodology of social science must explicitly recognize both fallibility and reflexivity and the Knightian uncertainty they create. Empirical testing ought to remain a decisive criterion for judging whether a theory qualifies as scientific, but in light of the human uncertainty principle in social systems it cannot always be as rigorous as Popper's scheme requires. Nor can universally and timelessly valid theories be expected to yield determinate predictions because future events are contingent on future decisions, which are based on imperfect knowledge. Time- and context-bound generalizations may yield more specific explanations and predictions than timeless and universal generalizations.[1]

4. Financial markets

Financial markets provide an excellent laboratory for testing the ideas I have put forward in the previous sections. The course of events is easier to observe than in most other areas. Many of the facts take a quantitative form, and the data are well recorded and well preserved. The opportunity for testing occurs because my interpretation of financial markets directly contradicts the efficient market hypothesis, which has been the prevailing paradigm.

The efficient market hypothesis claims that markets tend toward equilibrium and that deviations occur in a random fashion and can be attributed to exogenous shocks. It is then a testable proposition whether the efficient market hypothesis or my theory of reflexivity is better at explaining and predicting events. I contend that my theory of reflexivity is superior, even in its current rudimentary stage of development for explaining and predicting financial markets in general, and historical events like the financial crisis of 2007–2008 and the subsequent euro crisis in particular.

4.1 My conceptual framework

Let me state the three key concepts of my approach, fallibility, reflexivity, and the human uncertainty principle as they apply to the financial markets. First, fallibility. Market prices of financial assets do not accurately reflect their fundamental value because they do not even aim to do so. Prices reflect market participants' expectations of future market prices. Moreover, market participants are subject to fallibility; consequently, their expectations about the discounted present value of future earnings flows are likely to diverge from reality. The divergence may range from the negligible to the significant. This is in direct contradiction of the efficient market hypothesis, which does not admit fallibility.

Second, reflexivity. Instead of playing a purely passive role in reflecting an underlying reality, financial markets also have an active role: they can *affect* the future earnings flows they are supposed to reflect. That is the point that behavioral economists have missed. Behavioral economics focuses on only half of the reflexive process: cognitive fallibility leading to the mispricing of assets; they do not concern themselves with the effects that mispricing can have on the fundamentals.

There are various pathways by which the mispricing of financial assets can affect the so-called fundamentals. The most widely used are those that involve the use of leverage – both debt and equity leveraging. For instance, companies can improve their earnings per-share by issuing shares at inflated prices – at least for a while. Markets may give the impression that they are always right, but the mechanism at work is very different from that implied by the prevailing paradigm.

Third, the human uncertainty principle turns what economic theory treats as timeless generalizations into a time-bound historical process. If agents act on the basis of their perfect understanding, equilibrium is far from a universally and timelessly prevailing condition of financial markets. Markets may just as easily tend away from a putative equilibrium as toward it. Instead of universally and timelessly prevailing, equilibrium becomes an extreme condition in which subjective market expectations correspond to objective reality. Theoretically such a correspondence could be brought about by either the cognitive or the manipulative function by itself – either perceptions can change to match reality or perceptions can lead to actions which change reality to match perceptions. But in practice such a correspondence is more likely to be the product of a reflexive interaction between the two functions. Whereas economics views equilibrium as the normal, indeed necessary state of affairs, I view such periods of stability as exceptional. Rather I focus on the reflexive feedback loops that characterize financial markets and cause them to be changing over time.

4.2 Negative versus positive feedback loops

Reflexive feedback loops can be either negative or positive. Negative feedback brings the participants' views and the actual situation closer together; positive feedback drives them further apart. In other words, a negative feedback process is self-correcting. It can go on forever and if there are no significant changes in external reality, it may eventually lead to an equilibrium in which the participants' views come to correspond to the actual state of affairs.

That is what rational expectations theory expects to happen in financial markets. It postulates that there is a single correct set of expectations that people's views will converge around and deviations are random – there are no systematic errors between participants' forecasts and what comes to pass. That postulate has no resemblance to reality, but it is a core tenet of economics as it is currently taught in universities and even used in the models of central banks. In practice, market participants' expectations diverge from reality to a greater or lesser extent and their errors may be correlated and significantly biased. That is the generic cause of price distortions. So equilibrium, which is the *central* case in mainstream economic theory, turns out to be an extreme case of negative feedback, a *limiting* case in my conceptual framework. Since equilibrium is so extreme that it is unlikely to prevail in reality, I prefer to speak of near-equilibrium conditions.

By contrast, a positive feedback process is self-reinforcing. It cannot go on forever because eventually the participants' views would become so far removed from objective reality that the participants would have to recognize them as unrealistic. Nor can the iterative process occur without any change in the actual state of affairs, because positive feedback reinforces whatever tendency prevails in the real world. Instead of equilibrium, we are faced with a dynamic disequilibrium, or what may be described as *far-from-equilibrium* situations.

There are myriad feedback loops at work in financial markets at any point of time. Some of them are positive, others negative. As long as they are more or less in balance they cancel out each other and market fluctuations do not have a definite direction. I compare these swings to the waves sloshing around in a swimming pool as opposed to the tides and currents that may prevail when positive feedbacks preponderate. Since positive feedbacks are self-reinforcing occasionally they may become so big that they overshadow all other happenings in the market.

Negative feedback loops tend to be more ubiquitous but positive feedback loops are more interesting because they can cause big moves both in market prices and in the underlying fundamentals. A positive feedback process that runs its full course is initially self-reinforcing in one direction, but eventually it is liable to reach a climax or reversal point, after which it becomes self-reinforcing in the opposite direction. But positive feedback processes do not necessarily run their full course; they may be aborted at any time by negative feedback.

4.3   Boom–bust processes

Building on these ideas, I have developed a theory about boom–bust processes, or bubbles (Soros, 1987, 2008). Every bubble has two components: an underlying trend that prevails in reality and a misconception relating to that trend (see Figure 4). A boom–bust process is set in motion when a trend and a misconception positively reinforce each other. The process is liable to be tested by negative feedback along the way, giving rise to climaxes which may or may not turn out to be genuine. If a trend is strong enough to survive the test, both the trend and the misconception will be further reinforced. Eventually, market expectations become so far removed from reality that people are forced to recognize that a misconception is involved. A twilight period ensues during which doubts grow and more people lose faith, but the prevailing trend is sustained by inertia. As Chuck Prince, former head of Citigroup said during the twilight of the super bubble: 'As long as the music is playing, you've got to get up and dance. We're still dancing.' Eventually, a point is reached when the trend is reversed, it then becomes self-reinforcing in the opposite direction. Boom–bust processes tend to be asymmetrical: booms are slow to develop and take a long time to become unsustainable, busts tend to be more abrupt, due to forced liquidation of unsustainable positions and the asymmetries introduced by leverage.

The simplest case is a real estate boom. The trend that precipitates it is easy credit; the misconception is that the value of the collateral is independent of the availability of credit. As a matter of fact, the relationship is reflexive. When credit becomes cheaper and more easily available, activity picks up and real estate values rise. There are fewer defaults, credit performance improves, and lending standards are relaxed. So, at the height of the boom, the amount of credit involved is at its maximum and a reversal precipitates forced

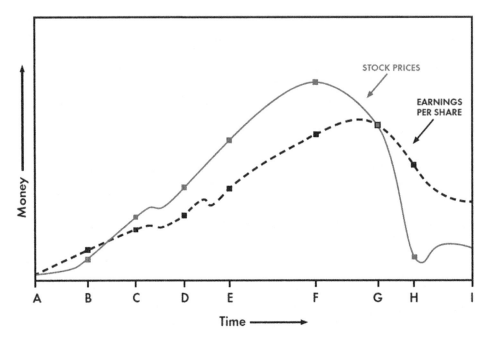

Figure 4.   A typical market boom–bust. In the initial stage (AB), a new positive earning trend is not yet recognized. Then comes a period of acceleration (BC) when the trend is recognized and reinforced by expectations. A period of testing may intervene when either earnings or expectations waiver (CD). If the positive trend and bias survive the testing, both emerge stronger. Conviction develops and is no longer shaken by a setback in earnings (DE). The gap between expectations and reality becomes wider (EF) until the moment of truth arrives when reality can no longer sustain the exaggerated expectations and the bias is recognized as such (F). A twilight period ensues when people continue to play the game although they no longer believe in it (FG). Eventually a crossover point (G) is reached when the trend turns down and prices lose their last prop. This leads to a catastrophic downward acceleration (GH) commonly known as the crash. The pessimism becomes over done, earnings stabilize, and prices recover somewhat (HI).

liquidation, depressing real estate values. Amazingly, the misconception continues to recur in various guises.

Other bubbles are based on different misconceptions. For instance, the international banking crisis of 1982 revolved around sovereign debt in which case no collateral was involved. The creditworthiness of the sovereign borrowers was measured by various debt ratios, such as debt to GDP or debt service to exports. These ratios were considered objective criteria, but in fact they were reflexive. When the recycling of petro-dollars in the 1970s increased the flow of credit to countries like Brazil, their debt ratios improved, which encouraged further inflows and started a bubble. In 1980, Paul Volcker raised interest rates in the USA to arrest inflation and the sovereign debt bubble burst in 1982.

Bubbles are not the only form in which reflexivity manifests itself. They are just the most dramatic and the most directly contradictory to the efficient market hypothesis, so they do deserve special attention. But reflexivity can take many other forms. In currency markets, for instance, the upside and downside are symmetrical so that there is no sign of an asymmetry between boom and bust. But there is no sign of equilibrium, either. Freely floating exchange rates tend to move in large, multi-year waves.

4.4   Markets versus regulators

One of the most important and interesting reflexive interactions takes place between the financial authorities and the financial markets. Because markets do not tend toward equilibrium, they are prone to produce periodic crises. Financial crises lead to regulatory reforms. That is how central banking and the regulation of financial markets have evolved. Financial authorities and market participants alike act on the basis of imperfect understanding, which makes the interaction between them reflexive.

While bubbles occur only intermittently, the interplay between authorities and markets is an ongoing process. Misunderstandings by either side usually stay within reasonable bounds because market reactions provide useful feedback to the authorities, allowing them to correct their mistakes. But occasionally the mistakes prove to be self-validating, setting in motion vicious or virtuous circles. Such feedback loops resemble bubbles in the sense that they are initially self-reinforcing but eventually self-defeating. Indeed, the intervention of the authorities to deal with periodic financial crises played a crucial role in the development of a 'super-bubble' that burst in 2007–2008 (Soros, 2008, 2009). The interplay between markets and regulators is also at the heart of the euro crisis.

4.5   The euro crisis

I have been following the euro crisis closely ever since its inception. I have written numerous articles that have been collected in a book (Soros, 2012). It would be impossible to summarize all my arguments for this essay; therefore, I shall focus only on the reflexive interaction between markets and authorities. Both acted on the basis of their imperfect understanding.

The design of the common currency had many flaws. Some of them were known at the time the euro was introduced. Everybody, for example, knew that it was an incomplete currency; it had a central bank, but it did not have a common treasury. The crash of 2008, however, revealed many other deficiencies. In retrospect, the most important was that by transferring the right to print to money to an independent central bank, member countries ran the risk of default on their government bonds. In a developed country with its own currency, the risk of default is absent because it can always print money. But by ceding or transferring that right to an independent central bank, which no member state actually controls, the member states put themselves in the position of third-world countries that borrow in a foreign currency.

This fact was not recognized either by the markets or by the authorities prior to the crash of 2008, testifying to their fallibility. When the euro was introduced, the authorities actually declared government bonds to be riskless. Commercial banks were not required to set aside any capital reserves against their holdings of government bonds. The European Central Bank (ECB) accepted all government bonds on equal terms at the discount window. This set up a perverse incentive for commercial banks to buy the debt of the weaker governments in order to earn what eventually became just a few basis points, because interest rates on government bonds converged to practically zero. This convergence in interest rates caused divergences in economic performance. The weaker countries enjoyed real estate and consumption booms, while Germany, which was dealing with the burden of reunification, had to adopt fiscal austerity and structural reforms.

After the Lehman bankruptcy European finance ministers declared that no other systemically important financial institution would be allowed to fail; Chancellor Merkel then insisted that the obligation should fall on each country individually, not on the European Union or the Eurozone collectively. That was the onset of the euro crisis. It took markets more than a year to react to it. Only when Greece revealed a much larger than expected fiscal deficit did markets realize that Greece may actually default on its debt – and they raised risk premiums with a vengeance not only on Greek bonds but also on the bonds of all the heavily indebted member countries.

A Greek default would have created a worse banking crisis than the Lehman bankruptcy. The authorities put together a number of rescue packages but they always did too little too late; so conditions in Greece continued to deteriorate. This set a pattern for the other heavily indebted countries such as Spain, Italy, Portugal, and Ireland as well. While the actions of the ECB have calmed the markets, the crisis is still far from resolved. Rather than an association of equals, the Eurozone became divided into two classes: creditors and debtors. In a financial crisis, the creditors call the shots. The policies they are imposing perpetuate the division because the debtors have to pay risk premiums, not only on government bonds but also on bank credit. The additional cost of credit, which is a recurrent burden, makes it practically impossible for the heavily indebted countries to regain competitiveness.

This is not the result of an evil plot. It was caused by a lack of understanding of an extremely complicated reality. In my articles, I put forward a series of practical proposals that could have worked at the time but became inadequate soon thereafter. Conversely, had the authorities adopted earlier some measures that they were willing to adopt later, they could have arrested the downtrend and then reversed it by adopting further measures. As it is, they have managed to calm the crisis, but failed to reverse the trend.

This analysis emphasizes the vital role that fallibility plays in shaping the course of history: there would have been no crisis without it. It also shows that in far-from-equilibrium conditions the normal rules do not apply. One of the reasons why the crisis persists is that the Eurozone is governed by treaties that were designed for near-equilibrium conditions. Obviously economists relying on the prevailing paradigm could not have reached this conclusion.

4.6 Fat tails

Both the super-bubble and the euro crisis are examples of far-from-equilibrium situations. A core difference between my approach and mainstream economics is that my framework can accommodate and explain such phenomena. Instead of declaring equilibrium as the outcome, I distinguish between near-equilibrium conditions that are characterized by random fluctuations and far-from-equilibrium situations that produce initially self-reinforcing but eventually self-defeating trends. Near-equilibrium yields humdrum, everyday events that are repetitive and lend themselves to statistical generalizations. In contrast, far-from-equilibrium conditions give rise to unique, historic events in which outcomes are uncertain but have the capacity to disrupt the statistical generalizations based on everyday events. Rules that can usefully guide decisions in near-equilibrium conditions can be misleading in far-from-equilibrium situations.

The financial crisis of 2007–2008 is a case in point. All the risk management tools and synthetic financial products that were based on the assumption that price deviations from a putative equilibrium occur in a random fashion broke down, and those who relied on mathematical models that had served them well in near-equilibrium conditions got badly hurt.

In the 1960s, the mathematician Mandelbrot (1963) discovered that the price movements of financial assets sometimes exhibit 'fat tails' – more extreme events than a normal Gaussian distribution would predict. This finding has since been confirmed by much research. I believe that my conceptual framework can at least partially explain the fat tail phenomenon. Reality feeds the participants so much information that they need to introduce dichotomies and other simplifying devices to make some sense of it. The simplest way to introduce order is binary division; hence, the tendency to use dichotomies. When markets switch from one side of a dichotomy to another the transition can be quite violent. The tipping point is difficult to predict but it is associated with a sharp increase in volatility, which manifests itself in fat tails.

4.7   Toward a new paradigm

One of the most powerful concepts for purposes of simplification is the concept of change. In my first philosophical essay (Soros, 1962, 2006) written under the influence of Karl Popper, I used the concept of change to build models of social systems and reflexively connect them to modes of thinking. I linked organic society with the traditional mode of thinking, open society with the critical mode, and closed society with the dogmatic mode.

It can be seen that my conceptual framework extends to a much broader area than that covered by economic theory. But financial markets provide the best laboratory for studying far-from-equilibrium situations at work because they manifest themselves in fat tails that can be clearly observed in the data. They can be studied in other fields as well, but only in the form of a historical narrative, as I have done in my analysis of the euro crisis, which weaves together politics with financial economics.

Reflexivity has been largely neglected until recently because it connects different fields studied by different disciplines. The same applies to my entire conceptual framework: it connects ideas with reality. Reality has been broken up into narrow fields of specialization. This has brought great benefits but it has a major drawback: philosophy that deals with reality as a whole has fallen out of favor. It needs to be rehabilitated.

Mainstream economics tried to seal itself off from reality by relying on postulates that turned out to be far removed from reality. The financial crisis of 2007/2008 and subsequent events exposed the weakness of this approach. The bankruptcy of Lehman Brothers was also the bankruptcy of the prevailing paradigm. There is urgent need for a new one.

This essay has shown that my interpretation of financial markets – based on my theory of reflexivity – is radically different from orthodox economics based on efficient markets and rational expectations. Strictly speaking, both interpretations are pseudo-scientific by Popper's standards. That is why I called my first book 'The Alchemy of Finance'. And that is why some proponents of the efficient market hypothesis still defend it in the face of all the evidence.

Nevertheless, I contend that my interpretation yields better explanations and predictions than the prevailing paradigm. How can I reconcile this claim with my starting contention that the future is inherently uncertain and financial markets are inherently unpredictable? By resorting to Popper's logic of scientific discovery. As a market participant, I formulate conjectures and expose them to refutation. I also assume that other market participants are doing the same thing whether they realize it or not. Their expectations are usefully aggregated in market prices. I can therefore compare my own expectations with prevailing prices. When I see a divergence, I see a profit opportunity. The bigger the divergence, the bigger the opportunity. Popper made a similar assertion about scientific hypotheses. Philosophers of science roundly criticized him for this on the grounds that the predictive power of scientific theories cannot be quantified. It may not work for scientific theories, but I can testify from personal experience that it does work in the alchemy of financial markets.

When the price behavior contradicts my expectations I have to re-examine my hypothesis. If I find myself proven wrong, I take a loss; if I conclude that the market is wrong, I increase my bet, always taking into account the risk that I am bound to be wrong some of the time. This works well in markets that are efficient in the sense that transaction costs are minimal; it does not work in private equity investments that are not readily marketable. My performance record bears this out. I was successful in markets but not in private equities. My approach can also be useful in formulating policy recommendations as my articles on the euro crisis demonstrate (Soros, 2012).

5. Conclusion

Ever since the Crash of 2008 there has been a widespread recognition, both among economists and the general public, that economic theory has failed. But there is no consensus on the causes and the extent of that failure.

I have argued that the failure is more profound than generally recognized. It goes back to the foundations of economic theory. Economics tried to model itself on Newtonian physics. It sought to establish universally and timelessly valid laws governing reality. But economics is a social science and there is a fundamental difference between the natural and social sciences. Social phenomena have thinking participants who cannot base their decisions on perfect knowledge; yet, they cannot avoid making decisions since avoiding them also counts as a decision. They introduce an element of indeterminacy into the course of human events that is absent in the behavior of inanimate objects. The resulting uncertainty hinders the social sciences in producing laws similar to Newton's physics. Yet, once we recognize this difference it frees us to develop new approaches to the study of social phenomena. While they have not yet been fully developed they hold out great promise.

The stakes could not be higher. The mistaken theories that allowed the 'super bubble' to build, the policy errors that were made in the wake of the crash, and the ongoing mishandling of the euro crisis highlight the human suffering that can result from a fundamental misunderstanding of the nature of economic systems. Recognizing the implications of our fallibility will be a great improvement in our understanding. Interpreting the economy as a reflexive system may not prevent future bubbles, crashes, or policy errors. But it may enable deeper insights into economic and socio-political phenomena and help humankind to better manage its affairs in the future.

I realize that my approach is still very rudimentary. For most of my life, I developed it in the privacy of my own mind. Only in recent years, did I have the benefit of substantive criticism. It remains to be seen whether my conceptual framework can develop into a new paradigm. Much depends on whether reflexive feedback loops can be properly modeled. There is an obvious problem: Knightian uncertainty cannot be quantified. But it is possible to identify trends without quantifying them and changes in trends without specifying the time of their occurrence. That is what I have done in my boom–bust model (Figure 4). We can also use volatility, which is quantifiable, as a substitute for uncertainty. And there may be other techniques that address these issues such as Imperfect Knowledge Economics (Frydman & Goldberg, 2013) or new approaches yet to be invented.

The new paradigm is bound to be very different from the one that failed. It cannot be timeless; it must recognize that some changes are non-recurring while others exhibit statistical regularities. Moreover, economic theory will not be able to seal itself off from other disciplines and from reality. It cannot confine itself to studying the allocation of limited means among unlimited alternative ends; it will have to take into account the impact the allocation may have on prevailing values and methods of production.

Obviously, I shall not be able to develop my ideas on my own. That is why I am so pleased that the *Journal of Economic Methodology* is publishing this special issue.

Note

1. *Postscript*: When I wrote this article I was troubled by drawing an overly sharp distinction between the natural and social sciences. Beinhocker's (2013) article in this symposium and a workshop at the Central European University on 8 October 2013 led me to modify my views on separating the two. I still think that the methodological convention I proposed is needed in the near term in order to break the stranglehold of rational choice theory, but I realize it could do more harm than good in the long term. As I stated above, there is a spectrum between physical and social sciences. Beinhocker is right in arguing that we should study the spectrum rather than attributing reflexivity exclusively to the domain of the social sciences. There are many similarities between human and non-human complex systems, which could be obfuscated by the proposed convention. Instead of denying the unity of science we ought to redefine scientific method so that it is not confined to Popper's model.

References

Beinhocker, E. D. (2013). Reflexivity, complexity and the nature of social science. *Journal of Economic Methodology, 20,* 330–342.

Frydman, R., & Goldberg, M. D. (2013). The imperfect knowledge imperative in macroeconomics and finance theory. In R. Frydman & E. S. Phelps (Eds.), *Rethinking expectations: The way forward for macroeconomics* (pp. 130–168). Princeton, NJ: Princeton University Press, Chapter 4.

Keynes, J. M. (1936). *The general theory of employment, interest, and money.* New York, NY: Harcourt Brace.

Knight, F. H. (1921). *Risk, uncertainty, and profit.* Boston, MA: Houghton Mifflin.

Mandelbrot, B. (1963). The variation of certain speculative prices. *Journal of Business, 36,* 394–419.

Merton, R. K. (1949). *Social theory and social structure.* New York, NY: Free Press.

Popper, K. (1935/1959). *Logik der Forschung.* Vienna. First English edition (1959) *The logic of scientific discovery.* London: Hutchinson Verlag von Julius Springer.

Popper, K. (1944). The poverty of historicism, II. A criticism of historicist methods. *Economica, 43,* 119–137.

Popper, K. (1945). *The open society and its enemies.* London: Routledge.

Popper, K. (1957). *The poverty of historicism.* London: Routledge.

Robbins, L. (1932). *An essay on the nature and significance of economic science.* London: MacMillan.

Soros, G. (1962). *Burden of consciousness.* (unpublished; revised version included in Soros (2006)).

Soros, G. (1987). *The alchemy of finance.* Hoboken, NJ: Wiley & Sons.

Soros, G. (1998). *The crisis of global capitalism: Open society endangered.* New York, NY: Public Affairs.

Soros, G. (2000). *Open society: Reforming global capitalism.* New York, NY: Public Affairs.

Soros, G. (2006). *The age of fallibility: Consequences of the war on terror.* New York, NY: Public Affairs.

Soros, G. (2008). *The new paradigm for financial markets the credit crisis and what it means.* New York, NY: Public Affairs.

Soros, G. (2009). *The crash of 2008 and what it means: The new paradigm for financial markets.* New York, NY: Public Affairs.

Soros, G. (2010). *The Soros lectures at the Central European University.* New York, NY: Public Affairs.

Soros, G. (2012). *Financial turmoil in the United States and Europe: Essays.* New York, NY: Public Affairs.

Reflexivity, complexity, and the nature of social science

Eric D. Beinhocker

Institute for New Economic Thinking at the Oxford Martin School, University of Oxford, Oxford, UK

In 1987, George Soros introduced his concepts of reflexivity and fallibility and has further developed and applied these concepts over subsequent decades. This paper attempts to build on Soros's framework, provide his concepts with a more precise definition, and put them in the context of recent thinking on complex adaptive systems. The paper proposes that systems can be classified along a 'spectrum of complexity' and that under specific conditions not only social systems but also natural and artificial systems can be considered 'complex reflexive.' The epistemological challenges associated with scientifically understanding a phenomenon stem not from whether its domain is social, natural, or artificial, but where it falls along this spectrum. Reflexive systems present particular challenges; however, evolutionary model-dependent realism provides a bridge between Soros and Popper and a potential path forward for economics.

1. Introduction

> I, however, believe that there is at least one philosophical problem in which all thinking men are interested ... *the problem of understanding the world – including ourselves, and our knowledge, as part of the world.*
>
> – Karl Popper, *The Logic of Scientific Discovery*

George Soros's mentor and inspiration Karl Popper wrote the above in the Preface to the first English language edition of his great work *The Logic of Scientific Discovery* (1959, p. xviii). Popper himself gave emphasis to the last part of the quote (which I have shortened) with italics. We cannot understand the world and ourselves separately from it – human beings and the knowledge they have – are intrinsically part of the world they are trying to understand. This embeddedness of human beings in the system they are seeking to understand, the limits to their knowledge of that system, the impact of their actions on the system's path, and the self-referential circularity this inherently creates all lie at the heart of George Soros's concept of reflexivity (Soros, 1987, 1998, 2000, 2006, 2008, 2009, 2010, 2012, 2013).

Unfortunately, however, Popper was wrong about one thing – not all 'thinking men' seem to be interested in this problem – not least of all economists. For roughly the past 140 years economics has taken another path. One that views the economy as an idealized mechanistic system and humans as detached rational analysts of that system rather than as embedded imperfect participants. This view claims to be 'scientific' but as Soros

(2013, pp. 315–320) argues it fundamentally misunderstands the nature of science – in particular social science – and the nature of the economy itself.

But in the wake of the 2008 financial crisis, there is now a growing community of economists and other scholars with an interest in the real functioning of the economy and a willingness to deviate from orthodox theory in order to attempt to explain that reality. Understanding the inherent reflexivity of the economy and the fallibility of the human beings that populate it must be a part of any post-crisis effort to reform and modernize economics.

In this essay, I will attempt to build on Soros's ideas to further specify what is meant by reflexivity, situate the concept in recent thinking on complex adaptive systems, and explore the fundamental issues it raises for epistemology and social science.

2. What are reflexive systems?

As Soros acknowledges, he did not introduce the term 'reflexivity' – it has a history of use in philosophy, sociology, and economics. The term has generally been used to describe processes where an observer is also a participant in a system and there is a two-way feedback between the participant/observer and the system. Soros's own definition of the terms reflexivity and fallibility is provided in his contribution to this symposium (Soros, 2013, pp. 310–311).

In this section, I will build on Soros's articulation and attempt to provide a definition that is both general and specific, situates reflexivity with other concepts such as cybernetic and complex adaptive systems, and helps distinguish reflexive systems from other kinds of systems.

2.1 Necessary conditions

I would propose that in order for a system to be 'reflexive' it must have the following elements:

- *Environment*: There is some setting or environment; it could be a physical environment, a socially constructed environment, or an artificial environment (e.g. in a computer).
- *Agent*: There must be at least one agent interacting with that environment and possibly multiple agents interacting with each other (for simplicity I will refer to agents in the plural as that is the more typical situation).
- *Goal*: The agents must have some goal or goals they are pursuing in that environment.
- *Cognitive function*: The agents must have some way of receiving information about their environment, perceiving the state of that environment, comparing that perceived state against the goal state, and identifying gaps between the perceived state and the goal state; Soros calls this the 'cognitive function.'
- *Manipulative function*: The agents must have some way of interacting with their environment in order to change or manipulate that environment in pursuit of their goal; Soros calls this the 'manipulative function.'
- *Internal model*: Each agent contains an internal model that connects its cognitive and manipulative functions; that model contains a mapping between states of the environment and possible actions and consequences.

This last point requires some further elaboration. In reflexive systems, agents have an internal model of their environment that enables them to move from perception via the cognitive function to action via the manipulative function in pursuit of their goal. This enables an agent to posit statements like '*If I perceive state A* (cognitive function) *and take action X* (manipulative function) *then state B will result, bringing me closer to (or farther from) my goal G'*. As we will see shortly, the inevitable flaws and shortcomings in any such model lead to the particular dynamics of reflexive systems.

The above list provides the *necessary but not sufficient* conditions for reflexivity. But it can also describe any simple feedback and control system. For example, a room thermostat can be thought of as an agent with a goal of keeping a room at a certain temperature, it perceives the state of the room through a thermometer, and takes action turning the heat on and off. Such dynamic feedback control systems, which I would *not* characterize as reflexive, have been well studied by scholars of cybernetics (Umpleby, 2007, 2010; Wiener, 1948) and system dynamics (Forrester, 1961; Sterman, 2000).

2.2   Distinguishing characteristics: internal model updating and complexity

There are two additional elements that I would argue distinguish a reflexive system from a dynamic feedback system:

- *Internal model updating*: The internal decision model of the agents is not fixed, but itself can change in response to interactions between the agent and its environment; thus, there is a feedback between the perception of the environment and the agent's internal model.
- *Complexity*: The system in which the agent is embedded in is complex in two senses: the system has *interactive complexity* due to multiple interactions between heterogeneous agents and
  the system has *dynamic complexity* due to nonlinearity in feedbacks in the system.

When these two elements are introduced, the system is no longer a simple dynamic feedback system, but it becomes a reflexive system. The thermostat in a room has neither internal model updating nor interactive or dynamic complexity. There are two reasons why these factors significantly change the nature of the system. First, when the internal model of the agents is no longer fixed, but can change in response to changes in the environment, then predicting future states of the system depends not just on understanding the rules of the internal model, but on fully understanding the process by which those rules update and accurately predict rule changes over time. In order to predict the future path of the system, we must know something about the agents' goals and internal model – the internal model cannot just be a black box.

I would further interpret Soros's definition to add that not only can models update through changes in model parameters (e.g. Bayesian updating), but also the rules or structure of the model itself might change [e.g. Holland, Holyoak, Nisbett, and Thagard (1986) provide an example of an updating model incorporating structural change, and Hommes (2013) shows experimentally how people can use mean-reverting rules in some circumstances, trend following rules in others]. It is important to note that in some cases an agent might 'learn' and its internal model might improve its performance in mapping perceptions and actions toward achieving the agent's goals. But it is also possible that model updating can worsen the performance of the model as well.

Second, rather than the simple environment of a single thermostat in a room, we now assume a more complex environment. Imagine if the room has multiple thermostat/heating systems, each with its own temperature goals and internal programs. The system would have multiple, interacting, heterogeneous agents – what might be called interactive complexity. Predicting the future path of the temperature in the room would suddenly become much more complex – one would have to know a lot about each agent thermostat, its goal, its internal program, the heating system it controls, time delays between actions by the thermostat and responses in temperature, etc. All sorts of behaviors would now be possible – the system could reach a stable equilibrium temperature, or it could oscillate between differing temperature goals, or it could engage in some complex nonperiodic pattern of temperature swings, or it might even exhibit chaotic behavior.

Likewise, if one or more of the thermostats had a rule where the room temperature was a nonlinear function of past temperature, this would introduce dynamic complexity into the system and make its future behavior even more difficult to predict. For example, if one of our thermostats had the internal rule $T_{t+1} = cT_t - cT_t^2$, where T_{t+1} is the room temperature for the next time period, T_t is the current temperature setting of the thermostat and c is a constant, then the system would have a very interesting range of behaviors. This simple nonlinear dynamic equation is known as the logistic map. Depending on the initial temperature and the value of the constant c, the system could do anything from going to a steady state, to regular oscillations, to swinging around chaotically. Such a system is sensitive to both initial conditions and path dependent. The key point is it is difficult or even impossible for an outside observer to predict the future path of a system with such a nonlinear relationship without both knowing the rule, its parameters and the initial conditions.

3.   Limits to knowledge and fallibility

The introduction of internal model updating and interactive and dynamic complexity then creates the central tension that defines reflexive systems: Internal model updating enables agents in the system to learn, but interactive and dynamic complexity makes it very difficult for agents in such a system to learn successfully.

It is this central tension that makes Soros's notion of fallibility inevitable. In order for an agent to successfully pursue its goals, it must have an accurate enough internal model of the system it is operating in so that its perceptions via its cognitive function lead to the correct actions through its manipulative function to move closer to its goals. But constructing such an accurate internal model and improving its performance through learning in a complex environment runs into fundamental limits to knowledge issues.

3.1   Flawed models in a complex world

If we assume that the agent or agents are not simply given the correct model of their environment a priori, but must discover, learn, or evolve their internal model through some process of observing data in the environment, then it is likely that the model the agent discovers will be flawed or inherently limited in some way. As Soros (2013, p. 310) notes, fallibility is core to his theory of reflexivity. Mathematicians and philosophers have discovered a number of results that fundamentally limit the knowledge that agents situated in complex systems can attain:

- *Difficulty discovering the correct model from finite data*: Agents only have access to finite amounts of data, but for high-dimensional systems there may never be enough data to discover the true underlying model.
- *Lack of knowledge of initial conditions and parameters*: Even if one has the correct underlying model, it may be impossible to predict the path of a nonlinear dynamic system without perfect knowledge of its initial conditions and key parameters (e.g. unknown Lyapunov exponent).

- *Inability to predict with finite computing time*: For some systems, there is no short cut or compressed model that allows forecasting future states without an infinite amount of computing power, one can only let the system run and play out over time (e.g. N-P complete problems).
- *No 'God's-eye view'*: It may be impossible for an agent embodied within the system to access information an agent outside the system with a 'God's-eye view' would have – this is related to Gödel's famous incompleteness theorem.

In any nontrivial setting of minimal complexity – i.e. almost any real-world economic situation – the true underlying model will not be given a priori to the agents, knowledge of initial conditions and parameters will be limited, data will be finite and noisy, computing power will be finite, and the agents doing the observing will also be participants in the system. This means that in almost any real-world situation the internal models of agents *must* be fallible. And that fallibility is also part of the system that the agents are trying to understand. We thus have the recursive loop that is at the center of Soros's concept: fallible agents try to understand and act in an environment of fallible agents trying to understand and act in an environment of fallible agents trying to understand .... Predicting the future path of such a system then requires perfect knowledge of the agent's own fallibility and the fallibility of all other agents – perfect knowledge of fallibility is truly a contradiction in terms.

Yet, it is precisely these limits to knowledge and the fallibility that they imply that the rational expectations hypothesis (REH) in economics assumes away (Lucas & Prescott, 1971; Muth, 1961). Under REH, agents live in a simple world without either interactive or dynamic complexity and with homogeneous and predictable agent model updating. Some may argue that REH incorporates reflexivity because it models two-way feedback between agent beliefs and the world. But REH does not incorporate any fundamental limits to knowledge in complex environments, the inevitable fallibility and heterogeneity such limits introduce, and the deep indeterminacy that reflexive interactions between fallible agents create.

3.2 Complex reflexive systems

In the above three sections, I have listed the necessary and sufficient ingredients for a reflexive system. I have briefly described how such a system differs from a cybernetic or dynamic feedback system. But one might ask whether this description differs from what are referred to as 'complex adaptive systems' (e.g. Anderson, Arrow, & Pines, 1988; Arthur, 1999; Beinhocker, 2006; Farmer, 2002; Miller & Page, 2007). The answer is they are close cousins but with some differences of emphasis. First, complex adaptive systems are generally thought of as multi-agent systems, but it is possible to imagine a reflexive system with one agent. Second, as noted, in reflexive systems internal model updating often involves not only changes in model parameters or weights, but changes in rules and model structure as well. Systems where agents have fixed rules but simply adjust rule parameters or weights in response to environmental feedback are often considered adaptive, but I would claim they are not necessarily reflexive in Soros's use of the term.

Thus, there is a high but imperfect degree of overlap between reflexive systems and complex adaptive systems. But given their close relationship, one might reasonably talk of 'complex reflexive systems' as a specific subset of the more general class of 'complex adaptive systems' which in turn is a subclass of the more general 'complex systems.'

4. Implications for social science

Space does not allow a full exploration of the many implications of Soros's ideas for epistemology, the philosophy of social science, and the future of economics. However, in this section, I will address one aspect of Soros's views: his arguments about the distinctions between natural and social science.

4.1 Timeless laws and prediction

Soros (2013, pp. 315–320) argues that one cannot create scientific explanations (at least in a Popperian sense) of human social systems because of the deep uncertainty and indeterminacy that reflexivity and fallibility introduce. Reflexive systems are inherently contingent and time bound, they do not have timeless universal laws, and one cannot make reliable predictions in such systems.

It is important to note, however, that all science is contingent and time bound – no science, not even physics has truly timeless laws. Chemistry has very empirically successful explanations and models of atomic interactions. Yet, atoms did not exist until 379,000 years after the Big Bang, so there was a period when the laws of chemistry did not exist. The regularities that chemistry describes are limited to a particular time and set of conditions. Likewise, the laws of evolution did not come into play until life was formed (whether on Earth or another planet). Some physicists even argue that time itself is not a fundamental property of the universe, but emerged as a post-Big Bang phenomenon too.

Rather than timeless, universal laws, what natural science describes is a process of the universe unfolding and creating itself after its origin, and new regularities and properties emerging at higher and higher levels of aggregation and complexity as that process proceeds. Those regularities may be universal for a period of time which may be very long, but any such regularities are nonetheless time bound and contingent. Seen from that perspective, both biological and social phenomena are merely at the end of a very long chain of growing complexity. So, the goal of science is not the discovery of timeless, universal laws – they don't exist. Rather, it is to explain time bound and contingent regularities in an empirically testable way.

Economics too has many regularities in need of explanation, for example, the power laws observed in financial volatility, Pareto distributions of income, the many regularities observed by behavioral economists, or the patterns of financial bubbles that Soros (2009, 2010, 2012) provides many insights into. These regularities in economic systems are dependent on a host of conditions and will not last forever – but neither will the laws of chemistry or biology and possibly even the laws of physics. The key is that the regularities are stable enough that they lend themselves to empirically testable explanation. Economics has many such stable regularities.

Soros (2013, p. 321) further argues that reflexivity destroys the ability to make 'determinate predictions' in social systems. Here, we must distinguish between prediction versus forecasting. Forecasting is a statement about the state of the universe at some future point in time. If Soros's claim is about forecasting then he is correct. As discussed in Section 1, reflexivity introduces indeterminacy and limits to knowledge that makes accurate forecasting in social systems often very difficult or even impossible.

But prediction, as it is used in a scientific sense, is a deductive logical consequence of a theory. A prediction does not necessarily have to take place in the future – the observation being predicted could take place now or in the past. For example, evolutionary theory cannot make accurate forecasts about the future evolution of individual species. The evolutionary process is too complex and suffers many of the same limits to knowledge issues characterized by reflexivity. But evolutionary theory has many testable, deductive consequences. For example, in 1859, Darwin wrote in the *Origin of Species* (Chapter 10) that his theory predicted fossils in pre-Cambrian rocks and if they were not found that it would be a strong argument against his theory – a kind of Popperian falsification test. In the 1950s and 1960s, with the help of more powerful microscopes such fossils were eventually found (Schopf, 2000). This was a prediction about past events, not a forecast of the future. Modern genetics has also validated many of the deductive implications of evolutionary theory in ways that Darwin himself could not have imagined.

Likewise, we may not be able to accurately predict future states of the stock market (though Mr Soros has an excellent record in this regard). But as noted there is a strong empirical regularity that price fluctuations are distributed according to a power law (e.g. Farmer & Lillo, 2004). Any theory of stock prices whose logical consequences included a distribution other than a power law would fail the Popperian test. Indeed, the efficient market hypothesis that predicts a random walk fails exactly this test.

Soros himself makes a number of testable predictions in his writings. For example, he has described in detail how reflexivity plays out in the laboratory of financial markets and how it underlies the dynamics of bubbles and crashes. Bubbles and crashes are an example of a persistent pattern or regularity. As Soros notes, bubbles cannot be forecast. But he shows how they can be explained and more deeply understood by this theory, and his theory predicts specific phases to bubbles that appear born out in the historical record. The predictions from reflexivity may be more qualitative than quantitative, but many natural sciences including evolutionary theory use descriptive and qualitative predictions very successfully.

4.2 A spectrum of complexity

Although the time frames of the regularities economics studies may be shorter than those in many physical systems, and forecasting may be difficult, neither of these disqualifies economics from potentially being a science. Instead, one can think of a spectrum of system complexity, stretching from basic mechanical systems (e.g. a ball rolling down a frictionless plane in a vacuum) to simple statistical systems (e.g. an ideal gas), to nonlinear, dynamic systems (e.g. a turbulent fluid), to systems with complex interactions (e.g. climate change), to complex adaptive systems (e.g. the human brain). Not only can physical systems be arrayed against such a spectrum, but so too can artificial and human social systems. Artificial systems range from the simple and mechanical (e.g. a pendulum swinging in a clock) to the mind-boggling complex (e.g. the Internet). Likewise, human social systems can be thought of along this spectrum – economics studies phenomena ranging from two people haggling over the price of a rug to the full complexity of the global economy.

Complex reflexive systems can be thought of as at the far end of this spectrum (on the right if one visualizes it stretching from left to right, see Figure 1). But a key question is whether reflexivity is limited to just human systems. Soros (2013, p. 311) defines reflexive systems as having 'thinking participants.' Numerous cognitive scientists and philosophers have felled many trees writing papers debating just what constitutes 'thinking' and whether thinking is something only humans can do. As Soros admits 'thinking' is hard to define and this creates a certain ambiguity in his definition. In my definition in Section 1, I have only generically referred to 'agents' whose models update, not specifically to humans. A bacterium swimming in a sugar gradient has a goal, a cognitive function, a manipulative function, an updating internal model, and two-way feedback with its

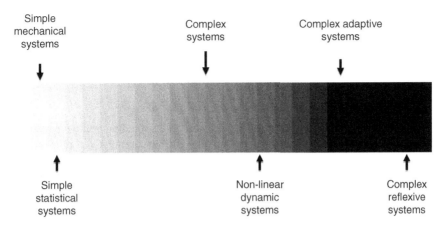

Figure 1.   A spectrum of complexity.

environment. Under my definition, it would be a single-agent reflexive system. An evolving forest ecosystem would be a multi-agent complex reflexive system. It is also possible for artificial systems to be reflexive. For example, the black-box stock trading robots now used by many hedge funds have arguably created an artificial reflexive market.

Of course, Soros is correct in asserting that there is something special about human systems. The internal mental models of humans are far more complex than other species or any current artificial system, and humans are the only species to use language. Human social structures and institutions are also more complex and enduring than those of other species. But again it is a matter of degrees, sliding up the spectrum from bacterium, to lizard, to primate, to human. Rather than a black and white distinction one can think of human reflexive systems as the far, far right end of the spectrum of complexity.

4.3   Common epistemological challenges

If one accepts the spectrum of complexity argument then it has important implications for the nature of social science. What defines the epistemological challenge of understanding a particular phenomenon is *where it sits on the spectrum of complexity, not its domain.* Understanding and explaining two people playing a simple game theory problem with an easily calculated unique Nash equilibrium has more in common with a simple mechanical equilibrium system than it does with trying to understand the effect of contagion in a banking crisis. But understanding the effect of contagion in a banking crisis has some striking similarities to understanding contagion in epidemiology, or the collapse of a food web in ecology (Haldane & May, 2011).

At the left (simple) end of the spectrum of complexity the epistemological challenges are few. There is a clear regularity to be explained, data are available, there are few nonlinearities, dynamics, or interactions, and the problem is amenable to standard analytical, statistical, or computational methods. The possibility of accurate forecasting (not just prediction) for such systems is high. At the right (complex) end of the spectrum the situation is reversed. The epistemological challenges are many and include the limits to knowledge issues outlined in Section 1. And while Popperian prediction and testing may be possible, highly accurate forecasting may not be.

Soros is thus correct that reflexive systems are very challenging to model and understand scientifically. I would argue that they are challenging *not* because there is a fundamental difference between physical and social systems, but because they are extremely complex – whether it is an ecosystem of human beings trading in a stock market, an ecosystem of sophisticated stock trading computer algorithms, or an ecosystem of interacting species (Farmer, 2002).

4.4 Evolution, good enough models, and muddling through

The epistemological challenges may be high for understanding reflexive systems, but fallible models, limits to knowledge, and the inherent indeterminacy of reflexive systems do not necessarily imply that all is lost and that we cannot gain insight into such systems. Biological systems, human systems, and various artificial systems all manage to function despite fallibility and limits to knowledge. The internal models of agents and their cognitive and manipulative functions may be 'good enough' for them to muddle through and make progress toward their goals. As the statistician George E.P. Box once said, 'Essentially, all models are wrong, but some are useful' (Box, 1987, p. 424).

Indeed, biological evolution depends on 'useful enough' models muddling through without the ability to forecast. Evolution picks up on regularities and through experimentation, selection, and amplification finds heuristics that are 'good enough for now' until something better comes along or something selects against them. There is a parallel with Popper's (1972, 1984) evolutionary views of science and epistemology, and in particular his view on the role of falsification in science. Success for a theory is always highly contingent and subject to future refutation while failure is generally fatal. This asymmetry is true for any evolutionary epistemological system where objective truth is inaccessible but increasingly successful approximations are possible. This has been the core idea of the evolutionary epistemology of theories program in the philosophy of science (Bradie, 1986; Campbell, 1960; Hull, 1988; Toulmin, 1972). And in such systems monotonic progress is not guaranteed – biological evolution, human social systems, and science can all experience blind alleys, reversals, and collapses. A model is shown to be wrong, and the search is on again for new and better ones. I would even claim that reflexive systems *require* evolutionary epistemological processes to deal with fallibility and limits to knowledge – there is simply no other way for such systems to function in a noisy, complex, difficult to forecast world.

I should also briefly note that while complex reflexive systems present a challenge due to their Knightian uncertainty, there is also an upside – their inherent indeterminacy creates space for novelty and creativity. In a perfectly deterministic system, there is no room for novelty to emerge. In a perfectly random system, there is insufficient coherence for novelty to matter. Complex reflexive systems are somewhere in between – they are hard to forecast and fallibility is inevitable, but there is nonetheless pattern and structure. This creates a space for novelty, experimentation, and in human systems creativity. One may even argue that there is a link between reflexivity and free will – reflexivity makes free will both possible and necessary.

4.5 Model-dependent realism: reconciling Soros and Popper

Reflexivity is not only consistent with an evolutionary view of epistemology, but also what the physicists Stephen Hawking and Leonard Mlodinow call 'model-dependent realism' (Hawking & Mlodinow, 2010). Under this view, there may or may not be an objective reality independent from us and the models we create. But whether there is or not does not matter because the only way we can access and perceive our world is via the models we create – whether it is the model of the room I am sitting in that my brain assembles from pixels of light coming through my eyes, or a mathematical physics model of an atom. One cannot separate reality from our models or say in any sense that a model is objectively true – all one can say is whether a particular model fits the data one has better than another model (in which case it is 'the best we have for now') or whether the data falsify the model. Such a pragmatic stance is an attempt to resolve the age-old debate in philosophy of science between 'realists' who argue that science is about discovering fundamental truths and explaining phenomena, and 'instrumentalists' who argue for more the more limited goal of creating tools that can make reliable and useful predictions.

If one combines evolutionary epistemology with model-dependent realism one comes to a view that science is about providing explanations of phenomena (realism), but such explanations are always mediated by our models and observations and thus cannot claim to be objectively and perpetually true (model dependency). Scientific explanations are formulated as models or theories which have deductive implications, some of which are observable and some are not (a model with no observable deductive implications is not scientific). Observable implications can then be used to make testable predictions. If those predictions are more congruent with empirical observation versus competing explanations, then the theory or model is 'the best explanation for now' (empirical adequacy), if it is falsified then it is thrown out (Popperian selection). Science is thus an evolutionary epistemological system of competing explanations, with the primary selection force being Popperian falsifiability (although, as many critics of Popper have argued, in real science falsifiability is rarely black and white and thus theory selection is often a complex mix of criteria – some empirically based and some more sociological, e.g. the power of authority figures in a field). The evolutionary process of competing explanations over time leads to the paradigmatic eras described by Kuhn (1962).

I believe that such an evolutionary, model-dependent realist epistemology is largely consistent with Soros's (2013) views. A passage from Hawking and Mlodinow (2010, Chap. 3) sounds almost as if it could have been written by Soros:

> Model-dependent realism applies not only to scientific models but also to the conscious and subconscious mental models we all create in order to interpret and understand the everyday world. There is no way to remove the observer – us – from our perception of the world, which is created through our sensory processing and through the way we think and reason.

As Soros (2013, pp. 316–317) observes, in reflexive systems agents do not have direct access to any objective reality – there is no ideal of the detached, objective observer. I would claim that in reflexive systems the best agents can do is to be evolutionary model-dependent realists and make judgments, using Popper's great insight of falsifiability, as to whether one model fits the finite, noisy, flawed data they observe better than competing models. In this way, inherently fallible agents muddle through with inherently imperfect models. Yet, these models may improve over time, even if they are only for a time, and in this way our knowledge grows.

5. A way forward for economics

Economies are certainly reflexive system and at the far end of the spectrum of complexity. Soros is correct in saying that the reflexivity of economic systems has been largely ignored by mainstream economics. For the past 130 years since Walras, economists have insisted on treating economies as simple mechanical or statistical systems. Economics is a diverse subject, but the core theories that have dominated the field and policy-making have been equilibrium theories derived deductively from axiomatic principles (Hausman, 1992).

However, much empirical work, particularly in behavioral economics, has shown that many of the core axiomatic assumptions of economic theory are flawed. Economics has what computer scientists call a 'garbage in, garbage out' problem – the logic of its proofs and equations may be flawless – but it is built on a base of empirically disproven assumptions and so the conclusions based on those assumptions are likely to be suspect as well (Beinhocker, 2006). This is born out by meta studies of empirical results in economics that conclude that the empirical credibility of economics is 'modest or even low' (Ioannides & Doucouliagos, 2013, p. 1).

To move forward and develop into what truly could be called a science, economics needs to embrace the philosophy of both Soros and Popper – as well as the toolkit of the modern science of complex systems. Economics needs to recognize that it made an ontological error when in the nineteenth century it categorized economies as equilibrium systems (Beinhocker, 2006; Mirowski, 1989). It was perhaps an understandable error as equilibrium analysis was the tool available at the time – but now we know better. Following Soros and categorizing economies as complex reflexive systems would end the false certainty of neoclassical theory and enable economists to embrace the inherent fallibility and Knightian uncertainty that characterizes real-world economic systems.

Soros (2013, p. 317) argues that economics has made an error in trying to be too much like the other sciences, but I would argue it has made too little effort. Economics has not been Popperian enough. It has developed an axiomatic, internally consistent, self-contained theory – more like theology than a science – and has developed a culture that is resistant to empirical testing and falsification (Ioannides & Doucouliagos, 2013). Theories such as rational expectations and the efficient markets hypothesis have been thoroughly discredited by decades of empirical work in behavioral, experimental, statistical, and financial economics – not to mention the real-world experiences of the 2008 financial crisis – and yet remain in current use in the field and in policy.

Economists must give up the myth that the economy is a simple mechanical equilibrium system. The field needs to embrace the economy in its full messy, uncertain, disequilibrium, complex reflexive reality. Approaches that can help give insight into such a system range from those found in the behavioral sciences, to experimental economics, network theory, nonlinear systems theory, complexity theory, evolutionary theory, and information theory. Economics is an inherently multi-disciplinary field and should draw ideas from across the social and natural sciences, as well as utilize a plurality of methods from analytical, to statistical, to computational, to qualitative and historical.

Soros has presented us with a major epistemological challenge, one that economics has not properly grappled with to date. Economics will never look like the Newtonian physics that Walras and many since have dreamed of. But neither does climate change science, neuroscience, evolutionary theory, or any other scientific field that studies highly complex phenomena. Human, complex reflexive systems may be another level more complex than these. Yet, we can be hopeful that although our ability to understand such systems may always be limited, our creativity in trying to will not be.

Acknowledgements

The author is grateful for the support of the Institute for New Economic Thinking (INET) and thanks the participants of the workshops on reflexivity at Central European University, Budapest, November 2011 and October 2013 for their comments and suggestions. The author also benefited enormously from George Soros's insights and his Popperian 'critical attitude.' All errors are the author's.

References

Anderson, P. W., Arrow, K. J., & Pines, D. (Eds.). (1988). *The economy as a complex evolving system*. Redwood City, CA: Addison-Wesley.

Arthur, W. B. (1999). Complexity and the economy. *Science, 284*, 107–109.

Beinhocker, E. D. (2006). *The origin of wealth: Evolution, complexity and the radical remaking of economics*. Boston, MA: Harvard Business School Press.

Box, G. E. P., & Draper, N. R. (1987). *Empirical model building and response surfaces*. New York, NY: Wiley.

Bradie, M. (1986). Assessing evolutionary epistemology. *Biology and Philosophy, 1*, 401–459.

Campbell, D. T. (1960). Blind variation and selective retention in creative thought as in other knowledge processes. *Psychological Review, 67*, 380–400.

Farmer, J. D. (2002). Market force, ecology, and evolution. *Industrial and Corporate Change, 11*, 895–953.

Farmer, J. D., & Lillo, F. (2004). On the origin of power law tails in price fluctuations. *Journal of Quantitative Finance, 4*, C7–C11.

Forrester, J. (1961). *Industrial dynamics*. Waltham, MA: Pegasus.

Haldane, A. G., & May, R. M. (2011). Systemic risk in banking ecosystems. *Nature, 469*, 351–355.

Hausman, D. M. (1992). *The inexact and separate science of economics*. Cambridge: Cambridge University Press.

Hawking, S., & Mlodinow, L. (2010). *The grand design*. New York, NY: Bantam Books.

Holland, J. H., Holyoak, K. J., Nisbett, R. E., & Thagard, P. R. (1986). *Induction: Processes of inference, learning, and discovery*. Cambridge, MA: MIT Press.

Hommes, C. (2013). Reflexivity, expectations feedback and almost self-fulfilling equilibrium: Economic theory, empirical evidence and laboratory experiments. *Journal of Economic Methodology, 20*, 406–419.

Hull, D. L. (1988). *Science as a process: An evolutionary account of the social and conceptual development of science*. Chicago, IL: University of Chicago Press.

Ioannides, J., & Doucouliagos, C. (2013). What's to know about the credibility of empirical economics? *Journal of Economic Surveys, 27*, 997–1004.

Kuhn, T. S. (1962). *The structure of scientific revolutions*. Chicago, IL: University of Chicago Press.

Lucas, R. E., & Prescott, E. C. (1971). Investment under uncertainty. *Econometrica, 39*, 659–681.

Miller, J. H., & Page, S. E. (2007). *Complex adaptive systems: An introduction to computational models of social life*. Princeton, NJ: Princeton University Press.

Mirowski, P. (1989). *More heat than light: Economics as social physics, physics as nature's economics*. Cambridge: Cambridge University Press.

Muth, J. E. (1961). Rational expectations and the theory of price movements. *Econometrica, 29*, 315–335.

Popper, K. R. (1935). *Logik der Forschung*. Vienna: First English edition (1959) *The logic of scientific discovery*, London: Hutchinson Verlag von Julius Springer.

Popper, K. R. (1972). *Objective knowledge: An evolutionary approach*. Oxford: Clarendon Press.

Popper, K. R. (1984). Evolutionary epistemology. In J. W. Pollard (Ed.), *Evolutionary theory: Paths into the future* (pp. 239–254). London: Wiley.

Schopf, J. W. (2000). Solution to Darwin's dilemma: Discovery of the missing Precambrian record of life. *Proceedings of the National Academy of Sciences, 97*, 6947–6953.

Soros, G. (1987). *The Alchemy of finance*. Hoboken, NJ: Wiley.

Soros, G. (1998). *The crisis of global capitalism: Open society endangered*. New York, NY: Public Affairs.

Soros, G. (2000). *Open society: Reforming global capitalism*. New York, NY: Public Affairs.

Soros, G. (2006). *The age of fallibility: Consequences of the war on terror*. New York, NY: Public Affairs.

Soros, G. (2008). *The new paradigm for financial markets the credit crisis and what it means*. New York, NY: Public Affairs.

Soros, G. (2009). *The crash of 2008 and what it means: The new paradigm for financial markets*. New York, NY: Public Affairs.

Soros, G. (2010). *The Soros lectures at the Central European University*. New York, NY: Public Affairs.

Soros, G. (2012). *Financial Turmoil in the United States and Europe: Essays*. New York, NY: Public Affairs.

Soros, G. (2013). Fallibility, reflexivity and the human uncertainty principle. *Journal of Economic Methodology, 20*, 309–329.

Sterman, J. (2000). *Business dynamics: Systems thinking and modelling for a complex world.* New York, NY: McGraw Hill.

Toulmin, S. (1972). *Human understanding: The collective use and evolution of concepts.* Princeton, NJ: Princeton University Press.

Umpleby, S. (2007). Reflexivity in social systems: The theories of George Soros. *Systems Research and Behavioral Science, 24*, 515–522.

Umpleby, S. (2010). From complexity to reflexivity: Underlying logics used in science. *Journal of the Washington Academy of Sciences, 96*, 15–26.

Wiener, N. (1948). *Cybernetics or control and communication in the animal and machine.* New York, NY: Wiley.

Reflexivity unpacked: performativity, uncertainty and analytical monocultures

Richard Bronk

London School of Economics and Political Science, European Institute, London, UK

This paper analyses Soros' theory of reflexivity by breaking it down into several component concepts that are individually well analysed in existing literature – including performativity, self-reinforcing feedback loops and uncertainty. By focusing on the cognitive myopia implied by analytical monocultures and on the indeterminacy implied by innovation, it helps establish boundaries of applicability for reflexivity (as opposed to standard economic) models. It argues that Soros largely ignores a key element in the formation of self-reinforcing delusions or market bubbles – the role played in conditions of uncertainty by homogeneous social narratives and shared mental models. This paper also examines how social learning, rhetoric, power, emotional contagion, the discourse of 'best practice', 'and Keynes' beauty contest may lead to such shared narratives and analytical homogeneity in markets. It concludes that market instability results when there is insufficient cognitive diversity or heterogeneity of beliefs among actors to enable them to spot anomalies and novelties.

Introduction

By his own admission, Soros' theories of 'reflexivity', 'fallibility' and the 'human uncertainty principle' have largely been developed in his own mind (2013, p. 328) rather than standing on the shoulders of scholars in economics and related disciplines. This may account for the boldness of the challenge he presents to standard economic theories, but also for some lack of nuance. There is room to add intellectual value by relating Soros' practical insights to well-developed theories in the literature. For example, Soros' emphasis on human fallibility and the central importance of uncertainty is less foreign to economics than his writings sometimes suggest. Not only Knight (1921), but also Keynes (1936), Hayek (1948) and Shackle (1992 [1972]) saw uncertainty and the precariousness of knowledge as central facts about markets; modern information economics starts from the assumption of asymmetric information; and Kahneman and Tversky (2000) stress the importance of contingent mental frames.

Soros sometimes defines 'reflexivity' broadly as a 'new label for the two-way interaction between thinking and reality' (1998, p. 10). Elsewhere he uses the term in a more specific sense to refer to the influence of contingent biases and distortions in beliefs (or theories) on the course of events they are supposed simply to reflect (or predict) and to the feedback loops by which the events so structured then influence in turn the beliefs (or theories). Crucially, these feedback loops are seen as sometimes becoming self-reinforcing and leading financial markets far from equilibrium. Again, at the level of component ideas, little of this is new. Even standard economics, for example, frequently assumes that its theories can be 'performative' in the sense of helping design 'perfect' markets, and likewise (e.g. the Lucas critique) that expectations influence behaviour, while behavioural economists look at the contingent effects of framing biases. At the same time, economic journals and the writings of complexity theorists (e.g. Arthur, 1994) are replete with analysis of increasing returns, path dependence, punctuated equilibria or dynamic disequilibrium. Soros' main achievement is perhaps to link the importance of self-reinforcing feedback loops to imperfect knowledge and to see them both as particularly prevalent in financial markets. For, this is the one area that until recently was seen as relatively safe territory for pure rationality and equilibrium assumptions, thanks to posted prices, frequent trades, standardised products and electronic information feeds. But here, too, Soros has illustrious antecedents. For example, Minsky (2008 [1986]) analysed the instability of financial markets, where market reactions appear to validate early forays into speculative finance leading to euphoric excesses.

Soros' theory shares at least one feature with the standard economics of rational expectations and equilibrium thinking he decries: it is drawn up as a universal theory and one that is almost a mirror image of the standard theory that prices reflect *all* available information and that expectations tend on average to be correct in competitive markets. For Soros, market prices 'do not accurately reflect' fundamental value; 'participants' views of the world never perfectly correspond to the actual state of affairs'; and expectations 'are likely to diverge from reality' (2013, pp. 310, 322). He does allow that 'negative feedback' may on occasion lead to equilibrium by causing beliefs 'to correspond to the actual state of affairs', but he sees this standard economic assumption as an extreme and '*limiting* case' (2013, p. 322f). Even if Soros is correct on this last point, his own equally polarised view of (nearly) universal fallibility is similarly unconvincing. For while, as recent history shows, mass price distortions and market bubbles are important and life-changing events, Hayek (1948) is also correct that, in many types of market, the marvel is rather how much information is widely conveyed in abbreviated form by the price mechanism. It is this 'wisdom of prices' emerging from the continuous process of market interaction that individuals can often use to supplement their own limited local knowledge in order to coordinate their actions successfully with others (Bronk, 2013). This paper therefore follows Willett (2010) in arguing that Soros should not aim for a comprehensive new paradigm to replace either standard or (the rather different) Hayekian economics, but instead should acknowledge that both they and his own theory capture certain important but partial truths about markets. The crucial task then becomes to work out the boundaries of applicability of each approach. To do this, we need to re-examine the nature and prevalence of uncertainty and the epistemic and market mechanisms that sometimes (but not always) lead to destabilising self-reinforcing feedback loops between beliefs and actions. But first it is helpful to examine two distinct if complementary kinds of reflexivity – the performative impact of theory (or beliefs) on behaviour, and the theoretical construction of data used to test the same theories.

Two kinds of reflexivity

Soros argues that social phenomena are influenced by theories used to explain them; and he argues that, when we face uncertainty, our guesses as to how the future will unfold find expression in stock prices, and these 'stock prices have a way of affecting the fundamentals' by altering the cost of capital (1998, p. 49). In this way, theories and beliefs may be self-fulfilling, and, as reality catches up with beliefs or theoretical expectations, it serves to reconfirm them. These self-reinforcing belief–behaviour–belief feedback loops are the essence of Soros' definition of reflexivity. MacKenzie (2008, p. 12) argues similarly that financial economics theory has to some extent formatted and structured markets in its own image, acting as 'an active force transforming its environment, not a camera passively recording it'. He distinguishes between 'Barnesian performativity', where use of an economic model (e.g. by arbitrageurs) alters outcomes in such a way that they 'better correspond to the model' (with resulting 'self-validating feedback loops'), and 'counterperformativity', where practical use of theory leads to outcomes that 'conform less well to the theory or model' (2008, p. 19). It is tempting to reinterpret the two stages of Soros' bubble scenario in terms of these two forms of performativity in sequence: a dominant narrative or model creating outcomes in its own image that serve to increase confidence in the narrative or model, until the point when its inherent contradictions lead to a sharp unravelling of widespread positions and beliefs. What is not clear is why Soros assumes that Barnesian performativity always leads to tears in this way. While he argues that equilibrium is a 'deceptive concept' and that the fundamentals are altered by beliefs (Soros, 1998, p. 49), there is lurking in his thought a residual equilibrium notion of reversion to fundamentals – of an inevitable and growing divergence between perceptions and reality that must be resolved. In fact, performativity is so tricky for economic actors precisely because it creates a new knowledge problem: we cannot know *ex ante* to what extent having a novel idea will make it happen. From time to time, new ideas do change the world forever, and it is this fact that leads many to dream that a new era is dawning when none exists – when beliefs have merely led to short-term moves in line with predictions.

Performativity (belief–behaviour–belief feedback loops) is only one form of reflexivity. To explain why economic actors fail to spot anomalies and contradictions until it is too late and fail to converge on the right theory, we need to articulate another 'epistemic' version of reflexivity – one that is at best implicit in Soros' observation that the mental constructs we use in making sense of the world inevitably lead to distortions. Soros focuses on the performative impact of these distortions in shaping the world. But models and metaphors have another insidious effect: the inevitable distortion of their particular focus and conceptual frameworks structures the very data and facts we use to assess theories and beliefs. As post-Kantian and postmodern philosophy argues, the world-as-we-see-it is partly constructed by the theories and narratives that act as our cognitive spectacles (Bronk, 2009). This means that if we all come to rely on *one* modelling framework, narrative or set of beliefs, we all tend to see things in the *same* way and 'to share the *same* cognitive myopia' (Bronk, 2013, p. 96). As Green and Shapiro (1994, p. 42) put it, our theoretical commitments can 'contaminate the sampling of evidence' and make us less likely to spot or interpret evidence in a way that will challenge rather than confirm these theoretical commitments. This epistemic version of reflexivity (theory–data–theory feedback loops) makes theories or narratives more invulnerable to anomalies and plays a crucial role in explaining financial bubbles. For example, prior to 2007, key players were in the grip of an analytical monoculture, and had so internalised one set of efficient market models, that 'they were simply not predisposed to see problems that were emerging because their theoretical and conceptual framework had no place for them' (Bronk, 2011, p. 15).

The indeterminacy of innovation and self-reinforcing feedback loops

Soros argues that the contingent distortions and errors of fallible thinking participants introduce an indeterminacy and path dependence in markets that make them unpredictable and subject to periodic self-reinforcing feedback loops. By contrast, rational expectations theory assumes that errors will be random (and tend to cancel out) because any systematic errors in forecasting will be eliminated in competitive markets. To understand under what conditions this intuitively plausible idea is likely to be mistaken and Soros' theory nearer the mark, we need to delve deeper than Soros does into the origins and prevalence of Knightian uncertainty.

Whenever future reality largely consists in 'given' options and preferences, known probabilities and an optimal outcome already 'out there' that can act as an anchor for expectations – upon which the beliefs of rational agents can converge thanks to competitive pressures – then the rational expectations hypothesis may be plausible. But very often the future is far from 'given'. Rather as Shackle (1979) points out, our imaginations inject novelty and hence an irreducible uncertainty into markets. We invent new options, new possibilities and new preferences. Such innovations make the future genuinely indeterminate. We cannot know *ex ante* the outcome of the novel choices we make, and 'this uncertainty is compounded by uncertainty about the second-order creative reactions of others' (Bronk, 2011, p. 9). Moreover, as Arthur (1994) argues, technological innovations tend to be subject to positive feedback and unpredictable threshold and lock-in effects. It is the ontological indeterminacy implied by novelty and innovation that ensures that our expectations must be partly the product of either individual imagination or shared narratives rather than rational calculation (Bronk, 2013; Shackle, 1992 [1972]), and it is this indeterminacy that removes any fixed anchor for competing beliefs and leaves scope for the performative impact of contingent narratives and beliefs to be transformative of our behaviour in unpredictable ways. Indeterminacy is thus a spur to destabilising self-reinforcing feedback loops as much as a result of them. It follows that financial markets may be prone to particularly high levels of instability (and to self-reinforcing new era stories) whenever innovation in financial products or in economic policy is high, as in the decade before 2007.

The destabilising role of homogeneous narratives and shared mental models

It is a standard assumption of economics that the preferences, beliefs and expectations of economic actors are revealed in actions and the prices willingly posted or paid and that these prices then lead to modifications in the beliefs and behaviour of other market participants. This weak form of the performativity of beliefs is normally assumed to be consistent with markets tending towards equilibrium. As we have seen, though, a tendency to equilibrium is likely to be absent in the indeterminate conditions of widespread innovation – when there is no pre-existing set of fundamentals on which beliefs and expectations can converge. But even in such indeterminate and uncertain conditions, performativity of beliefs need not lead to the sort of deceptive feedback loops and widespread price distortions that pre-occupy Soros. Rather, performativity will only normally lead to this outcome when a key pre-condition is met: when *all or most* actors come to share the *same or similar* beliefs, narrative or modelling framework. While Soros does speak of a 'prevailing bias' leading to a prevailing trend (1998, p. 52), and of correlated errors (2013, p. 322), he largely ignores this pre-condition for deceptive reflexive feedback loops to take hold.

Hayek (1948) argued that the price mechanism registers the market impact of the decentralised cognition, local tacit knowledge and diverse perspectives of all market participants. When this is true, mass delusions and market bubbles are unlikely, since there is a good chance that anomalies and novelties will be spotted by someone. Markets may not tend to an optimal equilibrium, but the summary message of market prices should at least be informative. As Keynes (1936, p. 154) pointed out, however, in conditions of uncertainty, we tend to resort to conventions and succumb to 'mass psychology' and 'waves of optimistic and pessimistic sentiment'. Faced with uncertainty, we adopt shared 'new era stories' that (together with levels of confidence) are subject to contagious transmission in the manner of epidemics (Akerlof & Shiller, 2009, p. 55f). The result is a growing (and unstable) homogeneity of stories and beliefs, and a tendency to '*groupfeel*' that undermines the cognitive diversity critical to the health of markets (Tuckett, 2011, p. 19). Since all narratives or conventional models have their weaknesses, the resulting analytical monoculture makes widespread cognitive myopia and unsustainable bubbles more likely. Of course, this sort of analytical homogeneity is not entirely irrational or unhealthy. Indeed, 'shared mental models' constructed in the face of uncertainty are partly the valuable product of indirect social learning and proven heuristics that reduce the costs of cognition; but their use is also likely to imply crisis-driven lumpy cognitive adjustments or re-evaluations, associated with 'punctuated equilibria', rather than smooth Bayesian updating (Denzau & North, 1994; Ferguson, 2013).

Even a cursory glance at the period leading up the post-2007 financial crisis suggests the presence of analytical monocultures in financial markets and that this did indeed lead to blindness to the unexpected and to persistent mispricing. Power (2007, p. viii), for example, argues that the entire financial industry and its regulators succumbed to a 'grand narrative of risk management' that confused uncertainty with measurable risk. VaR models that purported to measure the probability of failure calculated on the basis of data on the past became the homogeneous 'best practice' frame for managers and regulators alike. They promised, as Haldane (2009, p. 4) puts it, a 'new era' of 'simultaneous higher return and lower risk' as a result of 'a shift in the technological frontier of risk management'. In fact, of course, the widespread use of such Gaussian distribution-derived models implied a shared blindness to emerging 'fat tail' risks. Worse still, given the performativity of theory and beliefs, it led to homogeneity of business strategy and behaviour and to dangerously high correlations in markets (Bronk, 2011). In this way, it can be argued that it was the homogeneity of beliefs (rather than simply the fallibility and performativity of beliefs) that led to reflexive feedback loops and market instability.

Social and market mechanisms leading to analytical monocultures

If the dangers of analytical and modelling monocultures are clear, this still begs the question of how prevalent they are and what mechanisms (beyond the contagion and social learning effects already mentioned) might be responsible for their frequent emergence in financial markets.

Three social mechanisms are noteworthy. First, the whole discourse of 'best practice' implies that it is wise for all players to converge on a supposedly optimal set of models and beliefs. This ignores, of course, the ontological indeterminacy implied by innovation, which entails that we cannot know *ex ante* what best practice or the best model will be. What is more, the cognitive myopia implied by reliance on a single modelling or analytic framework ensures that we may be slow to question or update established best practice, even assuming the presence of institutional incentives to challenge the status quo. Second, a number of players use rhetoric to establish the hegemony of their favoured narrative or template for the future. For example, as Holmes (2009, p. 385f) argues, central banks devote enormous efforts to composing persuasive narratives that 'serve as an analytical bridge to the near future' and serve to align expectations with their chosen inflation, growth or financial stability target. If these narratives are credible, then they have a good chance of shaping reality in their own image – of being self-fulfilling prophecies. It may, of course, be that the narrative is so flawed that any initial credibility only sets up the conditions for a sharp market reaction when its flaws are revealed. But there is plenty of evidence that credible central bank narratives can have a permanent impact on the shape of the future. Lastly, the power to establish the dominance of one narrative or model is not only the preserve of rhetoric, credibility and government power. It is also a function of market power. Too little focus is given to how far the impact on prices of particular narratives, models or perspectives is a function of the market power or wealth of those to whom they belong (Bronk, 2013).

A further mechanism leading to self-reinforcing feedback loops in markets is described by Keynes (1936, p. 156) in his analogy of a newspaper beauty contest, where the prize goes to the competitor who best anticipates 'what average opinion expects the average opinion to be'. Financial market investors make money (at least in the short term) by second guessing what the dominant narrative or opinion will be. The risk in this process is that the efficient markets hypothesis view that prices reflect *all* available information then becomes particularly misleading. For, in Keynes' beauty contest, market participants have every incentive to free ride on the cognitive efforts of influential opinion formers and to assume that whatever emerges as the dominant narrative is sufficient for their ends. The result is prices that reflect a narrower cognitive base than would otherwise be the case (Bronk, 2013). In some ways, this process is similar to an 'information cascade', in which market participants assume that the crowd is likely to be right and end up economising on (or ignoring) their own cognition (Cassidy, 2009; Surowiecki, 2004). The result again is market prices that reflect a widely shared narrative or belief rather than the sum of decentralised perspectives or knowledge. In such circumstances, the chances of widespread mispricing and unpredictable market bubbles are much higher.

Conclusion: cognitive diversity as antidote to instability

This paper has argued that Soros under-theorises the conditions in which self-reinforcing feedback loops between beliefs and behaviour tend to become destabilising. These conditions are, first, the indeterminacy (or Knightian uncertainty) caused by innovation; and, second, the cognitive myopia implied by reliance across much of the market on a single analytical framework. Together these imply that when navigating the uncertain future, the best antidote to instability is cognitive diversity and constant questioning of best practice and consensus. Any single theory or idea has weaknesses, and homogeneity of belief therefore leads to highly correlated errors. Ideas can become 'too big too fail'.

There is, of course, a trade-off between the cumulative benefits of social learning as crystallised in shared mental models and the dangers of cognitive homogeneity. But because of the *epistemic* reflexive feedback loops by which a shared mental model influences the filtering and mental construction of data and evidence used to test it, and the *performative* reflexive feedback loops by which the same model influences behaviour (and vice versa), market participants are always at risk from self-reinforcing delusions and bubbles – unless they have access to the disruptive influence of alternative theory. As Feyerabend (2010 [1975], p. 20) puts it, there 'exist facts which cannot be unearthed except with the help of alternatives to the theory to be tested'. In order to spot anomalies and novelties that will challenge the validity of widespread beliefs, we need to display the sort of 'critical attitude' and constant 'self-doubt' that Soros (1998, p. 25f) sees as key to his investment record. We must display the 'organized dissonance' and marshal the 'heterogeneous perspectives' that Stark (2009, pp. 27, 147) argues are essential for entrepreneurial and investment success.

References

Akerlof, G. A., & Shiller, R. J. (2009). *Animal spirits: How human psychology drives the economy and why it matters*. Princeton, NJ: Princeton University Press.

Arthur, W. B. (1994). *Increasing returns and path dependence in the economy*. Ann Arbor, MI: University of Michigan Press.

Bronk, R. (2009). *The romantic economist: Imagination in economics*. Cambridge: Cambridge University Press.

Bronk, R. (2011). Uncertainty, modelling monocultures and the financial crisis. *The Business Economist, 42*, 5–18.

Bronk, R. (2013). Hayek on the wisdom of prices: A reassessment. *Erasmus Journal for Philosophy and Economics, 6*, 82–107.

Cassidy, J. (2009). *How markets fail*. London: Allen Lane.

Denzau, A. T., & North, D. C. (1994). Shared mental models: Ideologies and institutions. *Kyklos, 47*, 3–29.

Ferguson, W. D. (2013). *Collective action and exchange*. Stanford, CA: Stanford University Press.

Feyerabend, P. (2010 [1975]). *Against method*. London: Verso.

Green, D. P., & Shapiro, I. (1994). *Pathologies of rational choice theory*. New Haven, CT: Yale University Press.

Haldane, A. G. (2009). Why banks failed the stress test. Bank of England. Retrieved from http://www.bankofengland.co.uk/archive/Documents/historicpubs/speeches/2009/speech374.pdf

Hayek, F. A. (1948). *Individualism and the economic order*. Chicago, IL: Chicago University Press.

Holmes, D. R. (2009). Economy of words. *Cultural Anthropology, 24*, 381–419.

Kahneman, D., & Tversky, A. (Eds.). (2000). *Choices, values and frames*. New York, NY: Cambridge University Press.

Keynes, J. M. (1936). *The general theory of employment, interest and money*. London: Macmillan.

Knight, F. H. (1921). *Risk, uncertainty and profit*. Boston, MA: Houghton Mifflin.

MacKenzie, D. (2008). *An engine, not a camera: How financial models shape markets*. Cambridge, MA: MIT Press.

Minsky, H. P. (2008 [1986]). *Stabilising an unstable economy*. New York, NY: McGraw Hill.

Power, M. (2007). *Organized uncertainty: Designing a world of risk management*. Oxford: Oxford University Press.

Shackle, G. L. S. (1979). *Imagination and the nature of choice*. Edinburgh: Edinburgh University Press.

Shackle, G. L. S. (1992 [1972]). *Epistemics and economics: A critique of economic doctrines*. New Brunswick, NJ: Transaction.

Soros, G. (1998). *The crisis of global capitalism*. London: Little Brown.

Soros, G. (2013). Fallibility, reflexivity and the human uncertainty principle. *Journal of Economic Methodology, 20*, 309–329.

Stark, D. (2009). *The sense of dissonance: Accounts of worth in economic life*. Princeton, NJ: Princeton University Press.

Surowiecki, J. (2004). *The wisdom of crowds: Why the many are smarter than the few*. London: Abacus.

Tuckett, D. (2011). *Minding the markets: An emotional finance view of financial instability*. London: Palgrave Macmillan.

Willett, T. D. (2010). George Soros' reflexivity and the global financial crisis. *World Economics, 11*, 207–214.

George Soros: Hayekian?

Bruce Caldwell

Department of Economics, Duke University, Durham, NC, USA

This paper examines many similarities in the methodological and ontological views of George Soros and Friedrich Hayek.

The title is intentionally provocative. In his 2010 book *The Soros Lectures at the Central European University*, George Soros wrote that the Austrian Nobel laureate Friedrich A. Hayek 'became an apostle of the Chicago School of Economics, where market fundamentalism originated' (Soros, 2010, p. 22).[1] Given that Soros has long been a severe critic of market fundamentalism, it would seem that Hayek and he must be on opposite ends of the spectrum. For precursors, Soros looks to economists such as J.M. Keynes and Frank Knight, to the sociologist Robert Merton, and to the philosopher Karl Popper, all of whose writings in various ways anticipated certain key Sorosian ideas.

In the first two sections of this paper, I will show that in fact F.A. Hayek and George Soros share many views in common, some of them ontological (having to do with the nature of reality) and others methodological (having to do with the appropriate way to study and represent economic phenomena). I will then point out some differences between them, though we will see that, even here, they are closer than one might initially expect.

If at the end of the day George Soros still rejects the label of Hayekian, perhaps he will not mind if we instead describe Hayek as an ontological and methodological Sorosian, *avant la lettre*!

Some fundamental elements of the Sorosian vision

In his paper, George Soros offers an account of how humans make their way in the world. The starting point is to recognize that we inhabit a complex environment. We use various methods of simplification to try to make sense of the complex reality we face: 'generalizations, dichotomies, metaphors, decision rules, and moral precepts, just to mention a few' (Soros, 2013, p. 311). These mental constructs often take on a life of their own, which obscures our understanding of reality. The structure of our brain provides another source of distortion, something that Soros claims substantiates David Hume's insight that reason is the slave of passion (Soros, 2013, p. 311). Finally, there is the simple but significant observation that we cannot know what other people know; different people have different perceptions of the world. In the end, these limitations imply that the knowledge that humans possess is inherently fallible: our view of the world for a variety of reasons simply does not, and cannot, correspond with reality (Soros, 2013, pp. 310 and 311).

It is also the case, however, that our views of how the world works inform our actions, which can affect the world. This is captured through the concept of reflexivity. Soros describes thinking humans as possessing a cognitive function (which is operative when they try to understand the world in which they live) and a manipulative function (which is operative when they try to affect that world). The two functions can interfere with each other – when the actions of people affect the world, that interferes with our understanding of it; similarly, attempts to affect the world bring no guarantee of success, which may feed back into our knowledge. When the cognitive and manipulative functions collide, uncertainty increases.

The way that this plays out in the world is via feedback loops: 'participants' views influence but do not determine the course of events, and the course of events influences but does not determine the participants' views' (Soros, 2013, p. 312). Negative feedback loops bring the participants' subjective views ever closer in alignment with objective reality; the limiting case of this sort of process is captured by the notion of movement toward equilibrium. Positive feedback loops occur when the participants' subjective views become ever more removed from reality, yet are self-reinforcing. In this case, reality eventually intervenes, which produces a spiral in the opposite direction.

Soros' description of how the world works is obscured rather than being illuminated by the methods that the social sciences have adopted. Though Soros admires and respects the philosopher Karl Popper's emphasis on testing and the symmetry between explanation and prediction, he feels these insights apply most directly to the natural sciences, where reflexivity does not come up. They are less applicable to the social sciences, so Popper's unity of science thesis fails. Economists, hoping to imitate the successes of the physical sciences, adopted their methods. This is exemplified by constructs such as the efficient market hypothesis and the theory of rational expectations. These attempts to copy the methods of the natural sciences reflect little more than physics envy, or scientism. Soros first began to suspect that the models that economists were using were deficient when as a student he learned the theory of perfect competition, which seemed to have no connection to real competition as it exists in the world (Soros, 2013, p. 309).

All of this has implications for our understanding of financial market bubbles. If the efficient market hypothesis is correct, markets tend toward an equilibrium in which market prices reflect underlying objective reality. Positive feedback loops are ruled out by definition. But 'that postulate has no resemblance to reality':

> In practice market participants' expectations diverge from reality to a greater or lesser extent and their errors may be correlated and significantly biased. That is the generic cause of price distortions. So equilibrium, which is the *central* case in mainstream economic theory, turns out to be an extreme case of negative feedback, a *limiting* case in my conceptual framework. (Soros, 2013, pp. 322 and 323)

Crucially, the very *belief* that the efficient market hypothesis is true exacerbates the self-reinforcing positive feedback aspect of a bubble: reflexivity at work. Thus, those who believe in the hypothesis think that the system is self-stabilizing and that therefore no regulation of it is necessary. If regulators are among those who believe in it, this prevents them from taking steps to halt the bubble. When a bubble bursts, it typically leads to regulatory reform, but such reform is itself a reflexive process, because both market participants and regulators are plagued with imperfect information.

The theory of rational expectations is similarly problematical and misleading. Real market participants have to try to anticipate the future when they make decisions today. But the future is uncertain, and the decisions they make introduce further price distortions.

In short, current economic theory is of little use for understanding and counteracting financial bubbles. This is why economics requires new economic thinking.

Some fundamental elements of the Hayekian vision

As it was for Soros, the starting point for Hayek is that we live in a complex environment. Hayek's description of how humans interact with that environment also has many things in common with that of Soros.

First, there is the fact that humans (and indeed other animals) adopt often simple decision rules in trying to deal with a complex environment. As Hayek put it, 'Man is as much a rule-following animal as a purpose-seeking one' (Hayek, 1973, p. 11). Interestingly, Hayek would often invoke David Hume's writings about the limitations of reason in seeking the origin of some of these (and particularly the moral) rules: Hume's statement that 'The rules of morality are not the conclusions of our reason' is one of the three epigrams that Hayek chose to place on the title page of his last book, *The Fatal Conceit* (Hayek, 1988). Hayek also wrote about the structure of the brain and how its operation gives rise to the phenomenal or sensory order we experience, which natural science tells us is different from the underlying physical order (Hayek, 1952).

Perhaps most fundamentally, an essential element of the Austrian vision is its emphasis on subjectivism. In his appropriately named 'The Facts of the Social Sciences,' Hayek insisted that the concepts we employ in the social sciences

> refer not to some objective properties possessed by the things...but to views which some other person holds about the things. ...we could say that all these objects are defined not in terms of their 'real' properties but in terms of opinions people hold about them. In short, in the social sciences the things are what the people think they are. (Hayek, [1943] 1948, pp. 59–60)

The 'facts' of the social sciences, then, are all interpretations.

That our interpretations of reality may be different from objective reality is the starting point for Hayek's discussion of the problems of equilibrium theory in his 1937 piece, 'Economics and Knowledge.' In that seminal paper, Hayek notes that equilibrium theory assumes that all agents in the economy have the same, objectively correct knowledge. In reality, of course, different people have access to different bits of knowledge – knowledge is dispersed – and some of what people think they know is in fact incorrect, due to the subjectivity of our beliefs and to the fact that we base our actions in the present at least in part on what we expect to happen in the future. Hayek ties this all together by defining equilibrium in terms of compatibility of expectations:

> ...the concept of equilibrium merely means that the foresight of different members of society is in a special sense correct. It must be correct in the sense that every person's plan is based on the expectation of just those actions of other people which those other people intend to perform and that all these plans are based on the expectation of the same set of external facts... Correct foresight is then not, as it has sometimes been understood, a precondition which must exist in order that equilibrium may be arrived at. It is rather the defining characteristic of a state of equilibrium. (Hayek, [1937] 1948, p. 42)

Hayek recognizes that this is a very strict condition that raises more questions than it answers: 'the question why the data in the subjective sense of the term should ever come to correspond to the objective data is one of the main problems we have to answer' (Hayek, [1937] 1948, p. 39). To answer the question, we must examine the conditions under which a tendency toward equilibrium might exist, and also the process by which individual knowledge gets coordinated.

Significantly, in a later paper, Hayek pointed out that the dispersion of knowledge implies that the standard theory of perfect competition, because it assumes that market participants have access to complete, objectively correct knowledge, is unhelpful for understanding how actual markets work:

I shall attempt to show that what the theory of perfect competition discusses has little claim to be called 'competition' at all and that its conclusions are of little use as guides to policy. ... competition is by its nature a dynamic process whose essential characteristics are assumed away by the assumptions underlying static analysis. (Hayek, [1946] 1948, pp. 92 and 94)

Thus, Hayek too was dissatisfied with the theory of perfect competition, and contrasted it with the dynamic market process that represents competition as it exists in the real world.

Like Soros, Hayek was wary about the dangers of scientism, a phrase that he coined in his paper 'Scientism and the Study of Society.' And like Soros, he initially drew the contrast in terms of the differences between the natural and the social sciences, defining scientism as the 'slavish imitation' by the latter of the methods of the former (Hayek, [1942–1944] 2010, p. 80; cf. [1943] 1948, pp. 57 and 58).

Hayek was a great friend of Soros' teacher, the philosopher Karl Popper, and in the 1950s, Hayek began to accept Popper's argument about the unity of the sciences. This would seem to undermine Hayek's earlier argument that the social sciences must not try to imitate the methods of the natural sciences. As was mentioned earlier, Soros criticizes Popper's unity of science thesis in his paper, so surely here is an area where he differs from Hayek (and from Popper).

But as it turns out, that is not the case, for Hayek's position differs from that of Popper in just those points where Soros' does. In the 1950s, Hayek began to drop the natural science–social science distinction and instead began to differentiate among sciences that study simple versus those that study complex phenomena. Because it studies complex, structured orders, economics is one of the latter. For Hayek, all sciences follow the same method. But for those that study complex orders, prediction will be more difficult (only pattern predictions will be possible) and as a result the clean falsification of theories will be undermined (Hayek, [1955] 1967, [1964] 1967). So though Hayek endorsed the unity of science thesis, he also thought that fields that study complex orders are unable to follow the strict falsificationist philosophy that Popper had developed with the natural sciences in mind. In this regard, Hayek and Soros again agree about the limits of Popper's methodology when applied to social sciences such as economics that study complex phenomena.

By the end of his life, Hayek became more and more critical of equilibrium theory for explaining the workings of a market economy. In a talk he gave at the London School of Economics in February 1981 to mark the 50th anniversary of his 'Prices and Production' lectures there, Hayek said that the metaphor of a stream (or, rather, 'countless interlocking and intertwined flows') might be more apt for describing the structure of production in a market economy. At one point, he even states

The achievement of an equilibrium is strictly impossible. Indeed, in a literal sense, *a stream can never be in equilibrium*, because it is disequilibrium which keeps it flowing and determines its directions. (Hayek, [1981] 2012, p. 338, emphasis in the original)

Thus, Hayek shared Soros' concerns about the adequacy of equilibrium theory. As we saw above, Hayek also emphasized the importance of expectations and forward-looking behavior. He never wrote about the theory of rational expectations. But in general Austrians think of current market prices not as representing reality but merely as summaries of recent economic conditions, or recent economic history (see, e.g., Mises, [1934] 2012, p. 326). They also endorse the Knightian/Keynesian distinction between risk and uncertainty.[2]

So, Austrians would share George Soros' view that 'new economic thinking' requires that we go beyond the current mainstream theories. Where would they go? For Hayek, author of papers such as 'The Theory of Complex Phenomena' and 'Rules, Perceptions and Intelligibility,' (Hayek, [1962] 1967, [1964] 1967). I suspect that recent advances in complexity theory would be very attractive. Others working in the Austrian tradition have endorsed the comparative analysis of political and economic institutions, both economic and political, in search of those that are robust in the face of opportunistic behavior and the dispersion of knowledge (Pennington, 2011).

So where do they differ?

So, where do Soros and Hayek differ? The most stark difference concerns the notions of positive and negative feedback loops. Clearly Hayek, as distinct from Soros, focused more on the latter, in emphasizing the coordinative effects of changing (product) market prices. For Hayek, the price structure is a constantly changing panorama. Price changes signal market participants about recent changes in relative scarcities, but they are simultaneously the result of the daily decisions of millions of market participants, who are acting on the basis of their own 'knowledge of the particular circumstances of time and place' (Hayek, [1945] 1948, p. 80). Given the complexity of the system (which both Soros and Hayek recognize and emphasize), clearly people can be and often are wrong in their interpretations of and reactions to the ever-changing array of prices; mistakes are ubiquitous. But for Hayek, and the Austrians generally, when people are wrong, that presents a profit opportunity for others, and the actions of those who are alert to the opportunity tend to move the market in the 'right' direction. For the Austrians, there is no *systematic* tendency for entrepreneurial errors to persist (see, e.g., Kirzner, 1997, pp. 81 and 82).

It is quite different for Soros. The essential property of a positive feedback loop is that errors persist and indeed feed upon themselves. How can this happen? Soros discusses this in his paper, and to supplement his discussion, I would further recommend a recent article by Bronk (2013).

Bronk highlights the importance of narratives and mass psychology in situations of radical uncertainty, and how narratives that emphasize the coordinative function of prices can mislead people into thinking that price movements reflect actual relative scarcities rather than a bubble. In doing so, he refers to the work of the British economist G.L.S. Shackle on radical (Shackle's phrase was 'kaleidic') uncertainty in describing how things might go wrong. Shackle was for a time a student of Hayek's at LSE. A later 'Austrian' (whose heritage was actually German) economist, Ludwig Lachmann, used Shackle ideas to criticize Mises and Hayek for an over-emphasis on the coordinative tendencies of markets and specifically for failing to extend subjectivism to the formation of expectations (see, e.g., Lachmann, 1976). Lachmann's work led to his being labeled a 'radical subjectivist' by some Austrians; it led other scholars (the present author among them) to envisage a rapprochement of sorts between post-Keynesians and Lachmann-influenced Austrians in the 1980s, a movement that unfortunately came to naught.

When Hayek wrote about the coordinative aspects of markets, he had product markets in mind. He was not so sanguine about the effects of money and credit (as he put it more than once, money is a 'loose joint' in the market system; see, e.g., Hayek, [1960] 2011, p. 452) and fully understood the role they could play in creating cycles: the title of his first book, after all, was *Monetary Theory and the Trade Cycle* (Hayek, [1933] 2012). Hayek's early writings on the cycle utilized an equilibrium theory framework, and indeed his framework was identified as a precursor by Robert Lucas (Lucas, [1977] 1981). This could be the source of, or evidence for, the idea that Hayek shared certain views in common with Chicago School economists. Others, though, have pointed out the tensions between Hayek's writings on the cycle and his later work on complex phenomena (e.g., Rosner, 1994; Witt, 1997; for more on this, see Caldwell, 2004, pp. 224–230).

So Hayek was no Pollyanna when it came to the stability of the financial system. What policies did he favor? Hayek was good at describing his preferred policy in general terms: he wanted money to be neutral, so that changes in relative prices had the best chance of actually reflecting changing relative scarcities. Unfortunately, he was much less clear as to how this general dictum could be operationalized.

Given that the Austrian story about the origins of the cycle invoke low interest rate regimes that distort the structure of production, he was wary of policies that called for increasing the money supply to counteract the cycle, thinking that this would simply further delay the return to the appropriate structure. This is quite consistent with Soros' argument that 'the intervention of the authorities to deal with periodic financial crises played a crucial role in the development of a "super bubble" that burst in 2007-08' (Soros, 2013, p. 325). Other parts of Soros' account, though, are absent from Hayek's theory, such as the role of conventional narratives in contributing to the positive feedback loop that generated the bubble, and in particular the performative aspects of a belief in market fundamentalism.

Conclusion

I have shown that there are many compatibilities between the views of George Soros and Friedrich Hayek. But what of Hayek's alleged embrace of market fundamentalism? In his Central European University lectures, George Soros criticized the arguments that market fundamentalism makes against government intervention. Market fundamentalism

> ... could have argued that all human constructs are imperfect and social choices involve choosing the lesser evil, and on those grounds government intervention in the economy should be kept to a minimum. That would be a reasonable position. Instead, it claimed that the failures of government intervention proved that free markets are perfect. That is simply bad logic. ... I condemn market fundamentalism as a false and dangerous doctrine, but I am in favor of keeping government intervention and regulations to a minimum for other, better, reasons. (Soros, 2010, p. 86)

Hayek was no market fundamentalist. He insisted that there was a role for government in providing a framework in which a market system could operate. He did not think free markets were perfect, and he was no anarcho-capitalist. He would, in short, agree with Soros' statement in its entirety. I suspect Hayek's 'better reasons' for placing constitutional limits on government intervention and regulations might differ in some details from those of Soros. But given the points they share in common regarding ontological and methodological commitments, perhaps the difference here is small as well.

Notes

1. A similar sentence appeared in the first draft of his paper for JEM, but it was dropped in the final version. It may be that Soros at some point independently reached a similar view to the one that I advance in this paper!
2. The literature on the ways that the Austrians differ from the mainstream is vast; perhaps the best summary is Kirzner 1997.

References

Bronk, R. (2013). Hayek on the wisdom of prices: A reassessment. *Erasmus Journal for Philosophy and Economics*, 6, 82–107.
Caldwell, B. (2004). *Hayek's challenge: An intellectual biography of F.A. Hayek*. Chicago, IL: University of Chicago Press.

Hayek, F. A. ([1933] 2012). Monetary theory and the trade cycle. In H. Klausinger (Ed.), *Business cycles: Part I. The collected works of F.A. Hayek* (Vol. 7). Chicago, IL/London: University of Chicago Press/Routledge.

Hayek, F. A. ([1937] 1948). Economics and knowledge. *Individualism and economic order* (pp. 33–56). Chicago, IL: University of Chicago Press.

Hayek, F. A. ([1942–1944] 2010). Scientism and the study of society. In B. Caldwell (Ed.), *Studies on the abuse and decline of reason. The collected works of F.A. Hayek* (Vol. 13, pp. 75–166). Chicago, IL/London: University of Chicago Press/Routledge.

Hayek, F. A. ([1943] 1948). The facts of the social sciences. *Individualism and economic order* (pp. 57–76). Chicago, IL: University of Chicago Press.

Hayek, F. A. ([1945] 1948). The use of knowledge in society. *Individualism and economic order* (pp. 77–91). Chicago, IL: University of Chicago Press.

Hayek, F. A. ([1946] 1948). The meaning of competition. *Individualism and economic order* (pp. 92–106). Chicago, IL: University of Chicago Press.

Hayek, F. A. (1952). *The sensory order: An inquiry into the foundations of theoretical psychology.* Chicago, IL: University of Chicago Press.

Hayek, F. A. ([1955] 1967). Degrees of explanation. *Studies in philosophy, politics and economics* (pp. 3–21). Chicago, IL: University of Chicago Press.

Hayek, F. A. ([1960] 2011). The constitution of liberty. The collected works of F.A. Hayek. In R. Hamowy (Ed.), (Vol. 17). Chicago, IL/London: University of Chicago Press/Routledge.

Hayek, F. A. ([1962] 1967). Rules, perceptions and intelligibility. *Studies in philosophy, politics and economics* (pp. 43–65). Chicago, IL: University of Chicago Press.

Hayek, F. A. ([1964] 1967). The theory of complex phenomena. *Studies in philosophy, politics and economics* (pp. 22–42). Chicago, IL: University of Chicago Press.

Hayek, F. A. (1973). Rules and Order. *Law, legislation and liberty* (Vol. 1). Chicago, IL/London: University of Chicago Press/Routledge.

Hayek, F. A. ([1981] 2012). The flow of goods and services. In H. Klausinger (Ed.), *Business cycles, Part II. The collected works of F.A. Hayek* (Vol. 8, pp. 331–346). Chicago, IL/London: University of Chicago Press/Routledge.

Hayek, F. A. (1988). *The fatal conceit: The errors of socialism.* Chicago, IL/London: University of Chicago Press/Routledge.

Kirzner, I. (1997). Entrepreneurial discovery and the competitive market process: An Austrian approach. *Journal of Economic Literature, 35,* 60–85.

Lachmann, L. (1976). From Mises to Shackle: An essay on Austrian economics and the Kaleidic Society. *Journal of Economic Literature, 14,* 54–62.

Lucas, R. ([1977] 1981). Understanding business cycles. *Studies in business-cycle theory* (pp. 215–239). Cambridge: MIT Press.

Mises, L. (2012). Monetary and economic problems before, during, and after the Great War. In R. Ebeling (Ed.), *Selected writings of Ludwig von Mises* (Vol. 1). Indianapolis, IN: Liberty Fund.

Pennington, M. (2011). *Robust political economy: Classical liberalism and the future of public policy.* Cheltenham, UK: Edward Elgar.

Rosner, P. (1994). Is Hayek's theory of business cycles an Austrian theory? In J. Birner & R. van Zijp (Eds.), *Hayek, coordination, and evolution: his legacy in philosophy, politics, economics, and the history of ideas* (pp. 51–66). London: Routledge.

Soros, G. (2010). *The Soros lectures at the Central European University.* New York, NY: Public Affairs.

Soros, G. (2013). Fallibility, reflexivity and the human uncertainty principle. *Journal of Economic Methodology, 20,* 309–329.

Witt, U. (1997). The Hayekian puzzle: spontaneous order and the business cycle. *Scottish Journal of Political Economy, 44,* 44–58.

Reflections on Soros: Mach, Quine, Arthur and far-from-equilibrium dynamics

Rod Cross[a], Harold Hutchinson[b], Harbir Lamba[c] and Doug Strachan[a]

[a]Department of Economics, University of Strathclyde, Glasgow, UK; [b]Investec Bank plc., London, UK; [c]Department of Mathematical Sciences, George Mason University, Fairfax, VA, USA

We argue that the Soros account of reflexivity does not provide a clear-cut distinction between a social science such as economics and the physical sciences. It is pointed out that the participants who attempt to learn from refutations of conjectures in the Soros world are likely to be haunted by the Duhem–Quine problem of conjointness of hypotheses and unfocused refutation. On a more constructive note, we argue that models of inductive learning, in which participants form conjectures on the basis of strictly limited information sets, can capture the basic thrust of the Soros position. The conjectures are in motion, as the participants attempt to avoid those that are systematically wrong, and there is something vague and uncertain about what can be learned from experience and refutations. The only notion of market efficiency in this world is one contingent on the strictly limited and varied information sets in play. Finally we present a mathematical model and numerical simulations that help justify the causal relationship between reflexivity and far-from-equilibrium dynamics postulated by Soros.

It is not uncommon to hear those engaged in business or financial markets say that economic theories might be OK in theory, but not in practice. Not many of these practitioners open up a dialogue by saying precisely what is wrong with the theories in question, and how the theories might be reformulated to improve their alignment with practice. George Soros is a notable exception. 'Fallibility, Reflexivity and the Human Uncertainty Principle' (Soros, 2013) is a valuable addition to his earlier contributions to such a dialogue.

In what follows, we will attempt to be constructive in relation to aspects of the Soros position that we have selected for attention. A first section deals with the Soros guillotine between the physical and social sciences, considering the treatment of this issue by Mach (1883). Then we comment on the Popperian perspective underlying the views of Soros, using the lens of Quine (1980). A third section deals with the learning problems raised by the Soros position, using the El Farol bar attendance parable of Arthur (1994) as a vehicle for exposition. The following section considers the implications of the Baddeley (2004) concept of working memory for the Soros critique of the rational expectations hypothesis (REH) and efficient markets hypothesis (EMH). The final section uses the heterogeneous agent model of Lamba (2010; Preprint) (following from Cross, Grinfeld,

Lamba, & Seaman, 2005) to help clarify how far-from-equilibrium behaviour in the Soros world arises from the non-standard elements of reflexivity.

The Soros guillotine

Soros argues that there is a dichotomy between the physical and social sciences because the latter deal with decisions made by thinking participants.

> In natural science the outside observer is engaged only in the cognitive function... By contrast, in human affairs, thinking is *part* of the subject matter. The course of events leads not only from facts to facts but also from facts to the participants' perceptions (the cognitive function) and from the participants' decisions to facts (the manipulative function). (Soros, 2013, p. 317)

A *human uncertainty principle* arises from it not being possible for participants in social systems to know what other participants are thinking, what their interests and values are and so on. *Reflexivity* is taken to involve a two-way process whereby reality helps determine participants' views, and vice versa.

This Soros guillotine between the physical and social sciences relies on there being a compelling logic underlying scientific method that can be applied to the physical sciences. For Soros it is taken as an article of faith that Popper's falsificationist account of science holds. To uphold an account of science in terms of a logic of scientific method requires a clear distinction between theories and observational evidence. The Popper version of hypothetico-deductive logic is $H \rightarrow I \cdot \tilde{}o \rightarrow \tilde{}H$, where H stands for 'hypothesis', $\rightarrow$ indicates 'implies', $\cdot$ indicates 'conjoined with', I stands for 'implications', $\sim$ indicates 'not' and o stands for 'observational evidence'. Thus a hypothesis is demonstrated to be false if the observational evidence is inconsistent with the implications of the hypothesis.

In the Soros account, theories are independent of observational evidence in the physical but not in the social world. This is because of reflexivity, by way of the manipulative function of thought, in the social world.

> As we have seen, natural phenomena provide a genuinely independent criterion for judging the validity of generalizations relating to them, but the facts produced by social processes do not do so because they are influenced by theories held by participants. (Soros, 2013, p. 318)

Alternative accounts of the physical sciences do not rely on there being a compelling logic underlying scientific method, and involve something similar to the two-way interaction between theories and their subject matter that Soros takes to be confined to the social world. Mach's account of science is instructive in this respect. His work on physics is well known (Mach, 1883), but he was also a psychologist, working on the physiology of sensations (Mach, 1897), and so was well placed to formulate a philosophy of science that could encompass, if appropriate, the physical and human worlds. Samuelson (1992), a towering figure in economics in the second half of the twentieth century, deemed Mach's conventionalist account of science to be that most consonant with good practice in economics, and so is at least worthy of consideration (Cross, 2006).

The starting point for Mach is one of reality being a non-repeating mosaic of elemental qualities. As Heraclitus is reported to have said, in Plato's *Cratylus* dialogue, 'you do not put your foot into the same river more than once'. The key problem for human thought in this world of flux is survival. In this biological account of the origins of science, human thought plays cognitive and manipulative roles not completely dissimilar to those depicted by Soros. Memory plays a key role in economising on the effort needed to survive in the face of this Heraclitean flux, by imposing some order, or revealing disorder in, this external world. So, for example, memory allows recall of element types such as a 'red' colour, and can associate this with 'fading of light' in a 'not-completely occluded sky' to allow a 'red sunset' to be recognised, and maybe distinguished from the 'red' associated with, say, a meteorite collision. By using conventions or classifications, memory can pave the way for science by distilling regularities from less recurrent phenomena. So the human memory is in effect producing low-level theories to aid comprehension of the flux of otherwise unique phenomena.

Science, according to Mach, proceeds by applying an epistemological economy principle – Mach took the term 'okonomisch' from discussions with a friend, Hermann, who was a political economist – to the ontological classifications or associations that are now treated as 'facts'. So, for example, Snel's law is an attempt to provide an economical rule covering different types of light refraction.

> It is the object of science to replace, or save, experiences by the reproduction and anticipation of facts in thought ... science itself ... may be regarded as a minimal problem, consisting of the completest possible presentment of facts with the least possible expenditure of thought. (Mach, 1883, pp. 577, 586)

This allies the 'entities are not to be multiplied without need' common sense of Ockham's razor to 'the completest possible presentment of facts'. The distinction between theories and facts is labile, higher level theories treating lower level theories as facts.

In this Machian account of science the physical, as well as the social, world is interpreted by human thought as an aid to survival. In evolutionary terms, theories that do not provide a good 'reproduction and anticipation of facts in thought' will not be conducive to survival. This is the problem facing mainstream economic theories since the beginning of the financial crisis in 2007, and the subsequent great recession. Are the mainstream theories fit to survive? It is difficult to disagree with Soros that the answer to this question is 'no'.

It is not too difficult to find examples where thought in the physical sciences plays a manipulative function. Theories of DNA paved the way for genetic manipulation, changing the reality to be explained. Theories of human-made global warming have stimulated agreements to curb CO_2 emissions, precisely with the aim of changing the world to be explained. A Gestalt view of the physical sciences takes into account technology as well. Sometimes the technological manipulation comes before the theory, as in the case of heat engines and modifications to the laws of thermodynamics. On other occasions the theories stimulate the technology, as in theories regarding sub-atomic particles and the making of nuclear weaponry and power stations. A step outside the laboratory reveals more of the reflexive two-way interaction between the cognitive and manipulative aspects of thought that the Soros guillotine takes to be confined to social sciences such as economics.

The Duhem–Quine problem

The preceding section casts doubt on whether reflexivity is a key feature serving to separate physical sciences from social sciences such as economics. In this section we discuss the sketch Soros gives of a methodological approach that is appropriate to economics. This is based on analysing economic systems as composed of market participants who use Popper's logic of scientific discovery to learn from their mistakes.

> As a market participant I formulate conjectures and expose them to refutation. I also assume that other market participants are doing the same thing whether they realize it or not. Their expectations are usefully aggregated in market prices. I can therefore compare my own

expectations with prevailing prices. When I see a divergence, I see a profit opportunity. The bigger the divergence, the bigger the opportunity. When the price behaviour contradicts my expectations I have to re-examine my hypothesis. If I find myself proven wrong, I take a loss; if I conclude that the market is wrong, I increase my bet, always taking into account the risk that I am bound to be wrong some of the time. (Soros, 2013, p. 327)

Market participants attempting to be guided by the Soros vision of Popperian conjectures and refutations are likely to be haunted by the Duhem–Quine problem. A conjecture about the future market price is likely to be guided by conjunctions of hypotheses about various potential influences on the market price. If the actual market price produces a loss, in relation to the participant's conjecture, the refutation is unfocussed: it will not be possible for the participant to know for sure which of the constituent hypotheses underlying the conjecture is to blame.

It is worth quoting Quine's 'Two Dogmas of Empiricism' essay at some length.

The totality of our so-called knowledge or beliefs, from the most casual matters of geography and history to the profoundest laws of atomic physics or even of pure mathematics and logic, is a man-made fabric which impinges on experience only along the edges. Or, to change the figure, total science is like a field of force whose boundary conditions are experience. A conflict with experience at the periphery occasions readjustments in the interior of the field. Truth values have to be redistributed over some of our statements. Revaluation of some statements entails re-evaluation of others, because of their logical interconnections – the logical laws being in turn simply certain further statements of the system, certain further elements of the field. Having re-evaluated one statement we must re-evaluate some others, which may be statements logically connected with the first or may be statements of logical connections themselves. But the total field is so undetermined by its boundary conditions, experience, that there is much latitude of choice as to what statements to re-evaluate in the light of any single contrary experience. No particular experiences are linked with any particular statements in the interior of the field, except indirectly through considerations affecting the field as a whole. (Quine, 1980, pp. 42–43).

As pointed out in an earlier paper (Cross & Strachan, 1997), participants in financial markets in a Soros world are engaged in guesses about other participants' expectations or conjectures of the type depicted in Keynes' beauty contest analogy. Participants' conjectures about the conjectures of other participants are also likely to involve conjectures about how 'relevant' economic news, and policy makers' responses to such news, will affect the conjectures of other participants. Some participants, in foreign exchange (FX) markets for example, will have access to private information stemming from the customer-direct orders with end-user clients, so believing themselves to have an advantage in the guessing game. Participants making large deals may also feel grounds for having a higher degree of belief that the market price will move to their advantage. Should a refutation occur, the market price having not moved favourably in relation to the price conjectured by a particular participant, what can be concluded? As Duhem, the co-originator of the Duhem–Quine thesis, pointed out,

the physicist can never subject an isolated hypothesis to experimental test, but only a whole group of hypotheses: when the experiment is in conflict with his predictions, what he learns is that at least one of the hypotheses constituting this group is unacceptable and ought to be modified; but the experiment does not designate which one should be changed. (Duhem, 1914, p. 187)

And so with market participants.

The El Farol bar

We would not disagree with the Soros view that the axiomatic approach of mainstream economic theory, a formalisation of metaphors drawn from Newtonian mechanics in the neoclassical revolution of the 1870s (Mirowski, 1989), has produced 'an axiomatic system based on deductive logic, not empirical evidence... at least some of the postulates of economics, notably rational choice and rational expectations, are dictated by the desire to imitate Newtonian physics rather than real-world evidence' (Soros, 2013, p. 318). A paraphrase of the biblical 'by their deeds shall ye know them' should suffice in the explanation of how humans make economic decisions. We also concur that it is not the lot of human beings to know the future, and that economic theory should take on board the fact that economic decisions are made in the face of endemic uncertainty regarding not only the future, but also regarding the present knowledge and dispositions of other participants. In such an uncertain world, simple decision rules or heuristics tend to outperform more complex, state-contingent rules (Gigerenzer, 2013).

The question, then, is whether it is possible to say anything interesting about this Mammonite flux. Are there regularities, or irregularities, that can be classified in an economical manner? Or are we left with an impossibility theorem regarding economic science, there being no economical classifications, in the sense of Mach, to be found?

We also concur with Soros that a sensible point of departure is an approach based on observation and inductive learning. As Hume pointed out, there are no logical grounds to expect past regularities to recur. But knowledge of such regularities, and irregularities, might provide the best show of realism in town. In what follows we use Arthur's parable of attendance at the El Farol bar (Arthur, 1994) to illustrate how the inductive learning problems faced by participants in economic systems might be modelled.

The Arthur parable relates to the El Farol bar in Santa Fe, New Mexico, in which Irish music is played on a Thursday evening. The situation facing the $N = 100$ people who might attend the bar on a particular Thursday is that space is limited: the evening is only enjoyable if the bar is not too crowded, defined as less than 60 people attending. There is no communication between the potential bar participants, attendance decisions are taken to be unaffected by a participant's previous visits, and the only information available concerns how many people attended the bar in previous weeks. The problem is that there is no deductive model available to guide the participant in the decision as to whether to attend the bar, if fewer than 60 people are expected to attend; or stay away, if 60 or more people are expected to attend. If procedures such as coin tossing are ruled out, inductive rules, based on the number of people attending the bar in previous weeks, can be used to form expectations of attendance in the coming week and guide the participant's decision on whether or not to go.

Interestingly, in relation to mainstream economic models in which a single rational expectation is held, any commonality in expectations will be defied by the decisions made on the basis of that expectation. If all participants expect the bar to be too crowded, their decisions will lead the bar to be uncrowded; and vice versa. In the extreme this could lead to a flipping between 0 and 100 in bar attendance. Instead, Arthur postulates that participants use a variety of inductive conjectures about the coming week's bar attendance: using just the last bar attendance information, moving averages of past bar attendances and so on. In response to the revealed bar attendance, participants revise their expectations and move away from errant predictors.

> I believe that as humans in these contexts we use inductive reasoning: we induce a variety of working hypotheses, act upon the most credible, and replace hypotheses with new ones if they cease to work. Such reasoning can be modelled in a variety of ways. Usually this leads to a rich psychological world in which agents' ideas or mental models compete for survival against other agents' ideas or mental models – a world that is both evolutionary and complex. (Arthur, 1994, p. 411)

In the original Arthur model, participants are in motion regarding their selection of inductive predictors of bar attendance, but attendance tends to average 60 and the predictors tend to settle on a 60/40 ratio between not-too-crowded and too-crowded forecasts. Various modifications can be made to the original Arthur specification of how bar attendance decisions are made. In (Cross, Grinfeld, Lamba, & Pittock, 2005) the participants take account of their own history of bar attendance, and their psychological reaction to their experiences. The number of times the participants enjoyed being at the bar because it was uncrowded, the occasions in which disappointment arose from the bar being too crowded, and the lost opportunities to have a good time when the participants did not go, but the bar was uncrowded, are taken into account. Habit formation, and thence hysteresis in bar attendance, is also introduced. Attempting to make the El Farol bar a more recognisable place by these modifications disturbs the 60/40 ecology. Hysteresis, for example, has a noticeable effect in increasing the periodicity in bar attendance.

It is interesting that applications of the El Farol parable to the behaviour of financial markets cite Soros, and adopt the term reflexivity to describe the processes involved in such models (Arthur, Holland, leBaron, Palmer, & Tayler, 1997, p. 37, footnote 16).

> Asset markets, we argue, have a recursive nature in that agents' expectations are formed on the basis of their anticipations of other agents' expectations, which precludes expectations being formed by deductive means. Instead, traders continuously hypothesize – continually explore – expectational models, buy or sell on the basis of those that perform best, and confirm or discard these according to their performance. Thus, individual beliefs or expectations become endogenous to the market, and constantly compete within an ecology of others' beliefs or expectations. (Arthur et al., 1997, p. 15)

Soros does not mention such models in the essay under present consideration. It would be interesting to know whether or not he thinks that such models (Le Baron, 2006) incorporate his core ideas.

Working memory

In the Machian account of science considered earlier, memory plays a key role in allowing humans to survive in the world of flux they inhabit, and paves the way for scientific classifications of the regularities, and irregularities, in this world. Psychologists and neuroscientists have distinguished various types of memory: short-term, long-term, episodic and semantic long-term, implicit and explicit, and working memory (Baddeley, 2004, Chapter 1). For Soros,

> the complexity of the world in which we live exceeds our capacity to comprehend it … we are obliged to resort to various methods of simplification: generalizations, dichotomies, metaphors, decision rules, and moral precepts, to mention just a few … the brain is bombarded by millions of sensory impulses, but consciousness can process only seven or eight subjects concurrently … the impulses need to be condensed, ordered, and interpreted under immense time pressure, and mistakes and distortions can't be avoided. (Soros, 2013, p. 311)

The reference to 'can process only seven or eight subjects concurrently' presumably relates to the working memory model Baddeley and Hitch (1974), where the capacity limits have been estimated to be in the range of 5–9 pieces of transitory information that can be held concurrently in the brain and manipulated. The working memory is taken to be made up of a visuo–spatial sketch pad that stores information in a visual or spatial form for around 1–2 seconds, a phonological loop that allows the comprehension of spoken or written information, an episodic buffer that provides a link with long-term memory and a central executive that performs a communication and coordination task. (Baddeley, 2004, Chapter 3)

What insights can the capacity limitations in working memory provide in relation to explaining the decisions made by participants in economic systems? These limitations would certainly seem to rule out the EMH that the market prices of assets reflect all the information relevant to their determination. If participants can only hold less than 10 pieces of information in their working memories when making decisions, how is the full set of information be reflected in market prices? There would have to be a substantial variation in the information sets used in different participants' working memories for the full information requirement to hold. Such variation is ruled out in the representative agent assumption that is often used to underpin the EMH in mainstream economic models. The use of algorithms to design and execute trades can enhance the information sets used to inform trading decisions. Algorithms, however, have a survival problem in common with the non-algorithmic conjectures faced by humans. Even if an algorithm is used to choose between alternative algorithmic trading rules, a human has to choose the algorithm for algorithms. And that human will be faced with working memory capacity limits. The human eye operates by taking a small snapshot of the visual field, then jumping to another spot, and can perform only up to five such jumps per second (Coates, 2012, p. 63). This explains why traders typically operate with a small number of trading screens, often four, providing continuous information flows regarding the market in which they operate.

Soros argues that 'market prices of financial assets do not accurately reflect their fundamental value... there are various pathways by which the mispricing of financial assets can affect the so-called fundamentals' (Soros, 2013, pp. 321–322). If we take a Machian view of the world, the 'underlying fundamentals' are a mosaic of elemental qualities in flux that are interpreted by the participants in economic systems. These interpretations are likely to differ, so the notion of 'underlying fundamentals' has little or no meaning. All that market prices can reflect are the information sets used to shape active conjectures regarding market prices. Only in this very limited sense can markets be described as 'efficient'. To distinguish this world from that depicted in the EMH requires a different terminology. We would suggest contingent markets hypothesis (CMH), where the only notion of 'efficiency' is contingent on the varied and strictly limited information sets used by market participants when forming conjectures about the economic world.

Soros takes the REH to imply 'that there is a single correct set of expectations that people's views will converge around' (Soros, 2013, p. 322). In a CMH world it is 'rational' for participants to use limited information sets to construct conjectures about the economic world, and use the feedback from events to strengthen or weaken their beliefs in these conjectures, replacing them as needed with different conjectures. It is 'rational' to discard conjectures that are systematically wrong. The set of active conjectures will be in motion, and differ between participants. To distinguish this state of affairs from that depicted in the REH, we would suggest rational differentiated conjectures hypothesis (RDCH).

Far-from-equilibrium

In its current form, as applied to financial markets, Soros' theory lacks a mathematical or computational framework. The following agent-based market model, detailed in Lamba (2010; Preprint), was not developed with reflexivity in mind. Rather it was constructed to demonstrate, as simply as possible, how the equilibrium solutions in economic and financial models lose stability when the standard assumptions are violated. Nonetheless it is based around elements that closely correspond to fallibility, both cognitive and manipulative functions, and positive feedback. As shown below, these can indeed combine to destabilise equilibria resulting in boom-bust, far-from-equilibrium, fat-tailed dynamics at realistic parameter values. Although the simple model presented below does not incorporate any specific notion of market fundamentals or underlying trends (but see the end of this section), it reaches many of the same conclusions as Soros and may provide a stimulus for more accurate renderings of reflexivity.

Full details of the modelling assumptions can be found in (Lamba, 2010; Preprint) but, briefly, only market participants (agents) whose opinions and strategies change over timescales of several days or longer are directly simulated. At each time t, each agent is assumed to be in one of two states, either $+1$ or -1, that roughly correspond to positive or negative opinions about the future value of an asset that are then disseminated and/or traded upon. Any given agent switches state relatively infrequently – only when the current asset price $p(t)$ suddenly exceeds a threshold value defined by that agent's *evolving* expectations.

The average state of the agents is defined as the 'sentiment' σ that can take values between -1 and $+1$. Changes in the price $p(t)$ are due to both the arrival of new Brownian exogenous information $B(t)$ and changes in sentiment that are endogenous, i.e. generated within the market itself. Following (Lamba, Preprint), defining the log-price $r(t) = \ln p(t)$, and using the mathematical notation for differentials, we have

$$\mathrm{d}r = \mathrm{d}B + \kappa \mathrm{d}\sigma, \tag{1}$$

where $\mathrm{d}r$, $\mathrm{d}B$ and $\mathrm{d}\sigma$ represent the changes in log-price, exogenous information and endogenous sentiment, respectively. Larger values of the parameter $\kappa > 0$ imply a larger influence of endogenous dynamics upon the asset price.

The correspondence with Soros reflexivity is as follows. The term $\kappa \mathrm{d}\sigma$ in Equation (1) plays the role of the manipulative (or participating) function. If it is absent, then agents have no influence upon the system and the solution to (1) is just a price that follows the exogenously determined (equilibrium) Brownian motion in accordance with the very strongest versions of the EMH. Next, the cognitive functions of the agents correspond to the evolving expectations (threshold dynamics) of each agent. The following point is mathematically subtle but crucial (Lamba, 2010). If these cognitive functions are sufficiently independent/uncorrelated with each other, then agents' fallibilities will mostly cancel. This situation, which corresponds to small, essentially random, deviations of σ around 0 agrees with the assumptions underlying the REH. And, once more, the term $\kappa \mathrm{d}\sigma$ all-but-vanishes, leading to the equilibrium EMH Brownian pricing model. Soros correctly noted that '...without fallibility there would be no reflexivity', (Soros, 2013, p. 4) but this observation should be strengthened to refer to *systemic* (i.e. non-cancelling) fallibility.

Thus in order to proceed we need to identify at least one form of fallibility that destroys the mathematical independence between agents' opinions/actions. This allows for the possibility of deviations from equilibrium which induce positive feedbacks. An obvious candidate is the phenomenon of *herding,* where agents in the minority opinion are fooled or pressured into joining the majority. Some likely causes of herding include psychological effects, momentum-trading strategies or rational responses to perverse incentives (Lamba, Preprint) (such as the entirely understandable tendency for investment managers to 'chase the average' when their performance is being frequently judged against that of their peers).

It is a simple matter to introduce herding into the threshold dynamics. It is at this point that the reflexive nature of the model asserts itself – changes in the price and sentiment lead to changes in the threshold dynamics that lead to changes in the price and sentiment and so on. Estimates of the few critical parameters are easily established (Lamba, Preprint)

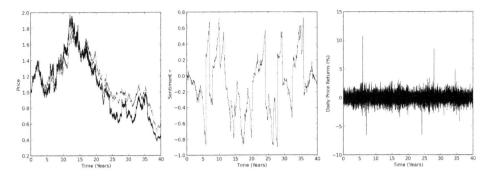

Figure 1. The left plot shows the output price of the model (thick line) and the Brownian equilibrium price (thin line) over a 40 year simulation. The difference between the two is caused by boom-bust endogenous effects that are approximately quantified by the deviations of σ from 0 (middle plot). The right plot shows daily percentage price returns with the largest values corresponding to the sudden collapse of positive-feedback deviations. Periods of increased price activity and false tops and bottoms can be observed as the extended mispricings come to their very violent but unpredictable end (note that for the corresponding equilibrium solution there is not even a single daily price change exceeding 2%). This minimal version of the model demonstrates that the unstable equilibrium solution is replaced by boom-bust dynamics at realistic parameter values. Incorporating additional effects (such as the asymmetries caused by leverage and margin-calls) improves the model's fit with more detailed real-world market statistics (see Lamba 2010; Preprint).

and the results of a typical numerical simulation (with parameters chosen for asset rather than currency markets) are shown in Figure 1 and compared with the equilibrium Brownian price over a (hypothetical) 40-year period. Even low levels of herding destabilise the equilibrium solution causing boom-bust dynamics in σ, and hence in the price via (1). The unpredictable but rapid cascade processes that suddenly reverse long boom phases are described mathematically in (Lamba, 2010) and can be explored interactively at (Lamba, 2013).

The reluctance of mainstream economics to seriously consider far-from-equilibrium descriptions of economic reality, such as Soros reflexivity, is due in no small part to two fundamentally flawed (but mathematically expedient) assumptions about economic systems. The first is that equilibrating negative feedbacks in economic systems operate near instantaneously [as (Soros, 2013) points out this is a limiting case of his framework]. However, the presence of participants with longer timescales, various forms of inertia/hysteresis/fallibility, and other limits to arbitrage can prevent this from happening. This delay in equilibration allows for positive-feedback effects to compete and sometimes dominate. Unfortunately such competition between positive and negative feedbacks can result in long periods that appear calm and predictable enough to be mistaken for a trend in the fundamentals of an equilibrium model.

However, even if equilibration were always instantaneous, there is a second flaw that relates to economists' understanding of 'balance of forces'. In their rush to emulate physics, they failed to appreciate that it is only in the simplest physical systems that a balance of forces implies the existence of a *unique* stable equilibrium, yet almost all neoclassical economics is imbued with this property. More complex systems (such as the above agent-based model or, say, a tectonic fault line) can support multiple internal configurations that correspond to different equilibria and gradual changes may cause unpredictable, sudden and irreversible shifts between them. Thus the portion of reflexivity that considers the effects of mispricing on fundamentals might plausibly be restated in terms of mispricings causing the system's internal state to shift to a different configuration – one that persists even after the mispricing has been corrected. Applying this concept precisely enough to usefully model changes in, say, the credit and regulatory environments of a financial system would be a formidable but potentially very valuable undertaking.

Concluding remarks

In the essay under review, George Soros provides a valuable exposure of the failings of mainstream theories in economics. On the negative side, we have argued that reflexivity does not provide a clear-cut distinction between a social science such as economics and the physical sciences; and that the Duhem–Quine thesis poses problems for a Popperian account of the way that participants might learn from refutations of conjectures, the latter being unfocused because of the conjointness of the hypotheses underlying the conjectures. On a more constructive note, we have argued that models of inductive learning by participants who make decisions on the basis of strictly limited and heterogeneous information sets can capture the basic thrust of the Soros view of the economic world. The conjectures are in motion as the participants use the feedback from the revealed world to try and avoid those that are systematically in error. The Duhem–Quine problem means that there is no necessary reason why any participants who initially held the same conjecture would draw the same conclusion from the feedback provided by the experienced world.

Somewhat surprisingly, in view of the intractable uncertainties faced by participants in a Soros world, there is very little discussion of the emotional and biological influences on decision taking. The language of conjectures and learning from refutations tends to paint the participants in terms of their cognitive, reasoning and calculating capacities. In Smith's *The Theory of Moral Sentiments,* passions or emotions are the main drivers of economic behaviour, with reason intervening when reflection is made on behaviour in the way an impartial spectator might (Smith, 1759). On financial markets, making profits has been found to be associated with a rise in testosterone levels, higher volatility with enhanced cortisol (Coates, 2012). Greed, fear, panic and euphoria are epithets often associated with financial markets. A more recognisable account of financial and other markets would incorporate the biological and emotional influences on the behaviour of the participants.

Finally, a mathematical model (Lamba, 2010; Preprint) with close structural similarities to reflexivity affirms the significant consequences of reflexivity which have been postulated by Soros both for financial markets and for equilibrium-based thinking in economics.

Acknowledgement

We are most grateful for the comments and assistance of Michael Grinfeld and Mrs Irene Spencer in the preparation of this paper.

References

Arthur, W. B. (1994). Inductive reasoning and bounded rationality. *American Economic Review*, *84*, 406–411.

Arthur, W. B., Holland, J. H., Le Baron, B., Palmer, R., & Tayler, P. (1997). Asset pricing under endogenous expectations in an artificial stock market. In W. B. Arthur, S. N. Durlauf, & D. A. Lane (Eds.), *The economy as an evolving complex system II, Santa Fe Institute*. Reading, MA: Addison-Wesley.

Baddeley, A. D. (2004). *Your memory: A user's guide*. London, UK: Carlton Books.

Baddeley, A. D., & Hitch, G. (1974). Working memory. In G. A. Bower (Ed.), *The psychology of learning and motivation* (*Vol. 8*, pp. 47–89). New York, NY: Academic Press.

Coates, J. (2012). *The hour between dog and wolf: Risk-taking, gut feelings and the biology of boom and bust*. London: Fourth Estate.

Cross, R. (2006). Paul Samuelson's Mach. In M. Szenberg, L. Ramrattan, & A. A. Gottesman (Eds.), *Samuelsonian economics and the twenty-first century* (pp. 330–341). New York, NY: Oxford University Press.

Cross, R., Grinfeld, M., Lamba, H., & Pittock, A. (2005). Frustration minimization, hysteresis and the El Farol problem. In M. P. Mortell, R. E. O'Malley, A. Pakrovskii, & V. Sobolev (Eds.), *Singular perturbations and hysteresis*. Philadelphia, PA: Society for Industrial and Applied Mathematics.

Cross, R., Grinfeld, M., Lamba, H., & Seaman, T. (2005). A threshold model of investor psychology. *Physica A*, *354*, 463–478.

Cross, R., & Strachan, D. (1997). On George Soros and economic analysis. *Kyklos*, *50*(4), 561–574.

Duhem, P. (1914). *The Aim and structure of physical theory*. (P. P. Wiener, 2nd French ed., 1981). New York, NY: Atheneum.

Gigerenzer, G. (2013). *Risk savvy: How to make good decisions*. New York, NY: Penguin Books.

Lamba, H. (2013). Far-from-equilibrium dynamics: What if financial and economic equilibria are actually unstable? http://math.gmu.edu/~harbir/market.html

Lamba, H., Implausible equilibrium solutions in economics and finance. Preprint, http://math.gmu.edu/~harbir/implausible.pdf

Lamba, H. (2010). A queueing theory description of fat-tailed price returns in imperfect financial markets. *European Physics Journal B*, *77*, 297–304.

Le Baron, B. (2006). Agent-based financial markets: Matching stylized facts with style. In D. Colander (Ed.), *Post walrasian macroeconomics*. New York, NY: Cambridge University Press.

Mach, E. (1959). *The analysis of sensations*. (C. M. Williams and S. Waterlow, Trans.). New York: Dover Books.

Mach, E. (1883). *The science of mechanics*. (T. J. McCormack, Trans., 1960). La Salle, IL: Open Court.

Mirowski, P. (1989). *More heat than light*. Cambridge: Cambridge University Press.

Quine, W. O. (1980). *From a logical point of view*. Cambridge, MA: Harvard University Press.

Samuelson, P. (1992). My life philosophy: Policy credos and working ways. In M. Szenberg (Ed.), *Eminent economists: Their life philosophies*. New York, NY: Cambridge University Press.

Smith, A. (1759). *The theory of moral sentiments*. (reprinted 1976). Oxford: Oxford University Press.

Soros, G. (2013). Fallibility, reflexivity and the human uncertainty principle. *Journal of Economic Methodology*, *20*, 309–329.

Soros's reflexivity concept in a complex world: Cauchy distributions, rational expectations, and rational addiction

John B. Davis[a,b]

[a]Department of Economics, Marquette University, Milwaukee, WI, USA; [b]Department of Economics, University of Amsterdam, Amsterdam, The Netherlands

George Soros makes an important analytical contribution to understanding the concept of reflexivity in social science by explaining reflexivity in terms of how his cognitive and manipulative causal functions are connected to one another by a pair of feedback loops (Soros, 2013). Fallibility, reflexivity and the human uncertainty principle. Here I put aside the issue of how the natural sciences and social sciences are related, an issue he discusses, and focus on how his thinking applies in economics. I argue that standard economics assumes a 'classical' view of the world in which knowledge and action are independent, but that we live in a complex reflexive world in which knowledge and action are interdependent. I argue that Soros's view provides a reflexivity critique of the efficient market hypothesis seen as depending on untenable claims about the nature of random phenomena and the nature of economic agents. Regarding the former, I develop this critique in terms of Cauchy distributions; regarding the latter I develop it in terms of rational expectations and rational addiction reasoning.

1. Soros's cognitive and manipulative causal functions

Soros's analysis explains reflexivity in terms of how cognitive and manipulative causal functions are connected to one another by a pair of feedback loops (Soros, 2013, pp. 311ff). The cognitive function concerns our knowledge of the world and the role that the world itself plays in determining our knowledge of it. The manipulative function concerns action and how people's motivations given their knowledge of the world determine their actions. His method of explanation is to have us first imagine each function *as if* it operated in isolation from the other, and then have us see how that function is modified by a feedback loop from the other function.

(i) In the case of the cognitive or knowledge function, the direction of *causation is from the world to the mind*. Taken in isolation, our knowledge of the world is determined by what the world is independently of us, *as if* what the world is were fully independent of our actions:

$$world \rightarrow mind \qquad (1)$$

Thanks go to Wade Hands and Cars Hommes for comments on an earlier version of this paper, and also go to the Central European University, George Soros, Eric Beinhocker, and participants in the Workshop on Reflexivity, 8 October 2013, where this paper was presented.

But in a complex reflexive world, the manipulative or action function interferes with the cognitive function because people act on what they know, action changes what the world is, and thus changes knowledge. Action thus has a feedback effect on knowledge so that

$$world \leftarrow mind \tag{2}$$

So it is incorrect to say as in (1) that the world is fully independent of us and independently determines our knowledge of it. The main direction of causation when we think of knowledge is still from the world to the mind, but the feedback loop from action in (2) produces a reverse causation that modifies the world and thus knowledge.[1] The cognitive function modified by manipulative function might thus be represented as

$$world \rightarrow mind \, [world \leftarrow mind]$$
$$or \tag{3}$$
$$'world \rightarrow mind'$$

(ii) In the case of the manipulative function, the direction of *causation is from the mind to the world*. Taken in isolation, people act on what they know *as if* their motivations in doing so were fully independent of their actions.

$$mind \rightarrow world \tag{4}$$

But the cognitive function interferes with this because acting on the world also produces knowledge about one's motivations for acting, so that the basis for action is changed.

$$mind \leftarrow world \tag{5}$$

So action depends not only on our motivations as in (4) but also on how our motivations change as we learn about them in acting upon the world as in (5), and so it is incorrect to say that the basis for action is independent of our actions. The main direction of causation is still from mind to the world – our motivations still basically drive our actions – but the feedback loop involving the reverse causation from knowledge gained in acting modifies motivation.[2] The manipulative function modified by cognitive function might thus be represented as

$$mind \rightarrow world \, [mind \leftarrow world]$$
$$or \tag{6}$$
$$'mind \rightarrow world'$$

(iii) Putting these two functions together with their respective feedback effects – the cognitive function modified by the manipulative one (3) and the manipulative function is modified by the cognitive one (6) – we have the following schema in a complex reflexive world:

$$'world \rightarrow mind' \, and \, 'mind \rightarrow world' \tag{7}$$

Thus, Soros explains reflexivity analytically by first isolating the two basic causal relationships concerning knowledge and action, and then showing how they are modified and interconnected by two separate feedback relationships.

2. A 'classical' world versus a complex reflexive world: the efficient market hypothesis

Soros reasons that what I call a 'classical' view of the world, in which knowledge and action are independent and can be investigated separately from one another, is an untenable simplification in a complex reflexive world of two-way feedback loops. His analysis offers two linked dimensions through which reflexivity can be investigated.

The first is an epistemological one in which the focus is the modified cognitive/knowledge function as in (3), and in which the main subject of investigation is the fallibility of scientific knowledge. Soros points out that there are multiple epistemic sources of fallibility associated with the complexity of the world and the structure of the brain. I associate the first with radical uncertainty (in the Keynes–Knight sense) and the latter with bounded rationality (in the Simon sense). But Soros's principle message in his contribution to this issue is that the reflexive feedback principle associated with how the manipulative function modifies the cognitive one is the fundamental source of the fallibility of scientific knowledge.

The second dimension of the analysis is an ontological one in which the focus is the modified manipulative/action function as in (6), and the main subject of investigation is how agents act in a world of radical uncertainty. Uncertainty is often seen as an epistemological concept associated with the impossibility of knowing the future.[3] But it also needs to be seen as an ontological concept associated with not having a basis for action.[4] Soros also points out that there are multiple sources of uncertainty, but again his principle message in his paper here emphasizes the special role of reflexivity, or how feedback from the cognitive function interferes with the manipulative one in unsettling the basis for action.

The 'classical' view of the world of standard economics, then, entails an epistemology and ontology in which knowledge and action are independent.[5] Since this is the world in which the efficient market hypothesis (EMH) applies, Soros's reflexivity analysis should show us why the EMH cannot apply in a complex reflexive world.

The EMH, whether in its strong, semi-strong, or weak versions, basically says that in financial markets, agents use 'all available information' about market prices efficiently. Behavioral finance economists generally argue this does not occur because people are subject to various psychological imperfections in reasoning or heuristics and biases that distort their information processing. Soros accepts this but for him the main reason the EMH is wrong is more fundamental: it ignores reflexivity. On the one hand, the EMH assumes traders' cognitive function is not modified by the manipulative function (1), and that accordingly 'all available information' can be reasonably taken to correspond to the way the world is. But, Soros tells us, the operation of financial markets affects what the world is because trading can distort the so-called underlying asset fundamentals which market prices are thought to reflect (2). So it is incorrect to say that 'all available information' corresponds to the way the world is independently of us. That is, traders' cognitive function is modified by their manipulative one (3). On the other hand, the EMH assumes traders' manipulative function is not modified by the cognitive function (4), from which it follows that traders are, as it were, motivationally complete (or have complete preferences). But, Soros tells us, turning points in boom-bust processes or other price cycles provide traders information about the consequences of their actions, which can change attitudes, and thus change traders' motivations. So it is incorrect to say that traders have 'all available information' when they set out to make any given set of trades since that information does not include information about how their motivations will change, or how their manipulative function is modified by their cognitive one (6).

The EMH is wrong, then, because it ignores the two-way feedback loops that operate on the two causal functions (7), because proponents of the EMH assume we live in a simple 'classical' world in which knowledge and action are independent of one another so that their effects can be investigated separately. This 'classical' thinking rests on two questionable ontological claims, one pertaining to the nature of random phenomena (the random walk hypothesis) and the other pertaining to the nature of economic agents (the expected utility conception). Consider first the claim about the nature of random phenomena.

2.1   The random walk hypothesis

The random walk hypothesis says that stock prices evolve in a random manner and thus cannot be predicted. Randomly distributed phenomena which are normally or bell-shaped distributed possess determinate means and finite variance, and these properties are needed to be able to say that economics agents can use all available information efficiently. So the random walk hypothesis requires normally distributed stock prices. In contrast, if random phenomena have a Cauchy distribution (a family of fat tail distributions), mean and variance are undefined, and it no longer makes sense to say that economics agents use all available information efficiently. The 'classical' view of the world and the EMH rules out Cauchy distributions by assumption, but the recent financial crisis seems to have shown that stock prices are not always normally distributed. That is, one of the clear lessons of the crisis is that fat tail 'extreme' events, that is, phenomena which are rare when we assume normal distributions, are somehow not all that rare after all.

Suppose, then, that stock prices can be Cauchy distributed with undefined means and variances. Why we might suppose this can be explained in terms of Soros's understanding of reflexivity in terms of the modified cognitive and manipulative functions (3 and 6). Soros's view is that the two functions are dominant causal processes that are only modified by feedback loops. Thus it can easily *appear* that the pure cognitive function (1) and the pure manipulative function (4) accurately represent the phenomena (particularly when methods of observation are imperfect). Note, then, that normal distributions presuppose the central limit theorem, which says that for a sufficiently large number of observations of a phenomenon, the distribution of the phenomena converges on a normal distribution. But when the cognitive and manipulative functions are modified by two-way feedback (7), in reality the phenomena are changed, and so there no longer are a large number of the identical phenomenon. Soros thus tells us that the fundamentals behind stock prices change in trading, but his view is actually more subtle. It is that fundamentals are most of the time only modestly changed by the action of traders so that they may well appear not to have changed at all (at least until boom and bust processes become undeniable). So it may appear that the phenomena are the same and unchanged, the central limit theorem applies, and random phenomena are normally distributed when in fact this is not the case.

Indeed, this deceptive combination of the appearance of normality and the emergence of crisis is reflected in the idea of a fat tail 'extreme' event occurrence. How can an 'extreme' event both be truly not rare (because it occurs more frequently than expected) and nonetheless still be regarded as 'extreme'? The answer is that reflexive worlds mask their rare but nonetheless very possible non-normal behavior with the appearance of normality, because feedback relationships only modify market actors' pure cognitive and pure manipulative functions gradually and often imperceptibly. Nonetheless these feedback effects can still be real and cumulative, and market phenomena – particularly where there are increasingly strong incentives for agents to act on their knowledge and affect the phenomena – should accordingly not be regarded as always normally distributed. Thus the EMH rests on a mistaken claim about random phenomena.

2.2   *The* **Homo economicus** *expected utility conception*

Now consider what the EMH requires about the nature of economic agents. There are two sides to the standard conception: the probabilities and knowledge side and the preferences and motivation side. On the former, the *Homo economicus* expected utility individual conception is objectivist about probabilities and knowledge. It assumes that learning occurs in a Bayesian way given common priors.[6] Everyone starts with the same knowledge of the world, and people acquire different posterior beliefs according to their differential experience. Furthermore, since expected utility depends on forecasts of future prices, and since forecasts are subject to error, the standard view crucially also assumes that *errors in forecasting are uncorrelated across agents*, so that one can aggregate individual expectations into a representative agent rational forecast – the rational expectations hypothesis – and say that people acquire objective knowledge about the world because on average they use probabilistic information efficiently (see Hommes, 2013). Bayesianism thus employs a pure cognitive function feedback analysis since the assumption that forecasting errors are uncorrelated leaves this up-dating process fully in the domain of probabilities and knowledge, and the cognitive function is unmodified by the manipulative one (1).

One way in which this view has been contested in reflexivity terms is through the development of bounded rationality agent conceptions employing expectations feedback systems with correlated forecasting errors. In terms of Soros's framework, expectations feedback systems with correlated forecasting errors show how agents' cognitive function – here their forecasting function – is modified by the manipulative one (3). If agents' forecasts are correlated, they do not balance out on average (ruling out the representative agent rational forecast), and what people do (the actions they undertake) changes the overall pattern of future forecasts. This rules out the 'classical' rational expectations view that knowledge and action are independent. It also rules out the important associated assumption that agents are independent with respect to knowledge. Soros brings out the latter assumption in his emphasis on interaction between multiple agents. Brock and Hommes (1997, 1998) have developed this framework in a systematic way by introducing heterogeneous expectations into expectations feedback systems with correlated forecasting errors, and by showing that when agents revise their forecasts of future prices, and switch back and forth between different forecasting rules based on their relative performance, excess volatility with bubbles and crashes in asset markets can result.[7]

But bounded rationality analysis strictly concerns knowledge and belief; that is, how the cognitive function is modified by the manipulative one (3). A quite different and often overlooked reflexivity analysis applies on the preferences and motivation side of the expected utility conception in which the issue is how the manipulative function is modified by the cognitive one (6). The *Homo economicus* conception, then, is objectivist about probabilities and knowledge, but subjectivist about preferences and motivation. Utilities are fully personal. In contrast to the common priors assumption on the knowledge and probabilities side, people's preferences have no common basis and are individual-specific (though people can accidentally happen to have the same preferences). This has meant for most standard economists that agents have no preference adjustment process, process of preference formation, or preference feedback system, analogous to expectations feedback systems. Generally speaking, saying preferences are subjective means, they have an exogenous character, or are given and unchanging.[8]

But looked at more closely, this is an odd conception. It assumes that a person's preferences constitute a finite set, and, according to the completeness axiom, are sufficient to evaluate all choice opportunities. People encounter new choices but since their preferences do not change, they must evaluate these new choices by means of the same preferences they employed to evaluate their past choices. Agents' given preferences, then, are not specific to the circumstance of choice, but have a kind of general, all-purpose nature or versatility for making an infinite number of possible choices. A particular preference x, that is, can be exercised to make any number of different choices $A, B, \ldots N$, though those choices can differ substantially due to differences in the person's information about the circumstances of choice. We might thus ask: why should preference x provide the means for making any particular choice versus any other choice? That is, what explains its versatility? The answer is that since preferences are subjective, that is, essentially unexplainable, this question simply cannot be raised.

One way, then, in which it may seem this view has been contested is in the analysis of fads, fashion, and related consumer phenomena as found in the recent literature on information cascades and 'herding' behavior (Banerjee, 1992; Bikhchandani, Hirshleifer, & Welch, 1992). But these models are explanations of 'rational' herding behavior, in which agents substitute public information for private information, and preferences are unaffected by choice. Thus they only concern a pure cognitive function (1), and tell us nothing about how the manipulative function is modified by the cognitive one (6) – which would seem to be the point of talking about fads and fashion.

Where the manipulative function has actually been the focus is in an older literature on endogenous preference. Preferences are endogenous and an intertemporal preference formation process – a preference feedback system – exists when individuals' preferences somehow depend on their past choices. Here, however, the standard analysis – the 'rational addiction' model (Becker & Murphy, 1988) – assumes that individuals' preferences are dynamically consistent across time in that their later preference sets are rationally derived from their earlier ones. This rules out the possibility that a person might have dynamically inconsistent preferences, and dissolve into a series of disconnected multiple selves, each associated with a different set of (present-biased) preferences. It essentially allows the endogenous preference feedback system to operate as if the person's preferences over time were the person's representative individual preferences.[9] This analogue or preference side representative individual conception also isolates the person's preference change process from the influence of other individuals, and thus essentially employs a pure manipulative function (4). Thus it also fails to get at Soros's understanding of reflexivity.

However, recent behavioral economics research provides strong evidence that people commonly employ hyperbolic rather than exponential time rates of discount, and thus exhibit present-bias in decision-making (Frederick, Loewenstein, & O'Donoghue, 2002). This implies that their preferences are dynamically inconsistent, that people effectively function as successions of multiple selves, and that a rational addiction representative individual assumption is not a reasonable way to model preference feedback systems and endogenous preference.[10] Thus, in the multiple selves time-inconsistent behavior literature (e.g., Laibson, 1997), no such assumption is employed, present-bias is interpreted as a lack of self-control (on the part of the representative individual planner self), and people are said to be reliant on external commitment devices, such as mandated 401(k) plans, to overcome present-bias. Recall that on Soros's understanding of how the manipulative function is modified by the cognitive one that the motivational basis for action is not independent of our actions; that is, we learn about ourselves when we act and this subsequently changes our motivations for acting. It might be argued, then, that generally people become aware of their present-bias and its sometimes unhappy consequences, and are then disposed to avail themselves of external commitment devices in forming future preferences. In this way the individual's preference feedback system functions in such a way that the manipulative function can be said to be modified by the cognitive one (6).

More certainly needs to be said about the nature of endogenous preferences to adequately explain preference feedback systems. But in closing this section, I simply note that replacing the expected utility individual conception with a reflexive individual conception depends on bringing together the two sides of the agent discussed above. That is, a full reflexivity account of agents would need to integrate expectations feedback systems and preference feedback systems by showing how each acts upon the other, and thus how both the cognitive and manipulative functions modify each another in a two-way feedback system.

3. Reflexivity and the EMH

Soros's analysis makes an important analytical contribution by explaining reflexivity as a two-way feedback system between knowledge and action. The basic idea is that people acquire knowledge, act on what they know, this changes the world and what they can know about it, and also changes what they know about the basis for action and how they will subsequently act. This means there are always both 'new' things true about the world and 'new grounds for action, and that time's arrow has a one-way direction.[11] This is ruled out in the 'classical' world of the EMH in which knowledge and action lack feedback channels. In standard economics, this is reflected in how the random walk hypothesis and the *Homo economicus* expected utility conception – the two pillars on which the EMH depends – assume that the phenomena of the world and economic agents constitute two bracketed-off ontologically independent domains.

$$\textit{Homo economicus} \quad \rightarrow \quad \text{EMH} \quad \leftarrow \quad \text{random walk}$$
$$\downarrow \qquad\qquad\qquad\qquad\qquad\qquad\qquad \downarrow$$
$$[\text{agents}] \qquad\qquad\qquad\qquad\qquad [\text{phenomena of the world}]$$

But in a complex economic world with reflexive feedback relationships between knowledge and action, agents and the phenomena of the world are ontologically interdependent and mutually influencing:

$$\text{agents} \quad \leftrightarrow \quad \text{phenomena of the world}$$

This is the vision Soros employs. Setting out this alternative ontological conception, then, is part of what is involved in explaining what reflexivity in economics entails.

Notes
1. Positive feedback effects of action on knowledge that reinforce knowledge have been termed self-fulfilling prophecies (Merton, 1948).
2. This second form of reflexivity is less commonly discussed, in no small part because it is associated with endogenous preferences, a subject assiduously left outside standard economics.

3.   As J. M. Keynes puts it:
     "The outstanding fact is the extreme precariousness of *the basis of knowledge* on which our estimates of prospective yield have to be made. Our knowledge of the factors which will govern the yield of an investment some years hence is usually very slight and often negligible. If we speak frankly, we have to admit that our *basis of knowledge* for estimating the yield ten years hence of a railway, a copper mine, a textile factory, the goodwill of a patent medicine, an Atlantic liner, a building in the City of London amounts to little and sometimes to nothing; or even five years hence." (1936, pp. 149 and 150; emphasis added)
4.   As Keynes also put it:
     "Most, probably, of our decisions to do something positive, the full consequences of which will be drawn out over many days to come, can only be taken as a result of animal spirits – of a spontaneous *urge to action rather than inaction*, and not as the outcome of a weighted average of quantitative benefits multiplied by quantitative probabilities." (1936, p. 161; emphasis added)
5.   The 'classical' view of the world entails a natural science view of social science. In natural science, human action does not change the laws of nature, so the cognitive function is unmodified by the manipulative one. Thus standard economics employs a natural science view of social science.
6.   See Morris (1995) for a critical discussion of the common prior probability distribution assumption.
7.   See Hommes (2013) for a discussion of the literature on expectations feedback systems as a response to rational expectations modeling. Note that agents change their mix of forecasting rules but do not change the motivational basis of their choices. The analysis is still reflexive in a way that Bayesianism is not because action feeds back onto belief. Hommes stresses the fact that in positive expectations feedback systems, non-rational almost self-fulfilling equilibria with correlated forecasts easily arise.
8.   Stigler and Becker (1977) influentially argued that preferences, like the 'Rocky Mountains' are just there, and thus essentially do not change. This assumption serves to isolate the effects of changes in prices and incomes on choice, and gives a market-driven analysis of choice. They also feared that if it were explained by changing preference, the explanation of choice would become hopelessly confused by competing theories of human psychology.
9.   In effect, it is as if the person's different preference sets over time are 'uncorrelated' in the sense of sustaining dynamic consistency of choice of the person's representative individual.
10. When individuals exhibit present-bias, their preferences are no longer uncorrelated over time but rather correlated around periods.
11. The arrow of time idea originates with Eddington (1928) as a property of entropy. As he puts it, 'If your theory is found to be against the second law of Thermodynamics I can give you no hope; there is nothing for it but to collapse in deepest humiliation' (1928, p. 74).

References

Banerjee, A. (1992). A simple model of herd behavior. *The Quarterly Journal of Economics, 107*, 797–817.

Becker, G., & Murphy, K. (1988). A theory of rational addiction. *Journal of Political Economy, 96*, 675–700.

Bikhchandani, S., Hirshleifer, D., & Welch, I. (1992). A theory of fads, fashion, custom, and cultural change as information cascades. *Journal of Political Economy, 100*, 992–1026.

Brock, W. A., & Hommes, C. (1997). A rational route to randomness. *Econometrica, 65*, 1059–1095.

Brock, W. A., & Hommes, C. (1998). Heterogeneous beliefs and routes to chaos in a simple asset pricing model. *Journal of Economic Dynamics & Control, 22*, 1235–1274.

Eddington, A. S. (1928). *The nature of the physical world*. New York, NY: Macmillan.

Frederick, S., Loewenstein, G., & O'Donoghue, T. (2002). Time discounting and time preference: A critical review. *Journal of Economic Literature, 40*, 351–401.

Hommes, C. (2013). Reflexivity, expectations feedback and almost self-fulfilling equilibria: Economic theory, empirical evidence and laboratory experiments. *Journal of Economic Methodology, 20*.

Laibson, D. (1997). Golden eggs and hyperbolic discounting. *Quarterly Journal of Economics, 112,* 443–477.

Keynes, J. M. (1936). *The general theory of employment, interest and money.* London: Macmillan.

Merton, R. K. (1948). The self-fulfilling prophecy. *Antioch Review, 8,* 193–210.

Morris, S. (1995). The common prior assumption in economic theory. *Economics and Philosophy, 11,* 227–253.

Soros, G. (2013). Fallibility, reflexivity and the human uncertainty principle. *Journal of Economic Methodology, 20,* 309–329.

Stigler, G., & Becker, G. (1977). De Gustibus non est disputandum. *American Economic Review, 67,* 76–90.

Hypotheses non fingo: Problems with the scientific method in economics

J. Doyne Farmer

Institute for New Economic Thinking at the Oxford Martin School and Mathematical Institute, University of Oxford, Oxford, UK

Although it is often said that economics is too much like physics, to a physicist economics is not at all like physics. The difference is in the scientific methods of the two fields: theoretical economics uses a top down approach in which hypothesis and mathematical rigor come first and empirical confirmation comes second. Physics, in contrast, embraces the bottom up 'experimental philosophy' of Newton, in which 'hypotheses are inferred from phenomena, and afterward rendered general by induction'. Progress would accelerates if economics were to truly make empirical verification the ultimate arbiter of theories, which would force it to open up to alternative approaches.

Introduction

There is a widespread feeling by many non-economists and a few rebels within economics that there is something fundamentally wrong with the culture for scientific discovery in the discipline of economics. This view is shared by George Soros, who has provided a substantial endowment to the Institute for New Economic Thinking and given it the mandate to transform the discipline of economics to develop more realistic and effective economic theories. To succeed in this endeavor it is essential to have a clear statement of what is wrong. This essay addresses this question, proposing that the fundamental problems are in the way the scientific method is practiced in economics, and suggests how this might be changed.

Before going further, let me clarify the connection between what I write here and the essay of Soros around which this volume is organized (Soros, 2013). I have already written elsewhere about reflexivity in Cherkashin, Farmer, and Lloyd (2009) where we studied it in the simple context of a game of chance such as a coin toss, in which the bias of the coin is influenced by how people place their bets. We obtained several interesting results, for example demonstrating how the rate of approach to efficiency depends on the subjectivity of the game. The rate of convergence to efficiency is always slow, even when the coin is unaffected by the betting, but it can become much slower when outcomes are affected by the betting. (Lack of efficiency in this context is measured relative to the returns of a hypothetical rational agent, who somehow knows the entire population of players and can make optimal bets.) Our results imply that in a strongly reflexive world, it will take a very long time for the market to ever become efficient, confirming Soros's intuition in this regard.

Here I would like to address another topic in Soros's essay, concerning his view that reflexivity demands a different version of the scientific method than that of the natural sciences. Stating a widely held view, Soros asserts that economics has tried too hard to be like physics.[1] This sounds very strange to a physicist, since to us economics does not seem at all like physics. It is true that both disciplines make substantial use of mathematics. However, the way in which mathematics is used to build theories and the way in which theories are proposed and tested is very different. These differences reflect larger epistemological issues that I will try to illuminate here. To us physicists the problem is not that economics is too much like physics, but rather that it is completely unlike it. While the difference is subtle, I hope I can convince you that it is nonetheless profound.

In Soros' words, '[Economics] is an axiomatic system based on deductive logic, not empirical evidence.'[2] In contrast, in a tradition that can be traced back to Galileo and Newton, physics is a non-axiomatic system using empirical evidence to inductively infer mathematical models. Economic theory takes a top down approach, in which models come first and empirical confirmation comes second, while physics takes a bottom up approach, in which data comes first and models follow. The difference is vital. Physicists have been humbled by nature and forced to become open-minded about their view of the world, where all too often economists have preconceived views into which they try to make the world fit.

It is important to stress that physical laws and phenomena come in a wide range of different flavors. The popular view of physics is based on the nearly perfect predictability of celestial mechanics rather than the messy unpredictability of fluid turbulence. Some branches of physics, such as statistical mechanics, have focused more on messy problems, and provide examples that have much in common with reflexivity. While reflexivity introduces some complications, I will argue that physics has been coping with similar problems of circular causality for a long time, and that we have the tools needed to address it.

In this essay I give the view of an outsider – someone who has been trained in physics but has spent the last 20 years working in economics. To this I add the perspective of someone who spent many years in the highly interdisciplinary environment of the Santa Fe Institute, where I was exposed to many other disciplines, including biology and other social sciences such as psychology, sociology and anthropology. I have gone to considerable effort to understand the main ideas in economics, as evidenced in the review I wrote with a leading general equilibrium theorist (Farmer and Geanakoplos, 2009).

Before proceeding with my critique, I want to acknowledge that things are changing in economics, in a good direction: it has now become respectable to perform economic experiments, which have solidly documented the variety of ways in which real people deviate from rationality or fail to selfishly maximize their own utility. Theoreticians are working hard to incorporate behavioral findings into models, even if equilibrium is still typically assumed at the outset, and the modeling style is still very much the same as that used for rational expectations models. In response to the great recession, many models have been built that make much more realistic institutional assumptions. These are all good developments that deserve to be acknowledged and applauded. They represent a positive trend. Nonetheless, I still believe it is worth taking a step back and asking why these developments have been so slow to take hold, what is still lacking, and how the agenda of producing more realistic models could be accelerated.

Cartesians versus Newtonians

Physicists spend very little time on history, but nonetheless, students are occasionally given historical tidbits, parables to help them think the right way. One such parable that is particularly relevant here is the debate that occurred nearly 300 years ago between the Cartesians and Newtonians concerning action at a distance.

Galileo's pioneering experiments, Descartes' mathematics and philosophy, and Newton's development of classical physics are familiar to most readers. What is sometimes forgotten, however, is that in his day Descartes was also widely regarded as what we would now call a physicist, and that his methods and theories contrasted sharply with those of Galileo and Newton. Bear in mind that Descartes (1596–1650) was more or less a contemporary of Galileo (1564–1642), and that his work preceded that of Newton (1642–1727), who was born in the year that Galileo died.

Descartes' *Principia Philosophiae* presented theories for such phenomena as the origin and mechanism of the solar system, the transmission of light, tides, and the power of magnets – many of the same phenomena later treated by Newton in his *Principia Mathematica*.[3] Descartes' core assumption was that the universe, including the ether, is built out of three types of corpuscles, which can be regarded as hypothetical atoms, but in a classical rather than quantum–mechanical mold. The imagination and mathematics were dazzling, some the explanations were intuitively appealing, and his ideas were very popular in their day. However, they also turned out to be completely wrong: none of the explanations he put forward has held up under the test of time. The problem is that Descartes' assumptions were completely qualitative, difficult to test, and not grounded in experiments. They did not follow what we would now call the scientific method. In trying to explain everything from first principles in one stroke, Descartes failed to explain anything.

This is in striking contrast to Newton, who builds on the earlier quantitative experiments of Galileo and developed classical mechanics. Newton realized that the motion of celestial bodies could be explained based on the very simple assumption that the gravitational force between two objects is proportional to the inverse square of their distance. This was a leap, what a physicist would now call an *ansatz*. There was no underlying reason it should be true, but it resulted in a theory that matched the data. Based on the measurements of Edmund Halley, the Royal Astronomer and Newton's clandestine companion in alchemy, Newton was able to predict the future motion of the comet that now bears Haley's name. (Unlike the elliptic motion of planets, predicting the hyperbolic orbits of comets had previously been impossible.)

It is worth noting that even after more than 300 years have elapsed, we still do not have a complete microscopic explanation for action at a distance. It is hypothesized that the gravitational interaction is mediated by a particle called a graviton, but it has never been observed because the energies required are impossible to obtain in a laboratory. There remain many physicists who do not believe that such a particle exists. The debate about the origin of action at a distance still continues, but with no bearing on our ability to predict the motion of the planets.

Hypotheses non fingo

Newton's theory of gravitation was strongly attacked by the followers of Descartes. The focus of their attack was the inverse square law. Because Newton had simply hypothesized that the law existed, without offering an explanation, this was deemed 'action at a distance'. It violated the key principle that they felt any theory must obey, namely that all material interactions must be mediated by the mechanical interaction of corpuscles. Without such an explanation, they felt, the theory should not even be considered.

Newton took their complaints seriously at first and, in an effort to justify his assumption, at various points offered contorted arguments along Cartesian lines about the nature of the ether. He eventually gave up, and in the edition of *Philosophiæ Naturalis Principia Mathematica* published in 1712 he made a bold declaration:

> I have not as yet been able to discover the reason for these properties of gravity from phenomena, and I do not feign hypotheses. For whatever is not deduced from the phenomena must be called a hypothesis; and hypotheses, whether metaphysical or physical, or based on occult qualities, or mechanical, have no place in experimental philosophy. In this philosophy particular propositions are inferred from the phenomena, and afterwards rendered general by induction.

In 'experimental philosophy', propositions are inferred from the phenomena, and afterwards rendered general by induction. This approach is drilled into physicists. It is dramatically reinforced when a student learns quantum mechanics, which is such a counter-intuitive theory that one cannot comprehend it without abandoning one's preconceptions and reforming one's intuition about the nature of the world. Physicists are taught to pay close attention to data, have weak priors about theoretical explanations, and to be open to accepting the dictates of any theory that works, even if its predictions are counter-intuitive. The approach is fundamentally bottom up.

In contrast, this is not the way economists are taught to think. Economists are taught a style of modeling in which models come from idealized conceptions about how the world works. These is less emphasis on inferring propositions from phenomena; historical precedents are far more important, and propositions often come loaded with philosophical implications.

I have labeled the above story about Newton and Descartes a 'parable' to emphasize that, while I am suggesting an analogy between Cartesian approach to physics and most economists' approach to economics, I by no means intend to imply that most economists are as unscientific as Descartes. I do mean to say, however, that contemporary economics has some Cartesian tendencies that inhibit scientific progress. In particular, I will single out several aspects of contemporary scientific culture in economics that (at least in the eyes of a physicist) inhibit its progress.

Economic content

A naive outsider might assume that a theory with 'economic content' is one that explains an important economic phenomenon. Within economics, however, this phrase has a very different meaning: a theory has 'economic content' only if it is based on the assumption that selfish individuals maximize their preferences. Theories that are not based on this assumption are difficult to publish in top journals; indeed, economists do not even call them theories.

In some circumstances it is very reasonable to assume that agents selfishly maximize preferences. Nonetheless, making this a prerequisite for something to be called 'Economics' is dysfunctional. There is a clear analogy to the Cartesian requirement that all theories of nature must be derived from corpuscles. The first problem is that, in a young field such as economics in which so few theories have strong empirical support, it is unwise to prematurely lock down the form of all theories. The second problem is that it sets the bar too high: if Newton had waited until he could explain action at a distance from first principles, we would still be waiting. Very few theories in physics are derived directly from quarks. The third problem is that it may turn out to be wrong in many cases.

I now elaborate on the last point. The typical economics paper assumes agents with given information who can take certain actions, such as setting prices. It then assumes that these agents have a given utility function (which is pulled out of the air). It then calculates the decision rule that will maximize the utility of the agents, and looks at some of the consequences for properties such as prices.

But suppose the utility function that is pulled out of the air has little or nothing to do with the utility that motivates real people? Suppose that real utility functions are highly complicated and state dependent? Furthermore, suppose that the situation is so complicated that the decisions that agents actually make are very different from those that a rational agent would make?[4] In this case, setting the problem up in the standard form, so that the theory has 'economic content', is just bad science. It may be much more effective to take other approaches that are closer to reality, for example to study the decision rules that people use and implement them directly in computational agent-based models.

Many economic phenomena require little or no economic content to explain. Some examples of this include the distribution of mutual fund size (Schwarzkopf & Farmer, 2010), the relationship between order flow and price setting in the continuous double auction (Smith, Farmer, Gillemot, & Krishnamurthy, 2003), or the functional form of market impact.[5] I could list many others, and given that most of these have been discovered in the last decade, I expect this list to grow with time.

Connecting models to data

The requirement that all theories must have economic content causes serious problems in connecting models to data. Economists work in one of two modes: econometrics is essentially like statistics, in that reduced form models are chosen for more or less ad hoc reasons and fit to data. Theoreticians, in contrast, posit fundamental axioms within a set-up in which agents selfishly maximize utility. Because of the problems mentioned above, such as the arbitrariness of utility functions, the resulting model is not expected to fit data very well, so the resulting testing process is usually qualitative. As a result, the tests are not very sharp.

A physicist will approach the same problem in an iterative fashion. This approach strives toward fundamental models, but seeks to do so in developmental stages: one begins with exploratory data analysis, then formulates a model, tests it against the data, and iterates the process based on the successes and failures of the models, without strong priors. This data analysis begins by analyzing the data with the goal of discovering any possible 'laws', i.e. regularities in the data. Models are typically less ambitious, merely attempting to connect phenomena, without necessarily deriving all results from first principles.

A good example is provided by market impact. When a new order arrives on the market, it changes the balance of supply and demand, which exerts pressure on the price. The execution of a new buy order drives the price up, while a new sell order drives it down. Market impact is the average relationship between the size of the order and change in price. Early work on market impact was content to make fairly qualitative statements, and to study the factors that influenced market impact without searching for a law. Physicists built on this earlier work by analyzing the data to see whether there was a consistent pattern. As a result the hypothesis emerged that market impact increases as the square root of order size. In parallel, simulations and theoretical analyses were done on the continuous double auction that suggested that the mechanical response of the market strongly constrains impact (Smith, Farmer, Gillemot, & Krishnamurthy, 2003). Based on this, theories were formulated explaining the square root relationship and making additional hypotheses.[6] This process proceeded through a back and forth process between theory and data analysis.

The difference in attitude is reflected in the way in which Nobel Prizes are awarded. In physics, Nobel Prizes are not awarded unless a theory is confirmed by observation. For example, Einstein never received a prize for general relativity because it was not considered sufficiently well confirmed in his lifetime. In contrast, many Nobel Prizes in economics are for work that is influential, but has little or no empirical support.

Math versus science: the undue influence of Bourbaki

Economists are proud of the fact that economics is both a social science and a mathematical science. Physics is also a mathematical science, but to a physicist the style in which math is used in economics is strange. Economics theory is presented in theorem–proof format. Physics papers, in contrast, may have lots of equations, but they are written in a relatively informal style; the typical paper presents calculations rather than proofs, and the emphasis is on intuition rather than rigor. Physicists make approximations; economists prove upper or lower bounds.

This discrepancy traces back to a cultural divide that appeared in the early part of the twentieth century, when physics separated from mathematics. Up until then the style of physics and mathematics was fairly similar. But in the middle of the twentieth century this changed when mathematicians initiated a movement to make mathematics more rigorous. This was epitomized by the Bourbaki school, a group of (mainly French) mathematicians who published a series called *Elements of Mathematics* under the fictional name of Nicholas Bourbaki. This is reputed to have been partially in reaction to Henri Poincare', who was prominent both as a physicist and a mathematician, and who advocated an informal style. Bourbaki put a much higher weight on rigor and created a whole new style of presentation. As an illustration of this, their books contained no illustrations or figures, which they viewed as a crutch encouraging sloppy thinking.

When economics became a mathematical science in the middle of the twentieth century, the invaders were mathematicians, not physicists, and they brought the Bourbaki style with them. Economics papers have axioms, theorems, and proofs. Physics, in contrast, has never been axiomatized, despite the efforts of formidable mathematicians such as John von Neumann. The influence of the Bourbaki school is seen in many subtle ways. For example, physical and natural science journals are typically published in two-column format, whereas economics papers are written in single column format. This is because physicists love figures, and two-column format more easily accommodates figures. In contrast economists love tables, which single column format more easily accommodates.

Economists put a strong emphasis on math as a criterion for quality. Physicists, in contrast, are taught to view math as a means to an end, a tool in their toolkit, but of little scientific value for its own sake. To a physicist, too much emphasis on math for its own sake warps the criteria for good science. If a paper succeeds because it has nice math, even though the underlying assumptions are far-fetched, or the conclusions are weak and qualitative, then it excludes other papers that might have more science but less math. Because of this emphasis, there are many well-respected economists who are good mathematicians but poor scientists. This would be fine except for the fact that it means that other less rigorous but more scientific work ends up being excluded.

Simulation

In physical science the advent of the computer has arguably been the biggest force driving scientific progress in the second half of the twentieth century. Physicists were early adopters of computers. While physicists appreciate models with closed form analytical solutions, when this is impossible, simulations are considered perfectly acceptable. This is particularly true for complex systems, in which interactions are typically nonlinear and solutions are typically intractable without simulation.

In contrast, economists use computers to store and analyze data, to do word processing, and even to do algebra, but simulation is not part of the standard toolkit. Simulations rarely appear in top economics journals. This is a matter of what is considered valuable – since math is considered to have value for its own sake, a paper that does not have interesting math starts out with several strikes against it, and is likely to be difficult to publish in a good journal, no matter how interesting or powerful its conclusions.

This prejudice is strongly reinforced by the use of models based on rational expectations equilibrium. It is difficult to find rational strategies. As a result, economics models must be kept very simple in order to be tractable, and the functional form of the building blocks of the models, such as utility, must be chosen based on expediency rather than realism. The resulting models are brittle and inflexible. The result is that models in economics are typically highly stylized, omitting many key features that cannot be included due to the constraint of tractability, which is mandated by the dictums of equilibrium and optimality, and the requirement that the solutions be presented in closed form.

The underlying difficulty is that the set of tractable models is of measure zero in the space of all models. Most interesting phenomena are nonlinear, and as soon as models become nonlinear, solvability is rare and fortuitous. By requiring that all models must have closed form solutions, economists have painted themselves into a very small corner. The strong prejudice against simulation is probably the biggest cause of unreality in economic models. Closed form analytic solutions are a straightjacket from which economics must free itself.

In contrast, physicists who work in economics often gravitate to approaches such as computational agent-based models, i.e. computer simulations in which the agents are simulated algorithmically and their interactions are simulated on a computer. This emerging field has great potential – but it still lives on the fringe of contemporary economics.

Conclusion

In comparing economics to physics, I do not mean to imply that it is possible to predict economic systems with the precision of the solar system – at best, we may be able to make temporal predictions with the precision that we can predict weather, and even that is highly ambitious. But theories do many things besides temporal prediction, and laws come in many types. A more appropriate analogy is to statistical mechanics, in which the focus is not on temporal prediction, but rather on relating one quantity to another. For example, the ideal gas law states a relationship between temperature, pressure, and volume, without making a prediction about any one of them behave in time. Proper social science theories should begin at the phenomenological level – rather than being based on first principles, they should attempt to link phenomena, based on assumptions that should be flexible, and whose form should not be circumscribed.

Soros has argued that the human ability to think implies that theory in social science must be fundamentally different than in physical science, and in particular that this may impose limits on the ability to cast a successful theory in the language of mathematics. I disagree with this. Of course it is true that, unlike atoms, human beings can think, and that this makes finding theories and laws much harder. But this does not mean that finding laws is impossible.

In fact there are already several good examples of laws in economics, which have much the same character as physical laws. As my collaborators and I showed in our papers on limit order books (Farmer, Patelli, & Zovko, 2005; Mike & Farmer, 2008; Smith, 2003), an economic institution such as the continuous double auction can strongly constrain behavior and can result in quantitative relationships between human actions (such as rates of order placement) and economic properties (such as the bid–ask spread or the volatility of prices), which are analogous to the ideal gas law. The market impact rule that I have mentioned earlier is an even stronger example: if empirical tests continue to confirm our theories, as long as the circumstances required for the assumptions of theory to hold prevail, the average market impact is described by a simple functional form. Market impact is closely related to excess demand, and understanding it is a central problem in economics (or should be). If we are right, this alone is sufficient to show that economics can have quantitative laws, just like physics.

Note that the law of market impact coexists comfortably with reflexivity. That is because this law and many other relationships in finance and economics are not altered if agents are aware of them – in fact, in many cases the relationships are only strengthened. The formulas for option pricing provide another good example: the more participants believe in these formulas, the better they hold.

Economics would be a more successful science if it were both more empirical and more open minded. These two go together: when empirical confirmation is the arbiter of success or failure, theories are judged on their merits rather than on their cultural lineage. Economists should be taught to be suspicious of everything in their world view that has not received strong empirical validation. If one were to go through any standard introductory economics textbook, and color every statement pink with weak empirical confirmation, most of the book would be pink. This is understandable – economics is a new field, and social science is intrinsically harder than physical science. It is fine to make hypotheses that do not turn out to be correct. The problem is when they are presented as facts. The danger is that too many economists believe that what they are taught is actually true.

If economists were to acknowledge the shaky foundations on which their field stands, they would automatically become less dogmatic about what a theory of economics should look like. They would then be forced to expand their toolkit to include new tools, such as simulation, that would allow them to more directly connect theory and reality. By focusing on explaining empirical facts instead of elegance and fancy math, they would make bigger strides toward basing the field on realistic assumptions, which would lead to useful predictions. In order to achieve this, however, the epistemology of the field needs to change.

Notes

1. See for example Mirowski (1989), Beinhocker (2006), or Lo and Mueller (2010).
2. While I agree with the spirit of this remark, it is of course true that economics does strive to get agreement with empirical data. The difference is the way in which this is done.
3. Descartes also asserted that blood was vaporized in the heart and recondensed in the lungs, and the the soul is located in the Pineal gland.

4. Galla and Farmer (2011) suggests that even in the context of game theory, when the players must learn their own strategies, this is often true.
5. The theory of Toth et al. (2011) explains the functional form of market impact using only market efficiency, stressing the consequences of diffusion. The theory of Farmer et al. (2011) derives a Nash equilibrium.
6. Farmer, Gerig, Lillo, and Waelbroeck (2011) and Toth et al. (2011).

References

Beinhocker, E. (2006). *The origin of wealth.* Harvard Business Press, Boston.

Cherkashin, D., Farmer, J. D., & Lloyd, S. (2009). The reality game. *Journal of Economic Dynamics and Control, 33,* 1091–1105.

Farmer, J. D., & Geanakoplos, J. (2009). The virtues and vices of equilibrium and the future of financial economics. *Complexity, 14,* 11–38.

Farmer, J. D., Gerig, A., Lillo, F., & Waelbroeck, H. (2011). *How efficiency shapes market impact.* Retrieved from http://arxiv.org/abs/1102.5457

Farmer, J. D., Patelli, P., & Zovko, I. (2005). The predictive power of zero intelligence in financial markets. *Proceedings of the National Academy of Sciences USA, 102,* 2254–2259.

Galla, T., & Farmer, J. D. (2011). Complex dynamics in learning complicated games. *Proceedings of the National Academy of Sciences, 108,* 9008–9013.

Lo, A. W., & Mueller, M. T. (2010). *Warning: Physics envy may be hazardous to your wealth.* Retrieved from http://papers.ssrn.com/sol3/papers.cfm?abstract_id=1563882

Mike, S., & Farmer, J. D. (2008). An empirical behavioral model of liquidity and volatility. *Journal of Economic Dynamics and Control, 32,* 200–234.

Mirowski, P. (1989). *More heat than light: Economics as social physics. Physics as nature's economics.* Cambridge University Press, Cambridge.

Schwarzkopf, Y., & Farmer, J. D. (2010). *What drives mutual fund asset concentration?.* Retrieved from http://papers.ssrn.com/sol3/papers.cfm?abstract_id=1173046

Smith, E., Farmer, J. D., Gillemot, L., & Krishnamurthy, S. (2003). Statistical theory of the continuous double auction. *Quantitative Finance, 3,* 481–514.

Soros, G. (2013). Fallibility, reflexivity and the human uncertainty principle. *Journal of Economic Methodology, 20,* 309–329.

Toth, B., Lemperiere, Y., Deremble, C., de Lataillade, J., Kockelkoren, J., & Bouchaud, J.-P. (2011). Anomalous price impact and the critical nature of liquidity in financial markets. *Physical Review X, 1,* 021006.

Fallibility in formal macroeconomics and finance theory

Roman Frydman[a,b,1,2] and Michael D. Goldberg[b,c,3]

[a]Department of Economics, New York University, New York, NY, USA; [b]INET Program on Imperfect Knowledge Economics, New York, NY, USA; [c]Peter T. Paul College of Business and Economics, University of New Hampshire, Durham, NH, USA

This note focuses on George Soros's challenge to macroeconomics and finance theory that any valid methodology of social science must explicitly recognize fallibility in a Knightian sense. We use a simple algebraic example to sketch how extant models formalize fallibility. We argue that contemporary theory's epistemological and empirical difficulties can be traced to assuming away fallibility in a Knightian sense. We also discuss how imperfect knowledge economics provides a way to open mathematical models to such fallibility, while preserving economics as an empirical science.

1. Introduction

In his 1987 book *The Alchemy of Finance* (p. 310), George Soros proposed a pathbreaking conceptual framework for understanding financial markets that rested on two principles: fallibility and reflexivity. Over the last three decades, Soros has refined these concepts and argued that because prevailing economic models ignore their fundamental importance and that, as a result, economists have failed to explain how financial markets work or to understand adequately the role of public policy in influencing outcomes. In the lead paper for this Symposium, Soros provides the latest articulation of his framework and discusses its methodological implications for economics and the social sciences more broadly.

In discussing his 'principle of fallibility,' Soros observes that

> in situations that have thinking participants, the participants' view of the world never perfectly corresponds to the actual state of affairs. People can gain knowledge of individual facts; but when it comes to *formulating theories* or forming an overall view, their perspective is bound to be either biased or inconsistent or both. (p. 310 emphasis added)[4]

Soros incorporates fallibility into his 'principle of reflexivity': market participants' '*imperfect views* can influence the situation to which they relate through [their] behavior' (emphasis added, p. 310). Thus, participants' fallibility serves as the core principle of Soros's approach. In its latest rendition, his formulation of fallibility is expansive and includes both probabilistic risk and Knightian uncertainty.

Recognition of non-probabilistic uncertainty, Soros argues, is crucial for understanding phenomena such as the boom–bust processes in asset markets. Accounting for such fluctuations has confounded prevailing models for decades. For example, in their magisterial work on the current state of international macroeconomics, Obstfeld and Rogoff (1996, p. 625) concluded that, 'the undeniable difficulties that international economists encounter in empirically explaining nominal exchange-rate movements are an embarrassment, but one shared with virtually any other field that attempts to explain asset price data.'

There is little doubt that economists recognize that their own understanding of how the economy works – and that of market participants – is imperfect. Nonetheless, a vast majority of academic economists have maintained models that formalize fallibility solely in terms of probabilistic uncertainty.

The reasons why a group of thinkers or scientists maintains the core premises of their approach are complex. In the case of prevailing macroeconomics and finance theory, the sole reliance on probabilistic uncertainty seems to stem in part from the difficulties inherent to opening up formal models to Knightian uncertainty.

In this note, we provide a formal representation of fallibility in the Knightian sense in the context of a model that is typically used in macroeconomics and finance theory. In doing so, we illustrate how economists have represented their own and market participants' understanding of the process driving outcomes.

For Soros,

> [s]ome forms [of fallibility] are subject to statistical analysis – human errors leading to road accidents for example, or the many biases and errors discovered by behavioral economists. Other aspects of fallibility fall under Knightian uncertainty – for example, probability analysis is not much help in understanding the misconceptions at the heart of the euro crisis. (p. 314)

However, our example highlights the difficulty inherent in lumping together probabilistic risk and Knightian uncertainty in a formal representation of fallibility. Probabilistic uncertainty portrays fallibility by specifying fully in advance all potential values of the discrepancies between a model's representation of outcomes and their actual realizations (and the likelihoods with which they might occur). Such formulations of fallibility – what Soros refers to as 'human error' – presume that fallibility is governed by an overarching probabilistic law. There is thus a fundamental tension between Soros's inclusion of probabilistic uncertainty in his formulation of fallibility and his bold postulate that '[a]ny valid methodology of social science ... must explicitly recognize *Knightian uncertainty*' (p. 321 emphasis added).

We use our example to sketch how extant models formalize fallibility. We focus here on three classes of models: rational expectations (RE), behavioral finance, and imperfect knowledge economics (IKE).[5]

We point out that RE and behavioral finance models formalize fallibility solely in terms of probabilistic uncertainty. Except for random deviations that average to zero, both classes of models assume away economists' imperfect understanding. RE models also assume away imperfect understanding of the process driving outcomes on the part of market participants.

By contrast, behavioral finance models recognize market participants' imperfect understanding, and we show that they do not reduce fallibility to a random error that averages to zero. However, because these models represent fallibility solely in terms of probabilistic uncertainty, they can recognize fallibility only by presuming that market participants forego obvious profit opportunities.

Epistemological and empirical difficulties, which are inherent to efforts to maintain models that assume away Knightian uncertainty, provide a compelling argument for Soros's call for an alternative approach that recognizes the importance of such uncertainty for understanding outcomes. Its significance reflects '[t]he complexity of the world ... [which] exceeds our capacity to comprehend it.' He also views '[t]he structure of the brain [as] another source of fallibility' (p. 311).

However, these sources of fallibility do not distinguish 'the social from the physical sciences.' What distinguishes them is 'the fact that in social systems fallible human beings are not merely scientific observers but also active participants in the system themselves' (p. 311). Indeed, we have argued that, from the standpoint of mathematical modeling of social processes, we must come to grips with the fact that individuals change how they understand and forecast outcomes at times and in ways that do not conform to an overarching probabilistic law.[6] In Frydman and Goldberg (2013c), we show how Karl Popper's insights concerning the role of the growth of knowledge for understanding historical change can serve as the basis for such formal models. In particular, we build on his proposition that '[i]f there is such a thing as growing human knowledge, we cannot anticipate today what we shall only know tomorrow' (Popper, 1957, p. xii).

Here, we sketch how IKE formalizes imperfect understanding and reflexivity by opening mathematical models to the growth of knowledge, that is, to unanticipated changes in participants' understanding of the process driving outcomes. IKE enables an economist to acknowledge his own imperfect understanding, as well as that of market participants.

IKE explores the possibility that individual behavior and market outcomes exhibit context-dependent regularities that begin and cease to be relevant at moments that no one can fully foresee. IKE partly opens its models to Knightian uncertainty by formalizing such regularities with qualitative and contingent conditions.

Opening macroeconomic models to Knightian uncertainty helps to resolve the epistemological difficulties of extant models. For example, in Frydman and Goldberg (2013c), we show that it enables an economist to rid macroeconomic models of obvious irrationality, which is inherent in behavioral finance models that represent fallibility solely in terms of probabilistic uncertainty.[7]

2. Probabilistic fallibility in RE and behavioral finance models

In representing decision-making, say, in an asset market, an economist typically relates a participant's supply of or demand for an asset to her forecasts of future prices and the variables and parameters of his model's other components – an individual's preferences and constraints, together with a decision rule governing how she selects among the available options. Aggregating participants' supplies and demands results in a representation, in semi-reduced form, of an aggregate outcome – for example, the market price.

The following semi-reduced form is typical of many macroeconomics and finance models:

$$P_t = bX_t + c\hat{P}_{t|t+1} + \varepsilon_t^{\mathrm{P}} \quad \text{for all } t, \tag{1}$$

where $\hat{P}_{t|t+1}$ is the market's time-t forecast of the price at $t+1$, (b, c) is a vector of parameters, X_t is a set of causal factors, and $\varepsilon_t^{\mathrm{P}}$ is a random disturbance, which is typically characterized as distributed independently of the causal factors included in the model with a mean-zero, time-invariant probability distribution. The relationship in (1) represents the price at time t, P_t, in terms of an economist's understanding of the price process,

$$P_t^{\mathrm{EU}} = bX_t + c\hat{P}_{t|t+1} \quad \text{for all } t, \tag{2}$$

where $\varepsilon_t^{\mathrm{P}}$ can be thought of as representing the economist's imperfect understanding.

Formal accounts of how individuals understand how the economy works also relate market outcomes to a set of causal factors, which portray the information (the 'facts') that market participants consider relevant. A representation of the understanding that underpins the market's forecast can be written as

$$\hat{P}_{t|t+1} = \beta Z_t \quad \text{for all } t, \tag{3}$$

where β is a vector of parameters and Z_t represents the union of causal factors that market participants consider relevant for understanding outcomes. These factors may include fundamental variables, such as interest rates and income, and/or psychological considerations, such as confidence.

In order to derive time-series implications from his model, an economist must specify how the causal factors unfold over time. To simplify the presentation, we follow much of the literature and portray these causal factors as random walks with drift:

$$X_t = \mu^x + X_{t-1} + \varepsilon_t^x \quad \text{for all } t, \tag{4}$$

$$Z_t = \mu^z + Z_{t-1} + \varepsilon_t^z \quad \text{for all } t, \tag{5}$$

where (μ^x, μ^z) are drifts and $(\varepsilon_t^x, \varepsilon_t^z)$ are vectors of independently distributed disturbances ('the news'), which is characterized by a time-invariant probability distribution with mean zero and a finite variance–covariance matrix. The functional forms of the relationships in (1), (3), their parameters, and the properties of the causal factors characterized by (4) and (5) constitute the structure of the economist's model and formalize his/her understanding of participants' forecasting strategies as well as his/her own understanding of the process driving the market price at a point in time.

Like a vast majority of macroeconomic and finance models, the structure of our example is constrained not to change over time. Because they disregard the possibility of any structural change altogether, time-invariant models are particularly constrained versions of the class of models that we have referred to as determinate.[8] Such models assume away the possibility that the process driving the price, and market participants' understanding of this process, may change at times and in ways that no one can fully foresee.

2.1 Fallibility in a determinate model

We have shown in our earlier work that standard RE and behavioral finance models are determinate. We will now sketch how these two classes of models formalize fallibility in terms of probabilistic uncertainty. From the point of view of Soros's formulation of fallibility, these classes of models exemplify representations of fallibility as 'human error' and represent this error with a single overarching probability distribution.

2.1.1 RE and behavioral finance models: representing economists' fallibility as a random noise

The random variable ε_t^P in (1) represents the discrepancy between actual realizations of the price process, P_t, and an economist's understanding of it. It thus represents the 'human error' to which Soros refers in his formulation of fallibility. But, because ε_t^P is typically characterized with a time-invariant probability distribution, such representations presume that an economist can fully specify in advance how his own, supposedly imperfect, understanding of the price process will unfold over time. Such formulations of fallibility specify in advance all potential values of an economist's error and the chances of their occurrence.

Because standard RE and behavioral finance models are determinate, they presume that an economist has a nearly perfect understanding of how the price process unfolds over time. These models imply that an economist can correctly predict (on average) the market price at all future times.[9]

This conclusion easily follows by substituting (3) into (1) and iterating the result forward. We then use (4) and (5) to express the distribution of the future price in terms of an economist's understanding of the price process and realizations of the causal factors at any time t. This yields the following conditional distribution as the model's representation of the price at any time $t + \tau$:

$$P_{t+\tau} = bX_t + c\beta Z_t + \mu^{(\tau)} + \varepsilon^{(\tau)} \quad \text{for all } t \text{ and } \tau, \qquad (6)$$

where, $\mu^{(\tau)} = \tau(b\mu^x + c\beta\mu^z)$ and $\varepsilon^{(\tau)} = \varepsilon_{t+\tau}^P + \sum_{j=0}^{j=\tau}(\varepsilon_j^x + \varepsilon_j^z)$.

Although RE and behavioral finance models have the same implications concerning the near-irrelevance of fallibility on the part of an economist, they differ sharply in terms of how they represent market participants' fallibility. This difference stems directly from the roles that models in each class accord market participants' forecasts: whereas RE models rule out an autonomous role for individuals' forecasts, the vast majority of behavioral finance models consider them to be one of the factors driving outcomes.

2.1.2 The irrelevance of market participants' fallibility in an RE model

The RE hypothesis represents participants' understanding of the process driving outcomes by setting the market's forecast equal to the mathematical expectation of the price process, P_t in (1), conditional on time t information, I_t:

$$\hat{P}_{t|t+1}^{RE} = E[P_t|I_t]. \qquad (7)$$

Applying (4) in (1) results in the following representation of the process driving the price and the market's forecast[10]:

$$P_t^{RE} = \frac{bc}{(1-c)^2}\mu^x + \frac{b}{1-c}X_t + \varepsilon_t^P \quad \text{for all } t, \qquad (8)$$

$$\hat{P}_{t|t+1}^{RE} = \frac{b}{(1-c)^2}\mu^x + \frac{b}{1-c}X_t \quad \text{for all } t. \qquad (9)$$

The expressions in (8) and (9) show that RE models represent participants' fallibility with a random error, $\varepsilon_{t+\tau}^P$. Thus, they presume that market participants, too, have a nearly perfect understanding of how the market price unfolds over time.

2.1.3 Fallibility as irrationality in a behavioral finance model

Behavioral finance models accord market participants' forecasts an autonomous role in driving outcomes. Although they represent fallibility in standard probabilistic terms, they do not reduce it to a random deviation that averages to zero. This follows immediately from behavioral finance models' representation of participants' forecast error:

$$FE_{t+1} = P_{t+1} - \hat{P}_{t|t+1} = \mu + bX_t + (c-1)\beta Z_t + \varepsilon_{t+1}, \tag{10}$$

where, $\mu = b\mu^x + c\beta\mu^z$ and $\varepsilon_{t+1} = b\varepsilon_{t+1}^x + c\beta\varepsilon_{t+1}^z + \varepsilon_{t+1}^P$.

Expression (10) represents participants' forecast errors as systematic and easily detectable: they have a non-zero mean and are correlated with participants' information set, Z_t. Thus, representing forecasts as autonomous in models that formalize fallibility in probabilistic terms presumes that market participants forego obvious profit opportunities endlessly. Thus, although behavioral finance models do not reduce fallibility to a mere white noise error, they can only recognize fallibility by introducing obvious irrationality into an economist's model.

3.   Opening macroeconomics and finance theory to Knightian uncertainty

An IKE model jettisons determinate restrictions on its representations of how the macroeconomy and market participants' forecasting strategies might change over time. By doing so, the model recognizes that participants' forecasts depend not just on the information that they use, but also on how they revise their strategies:

$$\hat{P}_{t+1|t+2} - \hat{P}_{t|t+1} = \beta_t \Delta Z_{t+1} + \Delta\beta_{t+1} Z_{t+1}, \tag{11}$$

where $\Delta Z_{t+1} = Z_{t+1} - Z_t$, and $\Delta\beta_{t+1} = \beta_{t+1} - \beta_t$.

Using (11) and (1), we can write the change in the market price as follows:

$$P_{t+1} - P_t = b_t \Delta X_{t+1} + \Delta b_{t+1} X_t + c\left[\beta_t \Delta Z_{t+1} + \Delta\beta_{t+1} Z_t\right] + \eta_{(t,t+1)}, \tag{12}$$

where change in the macroeconomy is represented by Δb and $\eta_{(t,t+1)} = \varepsilon_{t+1}^P - \varepsilon_t^P$.

These representations make clear that unless further restrictions on revisions of forecasting strategies are imposed, the representation in (12) has no empirical content: it is compatible with *any* time path of the market price and with *any* causal process that underpins them.

3.1   *Methodological extremes: animal spirits versus determinate accounts of outcomes*

Early macroeconomic analysis, particularly that of Keynes, is sometimes interpreted as claiming that mathematical representations of the process driving outcomes are unattainable, because economic behavior, especially decision-making by financial market participants, stems only from mercurial 'animal spirits.' Similarly, Knightian uncertainty is often interpreted to imply that there are no regularities in the way that market participants make decisions. Indeed, unless participants' forecasting strategies could be connected, at least during some time periods, to the causal factors observable by economists, no formal economic theory with empirical content would be possible. As Phelps (2008) has put it, 'animal spirits can't be modeled.'

Contemporary models, with their core premise that determinate causal accounts of individual decision-making and market outcomes, are within reach of economic analysis, occupy the opposite methodological extreme. Searching for such accounts, economists constrain their models severely: they fully prespecify structural change. Consequently, their models represent outcomes at each point in time – and thus how they unfold over time – with a single, overarching conditional probability distribution.

3.2 IKE's intermediate position

IKE recognizes the inherent limits of economists' understanding that arise from unanticipated changes in the process driving outcomes and market participants' understanding of this process. However, it does not adopt the extreme view that mathematical macroeconomics and finance theory are impossible. IKE stakes out an intermediate position between completely open, unrestricted models (which, by definition, cannot be formally confronted with empirical evidence), and determinate models (which can be formally tested, but have failed empirically).

Like their determinate counterparts, IKE macroeconomic and finance models are mathematical. Moreover, the key assumptions that impute empirical content to IKE models are those that characterize structural change, particularly in how market participants revise their forecasting strategies. IKE explores the possibility that in some contexts, individual decision-making, exhibits some regularity.

3.2.1 Formal representations of forecasting

Consider an IKE representation of market participants' forecasting. The expression in (12) shows that movements in the market's forecast depend on how participants revise their forecasting strategies and on how causal factors move over time, ΔZ_{t+1}. In order for the model to generate empirically relevant implications, it supposes that there are protracted stretches of time during which revisions and movements of the causal factors exhibit qualitative regularities.

In representing revisions in our recent work, we build on an idea that goes back to Keynes (1936). Faced with imperfect knowledge concerning the causal process driving market outcomes, a participant tends to revise in moderate ways her thinking about how fundamentals influence outcomes: there are stretches of time during which she either maintains her forecasting strategy or revises it only gradually. Psychological studies have also uncovered evidence that individuals revise their beliefs gradually in the face of new evidence.[11] But, unlike behavioral finance models, we formalize this regularity with a qualitative condition on $\Delta\beta_{t+1}$, rather than with a determinate rule.

3.2.2 The contingency of IKE's representations

One would not expect market participants to revise their forecasting strategies in moderate ways, or that fundamentals will continue to trend in the same direction forever. One would also not expect the way that these decisions translate into aggregate outcomes to remain unchanged even if characterized by qualitative conditions. Indeed, structural change in an IKE model is defined by conditions that are not only qualitative, but also contingent. IKE models, therefore, are open to unanticipated change and recognize the importance of the imperfect understanding that such change engenders. Thus, they formalize fallibility in the sense of Knightian uncertainty, but in ways that yield implications that can be confronted with time-series evidence.

The contingent and qualitative nature of the conditions that IKE models place on structural change is crucial to their ability to deliver empirically relevant accounts of swings in asset prices and risk. Qualitative regularities, like market participants' tendency to revise their forecasts in guardedly moderate ways for stretches of time, play a key role in an IKE model of persistent upswings and downswings. But, because these conditions are also contingent, they are consistent with the irregular structural change in macroeconomic and finance models. By specifying its models as qualitative and contingent, IKE accounts for the irregular asset-price swings that we observe in real-world markets.

4. Fallibility and rationality

We have shown that determinate models can recognize the relevance of participants' fallibility only by according their forecasting an autonomous role in driving outcomes. But doing so presumes that participants forego obvious profit opportunities endlessly. In order to rid their models of such obvious irrationality, Lucas and the vast majority of contemporary economists have relied on determinate models and RE, thereby jettisoning any autonomous role for participants' forecasting behavior and thus reducing fallibility to random noise in their models.[12]

RE models are widely thought to represent rational forecasting. Thus, when economists uncovered massive evidence that these models fail to explain outcomes, especially in financial markets, they concluded that market participants are irrational. We show in Frydman and Goldberg (2013c) that, because they rule out unanticipated changes in how market participants revise their understanding of how the economy works, RE models are abstractions of rational decision-making only in markets in which knowledge of market processes does not grow.

The behavioral school resurrected the importance of autonomous expectations for macroeconomic analysis. This enabled researchers to incorporate into their models important empirical findings concerning how individuals actually behave in market settings.[13] But the behavioral finance approach has formalized its empirical findings with determinate models. Behavioral researchers thus construct models that allow for fallibility on the part of market participants, but presume that market participants are obviously irrational.

This argument does not, however, imply that behavioral findings should be ignored in building macroeconomic models, as RE theorists typically do. Recognizing that individuals do not endlessly forego obvious profit opportunities does not mean that behavioral economists' emphasis on realism and the importance of psychological and social considerations are unimportant for understanding regularities in time-series data. Indeed, such considerations are crucial for understanding how rational individuals make decisions and how aggregate outcomes unfold over time.

In Frydman and Goldberg (2013c), we show how recognizing the growth of knowledge – and the Knightian uncertainty that it engenders on the part of economists and market participants – provides a way past what appears to be determinate models' insurmountable epistemological and empirical difficulties. However, although all IKE models are open to Knightian uncertainty, not all of them are compatible with rational decision-making. In Frydman and Goldberg (2013c), we formulate the contingent expectations hypothesis (CEH), which selects IKE models that can serve as the basis for representing conditional rationality in macroeconomics and finance theory.[14]

CEH incorporates Popper's insights regarding the importance of the growth of knowledge and thus rules out models that represent outcomes and fallibility solely in probabilistic terms. This hypothesis also builds on John Muth's (1961) and Robert Lucas's (1995, 2001) insights concerning the importance of imposing a coherence between the economist's understanding of the macroeconomy, as represented by his semi-reduced form, and his representation of how market participants understand and forecast market outcomes. An RE model imposes such coherence in quantitative terms. By contrast, a CEH model imposes coherence only in qualitative terms.

In Frydman and Goldberg (2013c), we develop a CEH model that relates an economy's inflation rate to the real interest rate. We argue that change in the macroeconomy, as represented by Δb, depends on policy and institutional factors that tend to remain largely unchanged or that change very little for protracted stretches of time. During these periods, we would expect moderate or no change in the inflation process from one point in time to the next. However, major shifts in policy, institutions, and other factors do eventually occur. We would thus expect that periods of moderate or no change in the inflation process would be punctuated by relatively large shifts. Such larger scale change can be anticipated only dimly, if at all. Consequently, no one can fully anticipate when time intervals of moderate or no change in the macroeconomy might begin or end.

We formalize this understanding of protracted intervals of moderate change with qualitative and contingent conditions on structural change in the model's semi-reduced form. CEH implies using this understanding in representing how market participants might revise their forecasting strategies. In doing so, it shows how Keynes's and behavioral economists' insights regarding market participants' tendency to revise their forecasting strategies gradually can be seen, conditional on the adequacy of the CEH model, as a symptom of their rationality rather than their irrationality.

More broadly, CEH provides a way to synthesize REH's focus on the importance of fundamental considerations in underpinning rational forecasting (for example, that inflation expectations depend on interest rates) with the two other major advances in macroeconomics over the last four decades. One is Phelps's et al. (1970) research program of basing aggregate relationships on micro-foundations that accord an autonomous role to participants' expectations, and the other is behavioral economists' use of empirical observation in representing individuals' decision-making. These advances are usually thought to be incompatible with the assumption that market participants do not forego profit opportunities or make decisions that conflict with their objectives. By recognizing the importance of the growth of economists' and participants' knowledge, CEH-based analysis can incorporate these advances into macroeconomics and finance models, and yet maintain the assumption of conditional rationality.

5. Knightian uncertainty and time-series implications of macroeconomics and finance models

CEH models do not yield exact probabilistic predictions. But, as Soros (p. 321) emphasizes, 'Time and context-bound generalizations may yield more specific explanations and predictions than timeless and universal ones.' The development and testing of IKE theory indicate that models that are partly open to Knightian uncertainty not only have time-series implications, but also can explain key features of movements in asset prices and risk that have confounded extant approaches for decades.

When the economics profession embraced the search for a determinate theory of market outcomes, Soros (1987) understood the epistemological and empirical flaws of such an approach. He adopted fallibility, in the sense of Knightian uncertainty, as the core premise of his portrayal of boom-and-bust processes in asset markets and appealed to his own trading experience as evidence for the empirical relevance of his framework. The paper in this Symposium urges economists to recognize that '[a]ny valid methodology of social science must explicitly recognize both fallibility and reflexivity and the Knightian uncertainty they create' (p. 321).

Acknowledgement

The authors are grateful to the Institute for New Economic Thinking (INET) for supporting this research.

Notes

1. http://www.econ.nyu.edu/user/frydmanr/
2. http://ineteconomics.org/research-program/imperfect-knowledge-economics
3. http://pubpages.unh.edu/~michaelg/
4. Unless otherwise noted, all references to pages without a citation are to Soros's (2013) paper for this Symposium.
5. The RE approach has been presented in many books and articles. For an early comprehensive exposition, see Sargent (1987), Lucas (1995) and references therein. Shleifer (2000) provides an overview of behavioral finance models. Frydman and Goldberg (2007, 2011) propose IKE and show how it can be used to explain swings in prices and risk in asset markets and other macroeconomic and finance phenomena.
6. Frydman and Goldberg (2007, 2011, 2013a, 2013b) and references therein.
7. Although IKE models are partly open to unanticipated change in the process driving outcomes, the qualitative conditions upon which they rely imply regularities that can be confronted with time-series evidence. For a recent exposition of such regularities, and how they can serve as the basis for defining rationality in macroeconomics and finance models, see Frydman and Goldberg (2013c).
8. Sometimes economists allow for change in a determinate model. But, when they do, they fully specify when and how the price process, and participants' understanding of it, might change. In Frydman and Goldberg (2007, chapter 6), we show that, like their time-invariant counterparts, such determinate models represent outcomes in all time periods with a single overarching probability distribution. This implies that the conclusions of this section also apply to determinate models that allow for change.
9. Of course, if the processes underlying the error terms in an RE or behavioral model were assumed to have large variances, the models would presume that the economist's understanding was associated with large prediction errors.
10. In general, the parameters and causal factors in the representations for the price process in (1) depend on the specification of non-expectational components of the model's microfoundations, that is, market participants' preferences and the constraints that they face.
11. See Edwards (1968). For an application in a determinate behavioral finance model, see Barberis et al. (1998).
12. See Frydman and Phelps (2013) for an extensive discussion of this turn in macroeconomic research, which has altered the field in the decades since. Despite recent attempts to move away from RE models, macroeconomists have continued to believe that RE does represent rational forecasting. The reason, at least in part, seems to stem from the continuing reliance on determinate models, even by those who have been attempting to develop alternatives to RE.
13. See Shleifer (2000) and Barberis and Thaler (2003) and references therein.
14. By conditional rationality, we mean rationality conditional on the empirical adequacy of an economists' model. Indeed, rationality in macroeconomics and finance theory, including both RE and IKE approaches, is actually conditional on such adequacy. For a rigorous analysis and discussion of this key point, see Frydman and Goldberg (2013c).

References

Barberis, N., Shleifer, A., & Vishny, R. (1998). A model of investor sentiment. *Journal of Financial Economics, 49*, 307–343.

Barberis, N. C., & Thaler, R. H. (2003). A survey of behavioral finance. In G. Constantinides, M. Harris, & R. Stulz (Eds.), *Handbook of the economics of finance* (pp. 1050–1121). Amsterdam: North-Holland.

Edwards, W. (1968). Conservatism in human information processing. In B. Kleinmuth (Ed.), *Formal representation of human judgement*. New York: John Wiley and Sons.

Frydman, R., & Goldberg, M. D. (2007). *Imperfect knowledge economics: Exchange rates and risk*. Princeton, NJ: Princeton University Press.

Frydman, R., & Goldberg, M. D. (2011). *Beyond mechanical markets: Asset price swings, risk, and the role of the state*. Princeton, NJ: Princeton University Press.

Frydman, R., & Goldberg, M. D. (2013a). The imperfect knowledge imperative in modern macroeconomics and finance theory. In R. Frydman & E. S. Phelps (Eds.), *Rethinking expectations: The way forward for macroeconomics* (pp. 130–168). Princeton, NJ: Princeton University Press.

Frydman, R., & Goldberg, M. D. (2013b). Opening models of asset prices and risk to non-routine change. In R. Frydman & E. S. Phelps (Eds.), *Rethinking expectations: The way forward for macroeconomics* (pp. 207–250). Princeton, NJ: Princeton University Press.

Frydman, R., & Goldberg, M. D. (2013c). *Contingent expectations hypothesis: Conditional rationality in macroeconomics and finance theory*. Mimeo. September 2013.

Frydman, R., & Phelps, E. S. (2013). Which way forward for macroeconomics and policy analysis? In R. Frydman & E. S. Phelps (Eds.), *Rethinking expectations: The way forward for macroeconomics* (pp. 1–46). Princeton, NJ: Princeton University Press.

Keynes, J. M. (1936). *The general theory of employment, interest and money*. New York: Harcourt, Brace and World.

Knight, F. H. (1921). *Risk, uncertainty and profit*. Boston, MA: Houghton Mifflin.

Lucas, R. E. Jr. (1995). The monetary neutrality. *The nobel lecture*. Stockholm: The Nobel Foundation.

Lucas, R. E. Jr. (2001). *Professional memoir*, mimeo. Retrieved from http://home.uchicago.edu

Muth, John F. (1961). Rational expectations and the theory of price movements. *Econometrica, 29*, 315–335.

Obstfeld, M., & Rogoff, K. (1996). *Foundations of international macroeconomics*. Cambridge, US: MIT Press.

Phelps, E. S. (2008, March 14). Our uncertain economy. *The Wall Street Journal*.

Phelps, Edmund S, Armen, A. Alchian, Charles, C. Holt, Dale, T. Mortensen, Archibald, G. C., Robert, E. Lucas, Leonard, A. Rapping (1970). *Microeconomic foundations of employment and inflation*. New York: Norton.

Popper, K. R. (1957). *The poverty of historicism*. London and New York: Routledge.

Sargent, T. J. (1987). *Macroeconomic theory*. New York, NY: Academic Press.

Shleifer, A. (2000). *Inefficient markets*. Oxford: Oxford University Press.

Soros, G. (1987). *The Alchemy of finance*. New York, NY: Wiley.

Soros, G. (2009). Financial markets. *Lecture 2 of the Central European University Lectures*, October. Retrieved from http://www.ft.com/cms/s/2/dbc0e0c6-bfe9-11de-aed2-00144feab49a.html

Soros, G. (2013). Fallibility, reflexivity and the human uncertainty principle. *Journal of Economic Methodology, 20*, 309–329.

Reflexivity and equilibria

Francesco Guala

Department of Economics, Management and Quantitative Methods, Università degli Studi di Milano, Milano, Italy

The failure of models based on rational expectations to explain the 'boom and bust' of financial markets does not support Soros' critique of mainstream economics or his call for a theoretical revolution. Contrary to what Soros says, standard rational choice theory has the conceptual resources to analyse reflexivity. The dynamic of feedback loops for example can be described by simple models based on multiple equilibria and informational cascades. The problem is that agents and theorists sometimes lack the information required to identify equilibria and tipping points.

1. Introduction

'Reflexivity' is a popular term in scholarly conversations. The fact that it is used in different fields has certainly contributed to its diffusion, but at the same time has generated confusion. Its core meaning comes from mathematics: a reflexive relation ('is equal to', for example) relates every element of a set to itself. In social theory, reflexivity has been mainly used in the context of causal, rather than logical or mathematical relations: in a reflexive causal relation, each event or variable is both a cause and an effect of another event or variable (X causes Y and Y causes X).

Most accounts of reflexivity emphasize the role of beliefs. In George Soros' words, 'the participants' views influence but do not determine the course of events, and the course of events influences but does not determine the participants' views' (2013, p. 312). An attraction of the term 'reflexive' is its relationship with the phrasal verb 'to reflect on', meaning 'to think carefully' on a given topic. Social phenomena are reflexive because people are reflexive in this sense.

Soros argues that economists' failure to predict and prevent economic crises is a consequence of economic theory's neglect of reflexivity. He also claims that a theory that takes reflexivity seriously will depart radically from mainstream models, causing a paradigm shift from current economic thinking. Although I agree with Soros on the importance of reflexivity, I think that his critique of mainstream economics is mistaken. Reflexivity plays a central role in economic thinking, and rigorous models based on this concept are unlikely to depart substantially from standard models based on Nash equilibria and equilibration processes.

The paper is structured as follows: in Section 2, I explain why the concept of reflexivity, as understood by Soros, is strictly related to the concept of equilibrium used in rational choice theory. Section 3 provides a simple example of how reflexivity, as well as 'negative' and 'positive' feedback loops, can be represented using simple models of equilibrium and informational cascades. Section 4 extends the discussion arguing that reflexivity and equilibria are key concepts to represent not only 'boom and bust' phenomena, but also the stability and persistence of social institutions. Section 5 summarizes and concludes the paper with some reflections on the future of economics.

2. Equilibrium

George Soros' views on reflexivity originate from his life-long study of financial markets. Reflexivity is a likely source of the disruptive 'boom and bust' cycles that unsettle financial markets from time to time, and economists and politicians do not seem to have found a way to immunize the economy from these cycles so far. So Soros' emphasis on reflexivity and his call for increased research effort are certainly welcome. Unfortunately, Soros misdiagnoses the causes of economists' failure, and as a consequence overstates their implications.

One source of misunderstanding is Soros' conflation of rational expectations theory and the efficient markets hypothesis (EMH) with economic theory. The EMH is not representative of economics as a whole: it is a particular, and highly contentious, application of the theory of rational choice that lies at the core of most neoclassical economic models. As a mere point of logic, the failure of EMH can hardly be imputed to economics in general.

Rational expectations models assume that market participants have correct (rational) beliefs about the main economic variables, and as a consequence that market prices do not diverge significantly from equilibrium. But such claims rely on the crucial underlying assumption that there is a unique equilibrium and that the equilibrium is efficient. Although such assumptions are ubiquitous in finance, other branches of economics routinely use models with multiple equilibria, some of which are inefficient. These models are well suited to capture the dynamics of reflexivity that Soros is concerned about, because equilibrium is itself a reflexive notion.

In the technical jargon of economic theory, a *Nash equilibrium* is a profile of actions such that the action of every individual is optimal given the actions of the other individuals: each action is a best reply to the actions of others. This does not mean, as every economist knows, that the overall outcome (the profile of actions) is efficient. It just means that no one can achieve a better outcome by changing her strategy unilaterally. An important property of this concept is that the beliefs of all individuals are true in equilibrium. I choose X because I believe (correctly) that you choose Y, and you choose Y because you believe that I choose X. Another way to put it is that the beliefs of all the agents form a gigantic self-fulfilling prophecy.

Soros describes this mutual consistency of actions and beliefs informally, using the concepts of 'manipulative function' and 'cognitive function' of human thinking. Roughly, these refer to the fact that human agents simultaneously try to represent the world but, through their actions (which are influenced by their representations), also determine the state of the world they are in. According to Soros this mutual influence raises a theoretical puzzle:

> when both the cognitive and manipulative functions operate at the same time they may interfere with each other. How? By depriving each function of the independent variable that would be needed to determine the value of the dependent variable. The independent variable of one function is the dependent variable of the other, thus neither function has a *genuinely independent variable*. (2013, p. 311)

Before Soros, other social theorists have been baffled by this apparent circularity. Oskar Morgenstern gave one of the earliest formulations of the problem in his 1928 dissertation on *Wirtschaftsprognose* (economic forecast). One of his famous examples concerns two individuals – Holmes and Moriarty – playing a game of 'hide and seek' (Morgenstern, 1928, p. 98). If Holmes decides to take the train to Dover, Moriarty will try to catch him at the terminal station; Holmes should anticipate this, and stop at an intermediate station; but a rational Moriarty should anticipate Holmes' anticipation, prompting Holmes to consider travelling all the way to Dover again, … and so forth for an infinite number of iterations. Morgenstern found this circularity – the fact that any move will provoke a symmetric defeating counter-move – extremely disturbing, and used it to draw pessimistic conclusions for the predictive ambitions of economic theory.

But economists have gone a long way since then, partly (ironically) thanks to Morgenstern himself. Any student of game theory now knows that seemingly unstable interactions such as these can and often do converge to an equilibrium (von Neumann & Morgenstern, 1944). Take the game of penalty kicks, a situation that mirrors the Holmes–Moriarty game and that is routinely played by strikers and goalkeepers on European football pitches. Contrary to Morgestern's intuition, such games have a perfectly rational and stable solution (an equilibrium) according to which the strikers shoot 60% of the time on their strong side and the keepers dive 60% of the time on the same side.[1] This is a *mixed-strategy* equilibrium, a pattern that is statistically predictable, is compatible with individual rationality and leaves a lot of uncertainty and fun for the fans who watch the game on TV.

The concept of equilibrium, as used in strategic models, has allowed rational choice theorists to tackle these reflexive dependencies in an analytical way. At times Soros seems to accept that equilibrium must play a role in a proper theory of reflexivity. But the latter, he argues, will have to go much beyond equilibrium, in order to provide adequate understanding: 'equilibrium, which is the *central* case in mainstream economic theory, turns out to be an extreme case of negative feedback, a *limiting* case in my conceptual framework' (2013, p. 323).

So the problem is that economics does not go far enough. Its narrow focus on a limiting case prevents it from giving an adequate account of *out-of-equilibrium* behaviour. This is what Soros has in mind when he says that 'reflexive feedback loops have *not* been rigorously analysed' (2013, p. 313). But what is it exactly that economists are missing, and how would a better theory look like? Soros is not shy and tries to give an informal account of reflexivity. His stab is based on the twin notions of negative and positive feedback: 'negative feedback brings the participants' views and the actual situation closer together; positive feedback drives them further apart' (2013, p. 322).

Now, is economics really impervious to such notions? In rational choice terms, a negative feedback loop is a process of belief revision that converges towards a Nash equilibrium, while a positive feedback loop moves away from it. In the next section I illustrate a simple model of these processes. The model is abstract, but to make it concrete we can dress it with an interpretation taken from Robert K. Merton's classic discussion of the self-fulfilling prophecy (Merton, 1948).

3. Equilibration

Merton's story begins with a bank that is financially sound. The bank has plenty of liquidity for its day-to-day business and no prospect of insolvency in the foreseeable future. One day, however, an unusual number of depositors appear at its desks to withdraw their savings. To make sense of this unexpected event, some other clients conjecture that the bank is in trouble, and decide to withdraw their money too. This causes more queueing in front of the desks and more withdrawals. Very soon the rumour becomes true – the bank *is* insolvent and goes bankrupt.

Merton highlights the common pattern in this and other cases of reflexivity: a *false* belief brings about events that turn it into a *true* belief. The bank was not unsound before the rumour spread. But because people came to believe it, the bank became unsound. As Soros would say, this is the 'principle of fallibility' in action.

To Merton, self-fulfilling prophecies are obvious aberrations and raise two sets of concerns. First, there is a policy problem: can we prevent them from occurring? It seems that we would all be better off if our financial system was invulnerable to the diffusion of unfounded rumours. But there is also a scientific problem: self-fulfilling prophecies are puzzling – they are 'peculiar to human affairs', 'not found in the world of nature', according to Merton – so we ought to find an explanation.

Although his essay remains a classic reference, Merton did not propose a satisfactory analysis of the mechanics of self-fulfilling prophecies. In the two decades that followed, however, economists devised simple tools to model such situations (Figure 1). To simplify, let us assume that each depositor can only choose one of two actions: to keep her money stored in the bank, or to withdraw it. On the horizontal axis, we represent the proportion of depositors who are expected to withdraw, on a scale that goes from zero to one. For simplicity, we interpret this parameter as an aggregate function of the individual beliefs of all depositors, something like the 'average' expectation in the population. On the vertical axis, we represent the proportion of depositors who *actually* withdraw (again on a zero to one scale). The diagonal line includes all the points in which the expected number of withdrawals is equal to the actual number of withdrawals – that is, the set of all possible correct beliefs.

The S-curve in the diagram is called the *propagation* function, because it represents how many people decide to withdraw, given their beliefs about the proportion of withdrawals. If we suppose that customers observe in real time each other's behaviour, we obtain a dynamic model known as a 'Schelling diagram', from the game theorist and Nobel Laureate Thomas Schelling (1978).

The propagation function in Figure 1 crosses the diagonal in three different points: e_1, e_2 and t. These are self-fulfilling prophecies: people's beliefs about withdrawals (and, a fortiori, the soundness of the bank) are correct. A dynamic model, however, allows more than simply identify self-fulfilling prophecies and beliefs. It also permits an analysis of the

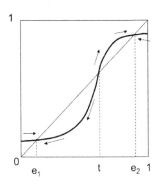

Figure 1.   A Schelling's diagram with three equilibria.

forces that lead individuals to adjust their behaviour as they update their beliefs. This analysis shows that over time some outcomes are more likely to occur. As Merton pointed out, certain self-fulfilling prophecies are very predictable – indeed, they appear inexorable. Looking at the model we can understand why.

Let us start from the bottom-left tip of the S-curve. In this corner of the box, we have those depositors who are going to withdraw their money no-matter-what. We can imagine these clients as people who need the money for some expense or investment, which was planned independently of any turmoil in the financial sector. Even if no one else withdraws, they will do it. All the other depositors instead condition their choices on their expectations regarding the proportion of withdrawals. Now, when the propagation function lies *above* the diagonal, we have a situation in which more people are withdrawing (vertical axis) than it was expected (horizontal axis). There is a contradiction between beliefs and behaviour that must be resolved. Once the lines begin to form in front of the bank, depositors process the new information and revise their beliefs accordingly. This corresponds to a shift towards the right in the diagram: a few more clients decide to withdraw their money from the bank. If we are still above the diagonal, the same sequence of observation, belief revision, and withdrawal continues until the propagation function meets the diagonal line.

Notice that when the reaction function lies *below* the diagonal, we have an adjustment in the opposite direction. Fewer people withdraw their money than expected. Again, customers process this new information and revise their beliefs accordingly, causing a shift towards the left-hand side of the box. These two dynamics jointly imply that the adjustment process tends towards e_1 or e_2 (see the arrows in the figure). Soros describes this equilibration process informally in these terms:

> A negative feedback process is self-correcting. It can go on forever and if there are no significant changes in external reality, it may eventually lead to an equilibrium in which the participants' views come to correspond to the actual state of affairs. (2013, p. 322)

He also points out that the system does not always return to the original equilibrium, though:

> Positive feedback loops are more interesting because they can cause big moves both in market prices and in the underlying fundamentals. A positive feedback process that runs its full course is initially self-reinforcing in one direction, but eventually it is liable to reach a climax or reversal point, after which it becomes self-reinforcing in the opposite direction. But positive feedback processes do not necessarily run their full course; they may be aborted at any time by negative feedback. (2013, p. 323)

This indeterminacy in the outcome of feedback processes is explained in the model by point t. By definition, e_1, e_2 and t are *all* self-fulfilling prophecies. Beliefs and behaviour are always consistent on the diagonal. But e_1 and e_2 are robust, in the sense that small deviations from these points will trigger processes that bring the system back to its previous state. Point t in contrast is very fragile: it is a 'tipping point', meaning that even the slightest deviation will start a dynamics that will make the system converge towards e_1 or e_2. Social scientists call these dynamics *informational cascades*, and use them to explain abrupt institutional changes such as political revolutions (Kuran, 1995). When a tipping point is crossed, there is no coming back – the gulf will increase and the fate of the bank is sealed.

How can it possibly happen? What triggers a run on a bank? Some event must push beliefs beyond the tipping point. If the system normally tends to gravitate around e_1, such an abrupt change can be brought about only by an external shock. This may be a new piece of information, such as, for example a report from a rating agency saying that the bank has falsified its accounts. Other abrupt events that may have the same effect include a declaration of war, or a sudden political crisis. The common feature of such events is that everyone has to form very quickly new beliefs about the behaviour of others, in unusual circumstances that they have never faced before. There is a lot of uncertainty, and people in such moments often go for the option that seems the safest – to withdraw their savings, for example. In these situations of panic, the whole system may crumble very quickly, and it is difficult to intervene before it is too late.

When beliefs are fluid, economic theory can have a stabilizing function. If the beliefs of a sub-class of individuals (economists or market analysts) enjoy a particular epistemic authority, they will tend to influence the views of other participants. This process of imitation is analogous to the dynamics described above, and may direct behaviour towards or away from a specific equilibrium. This is the sense in which social theorizing can influence reality, a feature that many philosophers – including Soros – consider truly distinctive compared to natural scientific theorizing.[2]

4. Social reality

Soros does not consider the possibility of multiple equilibria. His speaking of an 'objective reality' that 'reasserts itself', or of 'far-from-equilibrium situations' that persist over time suggests that he is in the grip of a key mainstream assumption: markets have a unique equilibrium. Once this assumption has been taken on board, feedback processes do appear puzzling and radically at odds with economic theorizing. But if multiple equilibria and tipping points are admitted, much of the mystery disappears. The problem becomes *practical* – how to model complex feedback processes adequately – rather than conceptual.

The practical problem is daunting, and explains social scientists' failures to forecast political and economic crises. The shape of the propagation function is usually unknown to agents and theorists alike. This implies that they are typically unsure about the existence and location of equilibria and tipping points. In times of uncertainty, forecasting becomes almost an impossible task. And reform, for the same reasons, is extremely difficult when people doubt that a superior equilibrium can be attained. Many aspects of the Euro crisis can be explained this way.

Is such a predicament inevitable for social science? Soros claims that equilibrium is 'an extreme condition', and stability is 'exceptional' (2013, p. 322). 'The human uncertainty principle implies that a perfect alignment would be the exception rather than the rule' (2013, p. 317). I think this is a misunderstanding, prompted perhaps by the uniqueness of equilibrium assumption. The truth is the opposite: equilibrium or near-equilibrium is the norm in social life. What may look like the persistence of far-from-equilibrium behaviour is often convergence towards *another* equilibrium that we had failed to consider before.

Equilibrium is the norm because radical uncertainty would make social life impossible. Human societies are enormously complex systems of coordination games, and coordination requires stability of behaviours and beliefs. This is not to deny the existence of coordination failures, or of systemic crises that occasionally affect large portions of society at once. During these periods of crisis, we tend to emphasize the fragility and unpredictability of the structure, forgetting the enormous resilience and consistency of expectations that make social life possible. Even simple actions like purchasing bread at the local baker's would be impossible if far-from-equilibrium behaviour was the norm.

Crossing the street would be a heroic feat without the equilibria of the rules of traffic; bartering with the baker would take an enormous amount of time without the equilibrium of a common currency.

Emphasizing the fragility rather than the robustness of social systems is like seeing the glass half empty or half full. This is why reflexivity elicits opposite reactions. Understandably, it has often been perceived a source of problems to be solved: if you are a scientist interested in explanation and prediction, reflexivity makes your life harder. But some scholars rejoice and celebrate feedback loops – like Douglas Hofstadter in his best-selling book on *Gödel, Escher, Bach* (subtitle: *An Eternal Golden Braid*). Loops may have creative, generative power. They may bring new kinds and phenomena into being. They may even bring about new ways of living – new human identities, as Ian Hacking has pointed out.[3] In general, feedback loops need not be disruptive.

Of course stability is not necessarily good in itself. There are different equilibria in our simple model of a bank run, and one of them (e_1) is intuitively better than others: it is the equilibrium in which the bank exists and it is financially sound. The situation in e_2 is quite different: although everyone is 'happy', in the sense that no one would like to change her behaviour unilaterally, each depositor regrets the demise of the bank. So it is possible that each individual is trapped in e_2 even though she recognizes that she would be better off in e_1.

The model of the run on a bank provides an important insight that should inform any social theory. The insight is that both states e_1 and e_2, where the bank is, respectively, sound and unsound, are self-fulfilling prophecies. A shift from e_1 to e_2 appears perverse because the new beliefs do not seem to reflect a change in the 'fundamentals' of the bank. But this is misleading: deposits are one of the fundamentals. So it is not irrational to withdraw, if the other customers are withdrawing. Since in e_2 all beliefs are correct and all preferences are satisfied (given these beliefs), the difference between e_1 and e_2 is not as deep than it may initially appear.

Another way to put it is that there is nothing weird or 'wrong' about reflexivity itself. Self-fulfilling prophecies may lead to equilibria that we like, as well as equilibria that we do not like (it depends on our preferences). But without reflexivity or self-fulfilling prophecies, a lot of important institutions that we love and respect would not exist. There would be no banks, for sure, but also no political leaders, no religious ceremonies, no football teams and so on and so forth. It took a long time for this simple truth to be appreciated by social scientists and philosophers.[4] The game–theoretic perspective on social institutions, which was developed independently and for other purposes, facilitates the construction of simple models of reflexivity. What is a sound bank? In equilibrium, I do not withdraw my money because I believe that you do not withdraw, because I believe that you believe that I do not withdraw, and I believe that you believe that I believe that you do not withdraw and so on. Social reality is constituted by beliefs about beliefs.

5.   Conclusion

Soros' reflections are driven by two different claims. One of them is correct: reflexivity is a key concept to understand the dynamics of market behaviour and of social phenomena more generally. The second thesis is that economic theory does not have the conceptual resources to deal with reflexivity. As I have shown in this paper, this claim is misleading. In part, it is based on the conflation of economic theory with a specific application, the EMH. The EMH is a particularly narrow rational choice model, and its failure does not have any implications for the prospect of economics to explicate reflexivity. As we have seen, the phenomena that Soros classifies as 'reflexive' can be easily represented using rational choice models such as Schelling's diagrams. The strategic interactions depicted in these models are admittedly simple, and economists face enormous difficulties when they try to explain the functioning of more complex systems such as real financial markets. But the very existence of these models demonstrates that the challenge is *practical*, rather than conceptual, in character. There is no deep flaw in economic theory that prevents it from capturing the essential features of 'negative' and 'positive feedback loops'. Soros claims that 'the new paradigm [based on reflexivity] is bound to be very different from the one that failed' (2013, p. 41). I think that the opposite is true: any theory that will succeed to model such phenomena will have to employ concepts that are very similar to equilibria and equilibration processes.

Once this has been clarified, other mistakes are easily avoided. Soros follows a long series of social theorists in identifying 'physics' envy' as a fundamental obstacle for the progress of social science. But physicists and biologists make extensive use of equilibrium models, and equilibrium is a reflexive notion. So physics' envy cannot be the problem. That neoclassical economic theory borrowed some analytical tools from Newtonian physics is a historiographic platitude.[5] Overall this may have been a bad or a good idea, but it has certainly not prevented economists from understanding reflexivity (if anything, the opposite is true). Newtonian physics did not dictate economists the theory of rational expectations or the EMH. Financial economists 'ended up' with such hypotheses for a number of contingent reasons, but their ignorance of reflexivity was not one of them. In fact the central modelling tools of rational choice theory, such as equilibria and belief revision, capture the essential features of reflexivity remarkably well. If reflexivity is a fundamental feature of social phenomena, as Soros contends, then the economic theory of choice is well equipped to explain social reality.

Of course this does not demonstrate that we should stick to rational choice theory. Perhaps we should really change strategy and abandon traditional models based on equilibria and equilibration processes. After all, we might never be able to understand, control and predict the behaviour of financial markets using such models. Perhaps a Copernican revolution is needed in this domain. But – paradoxically for Soros – any theory that will abandon equilibrium concepts will also abandon reflexivity. Because reflexivity and equilibrium models are so strictly related, they will stand or fall together in any future social theory.

Funding

This paper was written while I was supported by a MIUR grant 'Rientro dei Cervelli'.

Notes

1. Cf. Palacios-Huerta (2003). The 'strong side' of a striker is left for right-footed players, and right for left-footed players.
2. MacKenzie's (2006) narrative of the rise and fall of the Black-Scholes model of option pricing is based on this idea and provides a neat example of reflexivity in action.
3. See e.g. Hacking (1995, 1999) and Mallon (2003).
4. As far as I know, it was first noticed by the philosopher Daya Krishna, in a 1971 commentary on Merton's essay. For an influential early analysis of reflexivity along these lines, see also Barnes (1983).
5. See e.g. Ingrao and Israel (1987/1990) and Mirowski (1989).

References

Barnes, S. B. (1983). Social life as bootstrapped induction. *Sociology, 17*, 524–545.

Hacking, I. (1995). The looping effect of human kinds. In A. Premack (Ed.), *Causal cognition: A multidisciplinary debate* (pp. 351–383). Oxford: Clarendon Press.

Hacking, I. (1999). *The social construction of what?* Cambridge, MA: Harvard University Press.

Hofstadter, D. (1979). *Gödel, Escher, Bach: An eternal Golden Braid*. New York, NY: Basic books.

Ingrao, B., & Israel, G. (1987/1990). *La mano invisibile*. Bari: Laterza. [The invisible hand]. Cambridge, MA: MIT Press.

Krishna, D. (1971). The self-fulfilling prophecy and the nature of society. *American Sociological Review, 36*, 1104–1107.

Kuran, T. (1995). *Private truths, public lies*. Cambridge, MA: Harvard University Press.

MacKenzie, D. (2006). *An engine, not a camera: How financial models shape markets*. Cambridge, MA: MIT Press.

Mallon, R. (2003). Social construction, social roles, and stability. In F. F. Schmidt (Ed.), *Socializing metaphysics*. Lanham: Rowman and Littlefield.

Merton, R. K. (1948). The self-fulfilling prophecy. *Antioch Review, 8*, 193–210.

Mirowski, P. (1989). *More heat than light*. New York, NY: Cambridge University Press.

Morgenstern, O. (1928). *Wirtschaftsprognose, eine Untersuchung ihrer Voraussetzungen und Möglichkeiten*. Vienna: Springer Verlag.

Palacios-Huerta, I. (2003). Professionals play minimax. *Review of Economic Studies, 70*, 395–415.

Schelling, T. (1978). *Micromotives and macrobehavior*. New York, NY: Norton.

Soros, G. (2013). Fallibility, reflexivity and the human uncertainty principle. *Journal of Economic Methodology, 20*, 309–329.

von Neumann, J., & Morgenstern, O. (1944). *The theory of games and economic behavior*. Princeton: Princeton University Press.

Reflexivity, expectations feedback and almost self-fulfilling equilibria: economic theory, empirical evidence and laboratory experiments

Cars Hommes

CeNDEF, University of Amsterdam and Tinbergen Institute, Amsterdam, The Netherlands

We discuss recent work on bounded rationality and learning in relation to Soros' principle of reflexivity and stress the empirical importance of non-rational, almost self-fulfilling equilibria in positive feedback systems. As an empirical example, we discuss a behavioral asset pricing model with heterogeneous expectations. Bubble and crash dynamics is triggered by shocks to fundamentals and amplified by agents switching endogenously between a mean-reverting fundamental rule and a trend-following rule, based upon their relative performance. We also discuss learning-to-forecast laboratory experiments, showing that in positive feedback systems individuals coordinate expectations on non-rational, almost self-fulfilling equilibria with persistent price fluctuations very different from rational equilibria. Economic policy analysis may benefit enormously by focusing on efficiency and welfare gains in correcting mispricing along almost self-fulfilling equilibria.

1. Introduction

In his book *The Alchemy of Finance*, Soros (1987) introduced the principles of *fallibility* and *reflexivity* to describe the evolving state of financial markets and the economy. As a very successful market participant, Soros argued that standard economic theory built on the paradigm of rationality is a poor description of economic reality and has been of little help to guide investment behavior. Soros articulated the crucial role of expectations and feedback in the economy and the lack of a realistic description of these phenomena by the rational expectations (RE) paradigm. Soros' view has been updated and described elegantly in his recent contribution Soros (2013) to this special issue. Here, we discuss the relation between economic theory, especially the role of expectations and learning, and Soros' principles of fallibility and reflexivity emphasizing empirical and laboratory evidence.

Let me start by recalling the two principles *fallibility* and *reflexivity* and their central role in social science and economics in his own words (Soros, 2013, pp. 310–312):

> The first is that in situations that have thinking participants, the participants' view of the world never perfectly corresponds to the actual state of affairs. ... The second proposition is that these imperfect views can influence the situation to which they relate through the behavior of the participants ... it connects the universe of thoughts with the universe of events. ... Reflexive feedback loops between the cognitive and manipulative functions connect the

realms of beliefs and events. The participants' views influence but do not determine the course of events, and the course of events influences but does not determine the participants' views. The influence is continuous and circular; that is what turns it into a feedback loop.

Let me contrast this view with a quote from Muth's classical paper introducing RE. Muth was well aware that aggregation of individual expectations into a representative rational forecast depends critically on whether or not these individual expectations are *correlated* (Muth, 1961, p. 321, emphasis added):

> Allowing for cross-sectional differences in expectations is a simple matter, because their aggregate affect is negligible as long as the deviation from the rational forecast for an individual firm is *not strongly correlated with those of the others*. Modifications are necessary only if the correlation of the errors is large and depends systematically on other explanatory variables.

Who is right, Soros or Muth? I will review some recent theory, empirical evidence and laboratory experiments that shed some light on this debate.

2. Expectations feedback and bounded rationality

Soros recognizes the crucial difference between natural and social sciences: in social systems participants can think and affect actual events. Weather forecasts will not affect the probability of rain, but a forecast of the macroeconomic outlook by the president of the ECB may affect the likelihood of a recession. A dynamic economic model is an expectations feedback system, mapping individual beliefs into actions and market realizations, shaping new market expectations, etc. A simple form of an expectations feedback system is

$$p_t = F(p^e_{1,t+1}, p^e_{2,t+1}, \cdots p^e_{H,t+1}), \tag{1}$$

where today's realized market price p_t depends on the individual forecasts $p^e_{j,t+1}$ for tomorrow of all economic agents.

Traditional economics is built on the paradigm of RE introduced by Muth (1961) and popularized in macroeconomics by Lucas and Prescott (1971) and others. All agents are assumed to be perfectly rational using economic theory to form their expectations. All subjective beliefs then coincide with objective *model consistent* expectations, and the model can be solved for rational expectations equilibrium (REE), which is essentially a *fixed point* of the expectations feedback system. An important motivation contributing to the popularity of RE has been the Lucas critique (Lucas, 1976), that policy conclusions based on non-RE models are potentially misleading because changes in policy will alter individual behavior. In particular, expectations should not depend on exogenous parameters but should take policy changes into account.

Many economists today are well aware that RE imposes unrealistically high cognitive and informational assumptions on the agents in the economy and that some form of bounded rationality is needed. But which form? RE disciplines economic modeling in an elegant and convenient way. By imposing RE, all parameters of individual forecasting are removed from the model. Allowing for non-RE begs the question which errors the model should allow for. This leads to Sims' metaphor of the 'wilderness of bounded rationality': if agents are non-rational, there are a million ways of how individual agents may make mistakes.

One alternative approach to bounded rationality that is gaining some ground in macroeconomics is *adaptive learning*. Boundedly rational agents do not have perfect knowledge about the economy but act as econometricians or statisticians using an econometric forecasting model and updating the parameters over time as additional observations become available; see, for example, Sargent (1993) and Evans and Honkapohja (2001, 2013) for extensive surveys and references. The original motivation for this literature has been to study conditions under which learning converges to RE, in the hope that learning may enforce RE without assuming perfect knowledge of the expectations feedback system. Agents are then assumed to know the structural equations of the economy, but not the parameters which need to be learned over time as additional observations become available. Many examples, however, have been provided where learning does *not* settle down to RE, but to non-rational equilibria, explaining high persistence and excess volatility, as, for example, in the learning equilibria in Bullard (1994) or the self-fulfilling mistakes in Grandmont (1998). A *behavioral learning* approach based on simplicity and parsimony has been advocated by the so-called Restricted Perception Equilibria (Branch, 2006; Hommes & Zhu, 2013). Agents base their expectations on simple forecasting heuristics, such as an AR(1)rule, with the parameters pinned down by simple consistency requirements between beliefs and market realizations, for example, based on intuitive and observable quantities such as the mean and the first-order autocorrelation.

Another complementary approach to bounded rationality is *heterogeneous expectations* models as, for example, introduced in Brock and Hommes (1997, 1998) and Branch and Evans (2006). Agents endogenously switch between different forecasting rules, ranging from simple heuristics to more sophisticated strategies, based upon their relative performance. Notice that in both adaptive learning and heterogeneous switching models, the learning is *endogenous* and agents will adapt to policy changes, so that these models, at least to a first order approximation, mitigate the Lucas critique.

These recent approaches are much in the spirit of Soros' principles of fallibility and reflexivity. Agents do *not* know the correct model of the economy, but rather use some misspecified forecasting rules which may be heterogeneous across agents. This leads to a complex economic expectations feedback system. A REE may arise as a special case in which the equilibrium is exactly self-fulfilling, but often *almost self-fulfilling* behavioral learning equilibria will arise exhibiting excess volatility and deviating persistently from the rational benchmark. In what follows, we will discuss the empirical relevance of *almost self-fulfilling* equilibria.

3. A behavioral asset pricing model

We consider a stylized asset pricing model with heterogeneous beliefs, as in Brock and Hommes (1998), and fit a 2-type model to S&P500 data. Investors can choose between a risk-free asset paying a fixed return r and a risky asset (say a stock) paying uncertain dividends. Assume that investors have perfect knowledge of the exogenous cash flow process, and thus know the 'fundamental value' of the risky asset, but differ in their beliefs about the future price of the asset. Denote Y_t as the dividend payoff and P_t as the asset price. The market clearing pricing equation is given by

$$P_t = \frac{1}{1+r}\bar{E}_t[P_{t+1} + Y_{t+1}], \tag{2}$$

where $\bar{E}_t[.]$ denotes average expectations of the population of investors.

The dividend process follows a geometric random walk with drift:

$$\log Y_{t+1} = \mu + \log Y_t + \nu_{t+1}, \quad \nu_{t+1} \sim \text{IID}\left(0, \sigma_\nu^2\right). \tag{3}$$

Investors are assumed to have correct, model-consistent beliefs about the exogenous dividend process, $E_{i,t}[Y_{t+1}] = (1 + g)Y_t$, where $g \equiv e^{\mu+(1/2)\sigma_\nu^2}$ is the constant growth rate of dividends. This assumption has the convenient feature that the model can be written in deviations from a RE benchmark fundamental.

In the special case where *all* agents have RE about prices, the price equals its RE *fundamental value* given by the discounted sum of all future expected dividends[1]:

$$P_t^* = \frac{1+g}{r-g} Y_t. \tag{4}$$

Hence, under RE the price-to-dividend ratio is constant and given by $P_t^*/Y_t = (1+g)/(r-g) \equiv \delta^*$.

Figure 1 illustrates the S&P500 stock market index, the price-to-dividend ratio δ_t, and the fundamental value. The S&P500 index clearly exhibits *excess volatility*, as pointed out already in the seminal paper of Shiller (1981) and see also Shiller (2000). Boswijk, Hommes, and Manzan (2007) estimated a 2-type model using yearly S&P500 data from 1871 to 2003. More recently, Hommes and in't Veld (2013) updated the estimation of the 2-type model using quarterly data 1950Q1–2012Q3. In deviations from the fundamental value $x_t \equiv \delta_t - \delta^*$, the 2-type model is given by

$$x_t = \frac{1}{R^*}(n_{1,t}E_{1,t}[x_{t+1}] + n_{2,t}E_{2,t}[x_{t+1}]), \quad R^* \equiv \frac{1+r}{1+g}. \tag{5}$$

The asset pricing model has *positive expectations feedback*, i.e., the realized price deviation increases (decreases) when the (average) expected deviation increases (decreases). Consider the simplest form of heterogeneity with belief types which are linear in the last observation:

$$E_{h,t}[x_{t+1}] = \phi_h x_{t-1}. \tag{6}$$

Two types, $h = 1, 2$, are sufficient to capture the essential difference in agents' behavior: fundamentalists believe the price will return to its fundamental value ($0 \le \phi_1 < 1$) and chartists believe that the price (in the short run) will move away from the fundamental value ($\phi_2 > 1$).

The fractions of the two types are updated with a multi-nomial logit model based on their relative performance, as in Brock and Hommes (1997), with the *intensity of choice* β measuring how quickly agents switch strategies:

$$n_{h,t+1} = \frac{e^{\beta U_{h,t}}}{\sum_{j=1}^H e^{\beta U_{j,t}}}. \tag{7}$$

The performance measure $U_{h,t}$ is a weighted average of past profits and past fitness, with memory parameter ω:

$$U_{h,t} = (1 - \omega)\pi_{h,t} + \omega U_{h,t-1}. \tag{8}$$

Hence, consistent with empirical observations, agents tend to switch to strategies that generated higher profits in the recent past.

The econometric form of the endogenous switching model is an AR(1)-model with a time-varying coefficient:

$$R^* x_t = n_{1,t}\phi_1 x_{t-1} + (1 - n_{1,t})\phi_2 x_{t-1} + \epsilon_t, \quad R^* = \frac{1+r}{1+g}, \tag{9}$$

where ϵ_t represents an IID error term. The estimated parameter values in Hommes and in't Veld (2013) are as follows:

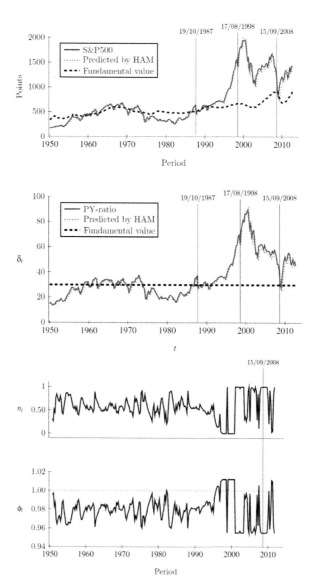

Figure 1. Time series of S&P500 and its fundamental value (top panel), price-to-dividend ratio and its (constant) fundamental (second panel), estimated fraction $n_{1,t}$ of fundamentalists (third panel), and the corresponding time varying market sentiment (bottom panel).

- $\phi_1 = 0.953$: type 1, therefore, are *fundamentalists*, expecting (slow) mean reversion of the price towards its fundamental value;
- $\phi_2 = 1.035$: type 2 are *trend-extrapolators*, expecting the price deviation from fundamental to increase by 3.5% per quarter;
- $\omega = 0.816$: implying almost 20% weight is given to the most recent profit observation and about 80% to past profitability.

Define the market sentiment as

$$\phi_t = \frac{n_{1,t}\phi_1 + (1 - n_{1,t})\phi_2}{R^*}. \tag{10}$$

Figure 1 shows the time series of the estimated fractions of fundamentalists and the market sentiment. The fraction of fundamentalists varies considerably, but gradually (due to memory) over time, with values between 0.25 and 0.9 until the 1990s, and more extreme values ranging from almost 0 to 1 after the dot com bubble. The switching model offers an intuitive explanation of the dot com bubble, as being triggered by economic fundamentals (good news about a new Internet technology) strongly amplified by trend-following behavior. Estimates of the market sentiment ϕ_t vary between 0.96 and 1 until the 1990s, showing near-unit root behavior. During the dot com bubble, the market sentiment ϕ_t exceeds 1 for several quarters, with the market being temporarily explosive. During the financial crisis, the market is mainly dominated by fundamentalists, indicating that the financial crisis has been re-enforced by fundamentalists, who expected a correction of asset prices back to fundamentals.

In this behavioral asset pricing model with heterogeneous beliefs, agents switch endogenously between a mean-reversion and a trend-following strategy based upon realized profitability and aggregate behavior is very different from the rational benchmark. Strategy switching driven by (short run) profitability leads to an almost self-fulfilling equilibrium with endogenously generated bubbles triggered by shocks to fundamentals ('news') and fueled by positive feedback from trend followers and market crashes re-enforced by negative feedback from fundamentalists.

4. Laboratory experiments

Laboratory experiments are well suited to study expectations feedback systems within a controlled environment. Hommes (2011) surveys the so-called Learning-to-Forecast Experiments (LtFEs), where subjects have to forecast a price, whose realization depends endogenously on their average forecast. The main goal of LtFEs is to study how individual expectations are formed, how these interact and which structure emerges at the aggregate level. Will agents learn to coordinate on a common forecast and will the price converge to the RE benchmark or will other aggregate behavior arise?

In the asset pricing LtFEs in Hommes, Sonnemans, Tuinstra, and van de Velden (2005), there are two assets, a risk free asset paying a fixed rate of return r and a risky asset, with price p_t, paying an uncertain dividend y_t. The asset market is populated by six large pension funds and a small fraction of fundamentalist robot traders. Six subjects are forecast advisors to each of the pension funds. Subjects' only task is to forecast the price p_{t+1} of the risky asset for 50 periods and, based on this forecast, the pension fund then computes how much to invest in the risky asset according to a standard mean–variance demand function. The fundamentalist robot trader always predict the *fundamental price p^f* and trades based upon this prediction. The realized asset price in the experiment is derived by market clearing and given by

$$p_t = \frac{1}{1+r}\left((1 - n_t)\bar{p}^e_{t+1} + n_t p^f + \bar{y} + \varepsilon_t\right), \tag{11}$$

where $\bar{p}^e_{t+1} = (\sum_{h=1}^{6} p^e_{h,t+1})/6$ is the average two-period ahead price forecast, $p^f = \bar{y}/r$ is the fundamental price, and ε_t are small shocks. Subjects do *not* know the underlying law of motion (11), but they do know the mean dividend $\bar{y}$ and the interest rate r, so they could use these to compute the fundamental price and use it in their forecast. The fraction n_t in (11) is the share of computerized fundamental robot traders, increasing as the price moves away from the fundamental benchmark according to

$$n_t = 1 - \exp\left(-\frac{1}{200}|p_{t-1} - p^f|\right). \tag{12}$$

The fundamental trader thus acts as a 'far from equilibrium' stabilizing force in the market, adding negative feedback when the asset price becomes overvalued. The negative feedback becomes stronger, the more price moves away from the fundamental. The overall expectations feedback system (11) has positive feedback, but the positive feedback becomes less strong (i.e., stronger mean-reverting) when price moves away from fundamental value.

Figure 2 shows time series of prices, individual predictions, and forecasting errors in three different groups with a robot trader. A striking feature of aggregate price behavior is that three different qualitative patterns emerge. The price in Group 5 converges slowly and almost monotonically to the fundamental price level 60. In Group 6 persistent oscillations are observed during the entire experiment, while in Group 7 prices fluctuate but the amplitude is decreasing.

A second striking result is that in all groups participants were able to *coordinate* their forecasts. The forecasts, as shown in the lower parts of the panels, are dispersed in the first periods but then, within 3–5 periods, move close to each other. The coordination of individual forecasts has been achieved in the absence of any communication between subjects, other than through the realized market price, and without any knowledge of past and present predictions of *other* participants.

The fourth group in Figure 2 shows a time series of prices, in a market *without* fundamental traders (Hommes, Sonnemans, Tuinstra, & van de Velden, 2008). In the absence of a far from equilibrium stabilizing force due to negative feedback from the fundamental robot traders, a long-lasting asset price bubble occurs with asset prices rising above 900, i.e., more than 15 times the fundamental price, before reaching an exogenously imposed upper bound of 1000 and a subsequent market crash.

These asset market laboratory experiments exhibit a strong degree of reflexivity. Markets do not converge to the perfectly self-fulfilling RE fundamental 60, but rather fluctuate persistently and exhibit expectations driven bubbles and crashes along almost self-fulfilling equilibria.

5. Positive versus negative feedback experiments

The asset pricing experiments are characterized by *positive expectations feedback*, i.e., an increase in the average forecast or an individual forecast causes the realized market price to rise. Heemeijer, Hommes, Sonnemans, and Tuinstra (2009) and Bao, Hommes, Sonnemans, and Tuinstra (2012) investigate how exactly the expectations feedback

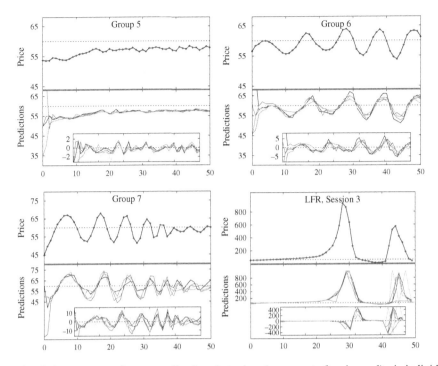

Figure 2. Laboratory experiments: realized market prices (upper part of each panel), six individual predictions (middle part of each panel), and individual errors (bottom part of each panel). Three asset markets with robot traders (upper + bottom left) and one asset market without robot traders (bottom right). Prices do not converge to the RE fundamental benchmark 60, but rather fluctuate. In the market without fundamental robot trader (bottom right), a long-lasting bubble arises. Individual expectations coordinate on almost self-fulfilling equilibria.

structure affects individual forecasting behavior and aggregate market outcomes. Their (unknown) price generating rules were as follows:

$$p_t = 60 - \frac{20}{21} \left[\left(\sum_{h=1}^{6} \frac{1}{6} p_{ht}^e \right) - 60 \right] + \epsilon_t, \quad \text{negative feedback,} \tag{13}$$

$$p_t = 60 + \frac{20}{21} \left[\left(\sum_{h=1}^{6} \frac{1}{6} p_{ht}^e \right) - 60 \right] + \epsilon_t, \quad \text{positive feedback,} \tag{14}$$

where ϵ_t is a small random shock to the pricing rule. The positive and negative feedback systems (13) and (14) have the same unique RE equilibrium steady state $p^* = 60$ and *only* differ in the sign of the expectations feedback map. Both are linear near-unit-root maps, with slopes $20/21 \approx -0.95$ resp. $+20/21$. Figure 3 (top panels) illustrates the dramatic difference in the negative and positive expectations feedback maps. Both have the same unique RE fixed point, but under near-unit-root positive feedback, as is typical in asset pricing models, each point is in fact an *almost self-fulfilling equilibrium*. Will subjects in LtFEs be able to coordinate on the unique RE fundamental price, the only equilibrium that is perfectly self-fulfilling?

Figure 3 (bottom panels) shows realized market prices as well as six individual predictions in two typical groups. Aggregate price behavior is very different under positive

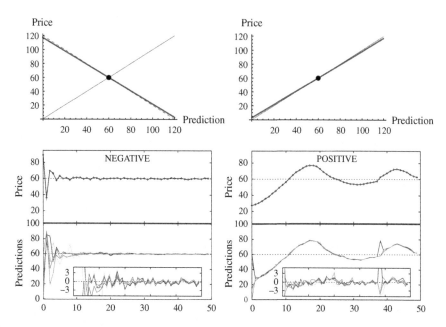

Figure 3. Negative and positive expectations feedback maps in Eq. 13 (top left panel) and Eq. 14 (top right panel). Laboratory experiments: realized market prices (upper part of each panel), six individual predictions (middle part of each panel), and individual errors (bottom part of each panel). Negative (bottom left) vs positive (bottom right) feedback experiments. In the negative expectations feedback market, the realized price quickly converges to the RE benchmark 60. In all positive feedback markets, individuals coordinate on the 'wrong' price forecast and as a result the realized market price persistently deviates from the RE benchmark 60.

than under negative feedback. In the negative feedback case, the price settles down to the RE steady-state price 60 relatively quickly (within 10 periods), but in the positive feedback treatment the market price does not converge but rather oscillates around its fundamental value. Individual forecasting behavior is also very different: in the case of positive feedback, coordination of individual forecasts occurs extremely fast, within 2–3 periods. The coordination, however, is on a 'wrong', i.e., a non-RE price. In contrast, in the case of negative feedback, coordination of individual forecasts is slower and takes about 10 periods. More heterogeneity of individual forecasts, however, ensures that the realized price quickly converges to the RE benchmark of 60 (within 5–6 periods), after which individual predictions coordinate on the correct RE price.

In his seminal paper introducing RE, Muth (1961) considered a negative expectations feedback framework of the cobweb 'hog-cycle' model. Our LtFEs show that under negative expectations feedback, heterogeneity of individual forecasts around the rational forecast 60 persists in the first 10 periods, and correlated individual deviations from the RE fundamental forecast do not arise (in line with Muth's observations as quoted in Section 1) and the realized market price converges quickly to the RE benchmark. In contrast, in an environment with positive expectations feedback our LtFEs show that, within 2–3 periods, individual forecasts become strongly coordinated and all deviate in the same way from the rational, fundamental forecast. As a result, in positive expectations feedback markets, at the aggregate level the market price may persistently deviate from the rational, fundamental price. Individual forecasts then coordinate on almost self-fulfilling equilibria, very different from the perfectly self-fulfilling RE price.[2]

6. A theory of heterogeneous expectations

The fact that qualitatively different aggregate outcomes arise suggests that *heterogeneous expectations* must play a key role to explain these experimental data. Anufriev and Hommes (2012), extending the model of Brock and Hommes (1997), fitted a simple heuristics switching model (HSM) with four rules to the asset pricing LtFEs.

Agents choose from a number of simple *forecasting heuristics*. The forecasting heuristics are similar to those obtained from estimating linear models on individual forecasting experimental data. *Evolutionary selection* or *performance-based reinforcement learning* based upon relative performance disciplines the individual choice of heuristics. Hence, the impact of each of the rules is evolving over time and agents tend to switch to more successful rules. The four forecasting heuristics are as follows:

$$\text{ADA}: \quad p^e_{1,t+1} = 0.65p_{t-1} + 0.35p^e_{1,t}, \tag{15}$$

$$\text{WTR}: p^e_{2,t+1} = p_{t-1} + 0.4(p_{t-1} - p_{t-2}), \tag{16}$$

$$\text{STR}: p^e_{3,t+1} = p_{t-1} + 1.3(p_{t-1} - p_{t-2}), \tag{17}$$

$$\text{LAA}: p^e_{4,t+1} = \frac{p^{av}_{t-1} + p_{t-1}}{2} + (p_{t-1} - p_{t-2}), \tag{18}$$

where $p^{av}_{t-1} = (1/t)\sum_{j=0}^{t-1}p_j$ is the sample average of past prices. *Adaptive expectations* (ADA) predicts that the price is a weighted average of the last observed price p_{t-1} and the last price forecast p^e_t. The *trend-following rules* extrapolate the last price change, either with a weak (WTR) or with a strong (STR) trend parameter. The fourth rule is an *anchor and adjustment* rule (Tversky & Kahneman, 1974), extrapolating a price change from a more flexible anchor.

The fractions of the four forecasting heuristics evolve according to a discrete choice model with *asynchronous updating*:

$$n_{i,t} = \delta n_{i,t-1} + (1 - \delta)\frac{\exp(\beta U_{i,t-1})}{\sum_{i=1}^4 \exp(\beta U_{i,t-1})}. \tag{19}$$

The fitness or performance measure of forecasting heuristic i is based upon quadratic forecasting errors, consistent with the earnings in the experiments:

$$U_{i,t-1} = -(p_{t-1} - p^e_{i,t-1})^2 + \eta U_{i,t-2}, \tag{20}$$

where $\eta \in [0, 1]$ measures the strength of the agents' *memory*. In the special case $\delta = 0$, (19) reduces to the *discrete choice model* with synchronous updating; δ represents inertia in switching as subjects change strategies only occasionally. The parameter $\beta \geq 0$ represents the intensity of choice measuring how sensitive individuals are to differences in strategy performance.[3]

Figure 4 compares the experimental data with the *one-step ahead predictions* made by the HSM. The one-step ahead simulations use exactly the same information available to participants in the experiments. The one-period ahead forecasts easily follow the different patterns in aggregate price behavior in all groups. The second and bottom panels show the

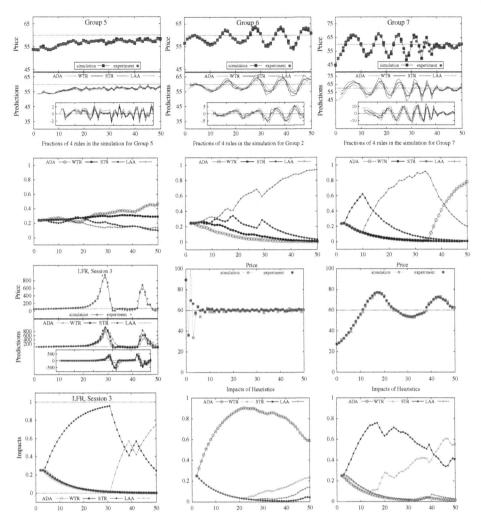

Figure 4. (Colour online) Simulated prices in laboratory experiments in different groups (red) with corresponding one-step ahead predictions of the HSM (blue), predictions and forecasting errors (inner frames) of four heuristics, and time series of fractions of each of the four heuristics ADA (purple), WTR (black), STR (blue), and anchoring adjustment heuristic (LAA, red). Two top panels correspond to three groups with robot traders; two bottom panels correspond to group without robot trader and large bubble (left panels) and negative and positive feedback groups. In the negative feedback market, the ADA rule dominates and enforces quick convergence to the RE fundamental price 60. In the positive expectations feedback market, the STR and the WTR trend-following rules perform well and reinforce price oscillations. In all the positive feedback groups, individual expectations coordinate on a non-RE almost self-fulfilling equilibrium.

corresponding fractions of the four heuristics for each group. In different groups, different heuristics are dominating the market, after starting off from an equal distribution.

In the monotonically converging group, the impact of the different rules stays more or less equal, although the impact of ADA gradually increases and slightly dominates the other rules in the last 25 periods. In the oscillatory group, the LAA rule dominates the market from the start and its impact increases to about 90% towards the end of the experiment. For the group with the dampened oscillations, one step ahead forecast produces a rich evolutionary selection dynamics, with three different phases where the STR, the LAA, and the ADA heuristics subsequently dominate. The STR dominates during the initial phase of a strong trend in prices but starts declining after it misses the first turning point of the trend. The LAA does a better job in predicting the trend reversal because of its more slowly time varying anchor and its impact starts increasing. The LAA takes the lead in the second phase of the experiment, with oscillating prices, and its share increases to almost 90% after 35 periods. But the oscillations slowly dampen and therefore, after period 35, the impact of ADA, which has been the worst performing rule until that point, starts increasing and ADA dominates the group in the last nine periods. In the asset market without a fundamental trader subjects coordinate on the strong trend-following strategy, thus explaining the large bubble in the experiment.

The HSM also matches aggregate price behavior in both the negative and the positive feedback experiments very well. The time series of the fractions of the different forecasting heuristics provide an intuitive explanation of how individual learning leads to different aggregate price behavior. In the negative feedback treatment, the ADA strategy performs the best and within 20 periods it captures more than 90% of the market, thus enforcing convergence towards the RE fundamental equilibrium price. In contrast, in the positive feedback treatment, the strong and weak trend-following rules dominate the market, amplifying price fluctuations. The difference in aggregate behavior is thus explained by the fact that *trend-following rules are successful in a positive feedback environment* reinforcing price oscillations and persistent deviations from the fundamental equilibrium benchmark price, while the trend-following rules are driven out by ADA in the case of negative feedback. Self-confirming coordination on trend-following rules in a positive expectations feedback environment has an aggregate effect with realized market prices deviating significantly and persistently from the RE benchmark.

7. Conclusions

The main conclusion to be drawn from the theoretical, empirical, and experimental work discussed above may be formulated as follows. In positive feedback markets, aggregate behavior is *not* well described by perfectly self-fulfilling REE. Instead, under positive feedback individuals tend to coordinate their expectations on *almost self-fulfilling equilibria*, very different from the exact rational self-fulfilling equilibria, and characterized by excess volatility and persistent price fluctuations.

The main finding, consistent with Soros principles of fallibility and reflexivity, is that under positive expectations feedback almost self-fulfilling equilibria provide a much better fit to individual and aggregate behavior in lab experiments and empirical data than the perfectly self-fulfilling REE in traditional models. This finding is also consistent with the view that the economy is a complex system with many interacting agents (Hommes, 2013). These interactions at the micro-level and the emergent structure arising at the aggregate macro-level are well described by a heterogeneous expectations agent-based model, either detailed or stylized, of the economy.

Macroeconomics assigns a central role for expectations in economic modeling. For example, in his standard work on monetary policy in modern New Keynesian macro, Woodford (2003) emphasizes the key role of 'managing expectations' for monetary policy. Policy analysis should focus more on managing almost self-fulfilling equilibria. The bounded rationality models discussed here, at least to a first order approximation, take into account the Lucas critique, as expectations and learning will adapt to policy changes.

Economic policy analysis may benefit enormously by focusing on efficiency and welfare gains in correcting mispricing along almost self-fulfilling equilibria.

Funding

Financial support from the Institute for New Economic Thinking (INET) grant for the project *Heterogeneous Expectations and Financial Crises* [INO1200026] is gratefully acknowledged.

Notes

1. This solution is known as the Gordon model.
2. In a recent paper, Asparouhova, Bossaerts, Roy, and Zame (2013) find similar results concerning coordination on almost self-fulfilling equilibria in their laboratory experiments based on Lucas asset pricing model.
3. In the following simulations, the parameters are fixed at the benchmark values $\beta = 0.4, \eta = 0.7, \delta = 0.9$, as in Anufriev and Hommes (2012).

References

Anufriev, M., & Hommes, C. H. (2012). Evolutionary selection of individual expectations and aggregate outcomes in asset pricing experiments. *American Economic Journal: Microeconomics, 4*, 35–64.

Asparouhova, E., Bossaerts, P., Roy, N., & Zame, W. (2013, May). *'Lucas' in the laboratory.* Caltech and UCLA Working Paper.

Bao, T., Hommes, C. H., Sonnemans, J., & Tuinstra, J. (2012). Individual expectations, limited rationality and aggregate outcomes. *Journal of Economic Dynamics and Control, 36*, 1101–1120.

Boswijk, H. P., Hommes, C. H., & Manzan, S. (2007). Behavioral heterogeneity in stock prices. *Journal of Economic Dynamics and Control, 31*, 1938–1970.

Branch, W. A. (2006). Restricted perceptions equilibria and learning in macroeconomics. In D. Colander (Ed.), *Post Walrasian macroeconomics: Beyond the dynamic stochastic general equilibrium model* (pp. 135–160). New York, NY: Cambridge University Press.

Branch, W. A., & Evans, G. W. (2006). Intrinsic heterogeneity in expectation formation. *Journal of Economic Theory, 127*, 264–295.

Brock, W. A., & Hommes, C. H. (1997). A rational route to randomness. *Econometrica, 65*, 1059–1095.

Brock, W. A., & Hommes C. H. (1998). Heterogeneous beliefs and routes to chaos in a simple asset pricing model. *Journal of Economic Dynamics & Control, 22*, 1235–1274.

Bullard, J. (1994). Learning equilibria. *Journal of Economic Theory, 64*, 468–485.

Evans, G. W., & Honkapohja, S. (2001). *Learning and expectations in macroeconomics.* Princeton, NJ: Princeton University Press.

Evans, G. W., & Honkapohja, S. (2013). Learning as a rational foundation for macroeconomics and finance. In Roman Frydman & Edmund S. Phelps (Eds.), *Rethinking expectations: The way forward for macroeconomics.* Princeton University Press, Chapter 2.

Grandmont, J.-M. (1998). Expectation formation and stability in large socio-economic systems. *Econometrica, 66*, 741–781.

Heemeijer, P., Hommes, C. H., Sonnemans, J., & Tuinstra, J. (2009). Price stability and volatility in markets with positive and negative expectations feedback. *Journal of Economic Dynamics & Control, 33*, 1052–1072.

Hommes, C. H. (2011). The heterogeneous expectations hypothesis: Some evidence for the lab. *Journal of Economic Dynamics & Control, 35*, 1–24.

Hommes, C. H. (2013). *Behavioral rationality and heterogeneous expectations in complex economic systems.* Cambridge University Press.

Hommes, C. H., Sonnemans, J., Tuinstra, J., & van de Velden, H. (2005). Coordination of expectations in asset pricing experiments. *Review of Financial Studies, 18*, 955–980.

Hommes, C. H., Sonnemans, J., Tuinstra, J., & van de Velden, H. (2008). Expectations and bubbles in asset pricing experiments. *Journal of Economic Behavior & Organization, 67*, 116–133.

Hommes, C. H., & in't Veld, D. (2013, July). *Behavioral heterogeneity and the financial crisis.* CeNDEF Working Paper, University of Amsterdam.

Hommes, C. H., & Zhu, M. (2013, June). *Behavioral learning equilibria.* CeNDEF Working Paper, University of Amsterdam.

Lucas, R. (1976). Econometric policy evaluation: A critique. In K. Brunner & A. Meltzer (Eds.), *The Phillips curve and labor markets*, Carnegie-Rochester Conference Series on Public Policy (vol. 1, pp. 19–46). New York, NY: American Elsevier.

Lucas, R. E., & Prescot, E. C. (1971). Investment under uncertainty. *Econometrica, 39,* 659–681.

Muth, J. E. (1961). Rational expectations and the theory of price movements. *Econometrica, 29,* 315–335.

Sargent, T. J. (1993). *Bounded rationality in macroeconomics.* New York, NY: Oxford University Press.

Shiller, R. J. (1981). Do stock prices move too much to be justified by subsequent changes in dividends? *American Economic Review, 71,* 421–436.

Shiller, R. J. (2000). *Irrational exuberance.* Crown Business.

Soros, G. (1987). *The alchemy of finance.* Hoboken, NJ: Wiley.

Soros, G. (2013). Fallibility, reflexivity and the human uncertainty principle. *Journal of Economic Methodology, 20,* 309–329.

Tversky, A., & Kahneman, D. (1974). Judgment under uncertainty: Heuristics and biases. *Science, 185,* 1124–1131.

Woodford, M. (2003). *Interest and prices: Foundations of a theory of monetary policy.* Princeton, NJ: Princeton University Press.

Soros and Popper: on fallibility, reflexivity, and the unity of method

Mark Amadeus Notturno

Interactivity Foundation, Washington, DC, USA

Let me begin by saying that I think that George Soros is right in identifying fallibility and reflexivity as important phenomena in economic life, and in social life more generally, and as phenomena that mainstream economic theory has largely ignored. I also agree with Soros that economics is an uncertain science. And I think that Soros himself, being one of the world's wealthiest men and most generous philanthropists, deserves credit for being ready and willing to think for himself. It would be all too easy for him to trot out conventional wisdom about market efficiency, privatization, and the like – safely under-written by economic science. It is much more difficult to question the conventional wisdom, let alone its theoretical foundations. Soros does both. Better yet, he takes the trouble to write down his ideas for public consideration and to respond to requests from academic journals to debate their significance – while he could just as easily be lounging on a yacht eating caviar for the rest of his days. Thus said, I do not agree with everything Soros says in his 'Fallibility, reflexivity, and the human uncertainty principle' and in what follows I will focus upon what I regard as misconceptions in what he says about fallibility, reflexivity, and scientific method. I will attribute these disagreements to misunderstandings of some of the ideas of our mutual mentor – Sir Karl Popper. In doing so, I hope to show that some of Soros' ideas may be closer to Popper's than Soros thinks, that reflexivity may not be as exclusive to social science as Soros thinks, and that it may not require a scientific method of its own. Getting clear about this may leave us with a somewhat different view of science.

Soros' project

Soros would like to replace such mainstream economic theories as Rational Choice Theory and the Efficient Market Hypothesis with his own understanding of economics as a reflexive system. But what does it mean to understand economics as a reflexive system? And why is it important?

Soros says that his conceptual framework is built on the twin principles of fallibility and reflexivity. I will begin by discussing each of them in turn.

Fallibility

Soros writes:

> In situations that have thinking participants, the participants' views of the world never perfectly correspond to the actual state of affairs. People can gain knowledge of individual fact, but when it comes to formulating theories or forming an overall view of the situation, their perspective is bound to be either biased or incomplete or both. That is the *principle of fallibility*. (Soros, 2013, p. 310)

But fallibility, at least for Popper, is the idea that we *can* be mistaken, not that we *actually* are – let alone that we *always* are. Soros says that the participants' views of the world *never* perfectly correspond to the actual state of affairs. But how can he know this? If the participants' views of the world *never* correspond to the actual state of affairs, perfectly or otherwise, then it would be difficult to see how we can gain knowledge of individual facts, as Soros says we can. And if the participants' views of the world *never* correspond to the actual state of affairs, then the principle of fallibility would allow us to reclaim certainty through the back door. For we could then know that a participant's view of the world is *always* false, regardless of what it might be. I sense a paradox lurking here. I think that Soros misunderstands fallibility and ignores the real problem that faces us – which is that we *can* always be mistaken, and can never know with certainty whether or not we actually are. Here, I fully agree with Soros that we do not, and cannot, have *complete* knowledge, and that there may always be something we do not know about a given state of affairs. I also agree that our views may be biased or incomplete or both. But the fact that they are biased or incomplete does not mean they do not perfectly correspond to the actual state of affairs, let alone that they *never* correspond to the actual state of affairs, or even that we cannot be certain about them.

Reflexivity is another matter.

Reflexivity

Soros writes:

> Imperfect views can influence the situation to which they relate through the actions of the participants. For example if investors believe that markets are efficient then that belief will change the way they invest, which in turn will change the nature of the markets in which they are participating (though not necessarily making them more efficient). That is the principle of reflexivity. (Soros, 2013, p. 310)

Popper called it 'the Oedipus effect', alluding to the Delphic Oracle's prediction that Oedipus would kill his father and marry his mother. He was concerned about the effect that a prediction might have upon a predicted event – whether it might bring it about or prevent it from happening – and upon the objectivity of the prediction itself:

> We are faced in the social sciences with a full and complicated interaction between observer and observed, between subject and object. The awareness of the existence of tendencies which might produce a future event, and furthermore, the awareness that the prediction might itself exert an influence on events predicted is likely to have repercussions on the content of the prediction; and the repercussions might be of such a kind as gravely to impair the objectivity of the predictions and of other results of research in the social sciences.

> A prediction is a social happening which may interact with other social happenings, and among them with the one which it predicts. It may, in an extreme case, even *cause* the happening it predicts: the happening might not have occurred at all if it had not been predicted. At the other extreme the prediction of an impending event may lead to its *prevention* (so that, by deliberately or negligently abstaining from predicting it, the social scientist, it may be said, could bring it about, or could cause it to happen). There will clearly be many intermediate cases between these two extremes. The action of predicting something, and that of abstaining from prediction, might both have all sorts of consequences. (Popper, 1957, pp. 14 and 15)

But Popper was also concerned that social scientists would become aware of this and try to manipulate events in ways they personally prefer:

> Now it is clear that social scientists must, in time, become aware of these possibilities. A social scientist may, for instance, predict something, foreseeing that his prediction will cause it to happen. Or he may deny that a certain event is to be expected, thereby preventing it.

And in both cases he may be observing the principle which seems to ensure scientific objectivity: of telling the truth and nothing but the truth. But though he has told the truth, we cannot say that he has observed scientific objectivity; for in making forecasts (which forthcoming happenings fulfill) he may have influenced those happenings in the direction that he personally preferred. (Popper, 1957, p. 15)

Soros says that reflexivity 'applies exclusively to situations that have thinking participants'. Hence his idea that it is essentially a feature of social science, which investigates phenomena in which there are thinking participants. But my own sense is that reflexivity is due not so much to someone's thinking about a situation, as his taking action to address it. And if we understand reflexivity in this way, then the great reflexive gap that Soros sees between social and natural science may disappear.

For suppose we predict, on the basis of our theory of planetary motion and initial conditions gleaned through observation, that an asteroid will hit the Earth at a certain date and time. This is about as naturally scientific a prediction as natural science makes. If we are powerless to act, then we will hope our prediction is not only fallible, but also false. But if we have the technology, and enough time, we might blow it to pieces with nuclear missiles – thereby ensuring that the prediction, which might otherwise have been true, is false, and changing the nature of the interplanetary space we observe. Here, Soros might object that thinking humans fired the missiles at the asteroid. True enough. But we have systems today that can do it without direct human intervention.

My point is that it is not merely Laius' and Oedipus' *thinking* about the oracle's prediction that triggered the reflexive effect – but the *actions* they took trying to avoid it. My point is that people apply scientific theories in real-life situations all the time and affect the world and how predicted events unfold in realty by doing so. This is as true of natural science as it is of social science. And it is what *applied* sciences such as engineering, medicine, and even climate science are all about.

This brings me to the unity of method.

The unity of method

Soros writes that 'Popper proclaimed what he called the 'doctrine of the unity of method,' by which he meant that both natural and social sciences should use the same methods and be judged by the same criteria' and that 'by proclaiming the doctrine of the unity of science, Popper sought to distinguish pseudo-scientific theories like those of Marx and Freud from mainstream economics' (Soros, 2013, p. 320). Soros is right that Popper proclaimed the unity of method. But he is not at all clear about what Popper was asserting, and defending, when he proclaimed it.

First, Soros slides from saying that Popper upheld *the unity of scientific method* to saying that he upheld *the unity of science*. But these are very different philosophical theses. And Popper was not proclaiming the unity of *science*. He was proclaiming the unity of *scientific method*.

Second, Popper did not say that there are no differences at all between the natural and social sciences. He said, on the contrary, that there are very clear differences in their *subject matters*, in the *problems* they try to solve, and in their scientific *achievements*. Nor did he want to suggest that there are no differences whatsoever between their methods. But he said that their methods are *fundamentally* the same – though he was quick to add that the methods he had in mind are very different from the methods that others have in mind when they proclaim the unity of scientific method:

I do not intend to assert that there are no differences whatever between the methods of the theoretical sciences of nature and of society; such differences clearly exist, even between the various natural sciences themselves, as well as between the various social sciences .... But I agree with Comte and Mill – and with many others, such as C. Menger – that the methods in the two fields are fundamentally the same (though the methods I have in mind may differ from those they had in mind). (Popper, 1957, pp. 130 and 131)

Here, Comte, Mill, the logical positivists, and others who argued for the unity of scientific method understood it to be the process of inductively inferring universal generalizations from observations of particular events. The unity of method for them went hand in glove with the unity of science – the idea that all of science can be based upon the same epistemological foundations – and, in the end, with the idea that scientific theories can be known with certainty, of one form or another, and that theories in the social sciences can be known with the same certainty as theories in the natural sciences.

This, however, is not how Popper understood scientific method or the unity of scientific method. Popper wrote that the methods of science:

> ... always consist in offering deductive causal explanations, and in testing them (by way of predictions). This has sometimes been called the hypothetical-deductive method, or more often the method of hypothesis, for it does not achieve absolute certainty for any of the scientific statements which it tests; rather, these statements always retain the character of tentative hypotheses, even though their character of tentativeness may cease to be obvious after they have passed a great number of severe tests.

> Because of their tentative or provisional character, hypotheses were considered by most students of method, as provisional in the sense that they have ultimately to be replaced by proved theories (or at least by theories which can be proved to be 'highly probable', in the sense of some calculus of probabilities). I believe that this view is mistaken and that it leads to a host of entirely unnecessary difficulties. (Popper, 1957, p. 131)

Popper, in fact, taught that there is no such thing as the scientific method over and above the method of conjecture and refutation, or trial and error.

Popper also taught that *all* scientific knowledge is conjecture, or guesswork. He taught that it is different from *mere* guesswork not because it is justified, or certain, but because it can be tested. And he held this to be true of both natural and social science.

It is in this ironic sense, *and only in this sense*, that Popper upheld the unity of method. He wrote that

> As a rule, I begin my lectures on Scientific Method by telling my students that scientific method does not exist. I add that I ought to know, having been, for a time at least, the one and only professor of this non-existent subject within the British Commonwealth. (Popper, 1983, p. 5)

Popper taught that science begins with problems and with hypotheses, or guesses, about how to solve them. He taught that what makes science *science* is not that our hypotheses are certain, or true, but that we can test them to find and eliminate their errors. And he taught that our tests never verify or even confirm the hypotheses, but typically lead to new problems. He developed his so-called tetradic schema

$$P_1 \rightarrow TT \rightarrow EE \rightarrow P_2$$

to encapsulate the idea. Here, P_1 is a problem, TT is a tentative theory offered to solve it, EE is our attempt to eliminate the errors in TT via experiment and criticism, and P_2 is a new problem that arises from EE. Popper thought that this is the 'method' of all science, natural and social, and indeed of all rational discussion. And it is, once again, in this ironic sense, *and only in this sense*, that he upheld the unity of method.

Soros, however, has something very different in mind when he chides Popper for upholding the unity of method. For Soros seems to think that natural science is certain – or at least much more certain than Popper did – and that this difference in certainty can be explained only by a difference in method.

This, so far as I can see, is Soros' only reason for saying that the methods of the natural and social sciences are or should be different.

Soros emphasizes that reflexivity introduces a new element of uncertainty and that participants in an event cannot act upon knowledge but only upon guesswork. Popper, however, would say that *all* scientific knowledge is guesswork and that the extent to which we act upon science is the extent to which we act upon guesswork.

But what, exactly, does the certainty or uncertainty of a theory have to do with scientific *method*? Why should we think that a difference in the *certainty* of a science should imply a difference in its *method*? And how, in any event, does Soros think the methods of the natural and social sciences differ?

Is it that social scientists do not try to explain phenomena they do not understand? Or that they do not deduce the events they try to explain from causal hypotheses and initial conditions? Or that they do not test them by deducing predictions of future events from those hypotheses and initial conditions and then checking to see if they actually occur?

And if some social scientists do not offer causal explanations, or fail to test them, does that mean that the methods of the social sciences are different from the methods of the natural sciences – or only that some social scientists (like some natural scientists) are doing it wrong?

Soros does not address any of these questions. So it is difficult to know exactly how he thinks the methods – as opposed to the subject matter or certainty – of natural and social science differ. But my own sense is that the differences that he is pointing toward when he talks about reflexivity are not so much differences in the methods of the natural and social sciences as differences between theoretical and applied science. So long as we stay within the realm of theory, reflexivity will not occur in either economics or physics. But once we begin to apply our theories, we may well encounter it in both.

Situational analysis

Popper, in any event, thought that we typically explain events in the social sciences through what he called 'situational analysis'. Situational analysis assumes that people always act adequately to their situation as they see it – and it then speculates about what beliefs, concerns, values, interests, goals, and desires would make their actions adequate to their situation. Popper called the idea that people act adequately to the situation 'the rationality principle'. But far from regarding it as timelessly true, he said that it is actually false, since people clearly do not always act adequately to the situation, even as they see it. But he also thought that we should continue to use it, instead of rejecting it as a false hypothesis, when the predictions we make to test our theories do not come true. He said that we should instead reassess the beliefs, concerns, values, interests, goals, and desires that our explanations and predictions attributed to the actors in the situation – and that we should do this partly because we already know the rationality principle is false, partly because we can learn a lot from seeing how far from the truth our explanations and predictions are by doing so, and partly because we otherwise would not be able to give a rational explanation of what we want to explain (see Popper, 1994).

Do mainstream economists really believe that we have perfect knowledge and perfect competition? There may be some that do. But my sense is that they generally believe that these are false but, for certain purposes, useful assumptions for modeling economic activity – that they give an oversimplified description of reality, but one that allows them to get a grip on something they might otherwise find too unwieldy to handle.

Soros, however, writes that the human uncertainty principle destroys the symmetry that Popper saw between explanation and prediction 'because the future is genuinely uncertain, and therefore cannot be predicted with the same degree of certainty as it can be explained in retrospect' (Soros, 2013, p. 316).

But this confuses matters.

We do not know when we make a prediction whether the predicted event will occur as predicted. And we do know when we explain an event that the event we are explaining has occurred. But in neither case do we know whether the *theory* we use in predicting and explaining the event is true. *That is the question in science.* The role of prediction, when it comes to science, is not so much to know the future, or to place a bet on it, as it is to test the truth of the theory that we use in trying to explain events that we do not yet understand.

It is not the *event* that we predict or explain that is scientific knowledge, but the *theory* we use to predict or explain it. And the theories in question when it comes to social science typically describe beliefs, concerns, values, interests, goals, and desires that the actors had when they acted in the situations that we are trying to explain.

But are economic theories and explanations empirically testable?

If it is really necessary to know all the relevant beliefs, concerns, values, interests, goals, and desires of every actor in an economic event in order to explain or predict it, then I do not see how understanding economics as a reflexive system would improve our ability to explain and predict economic phenomena, let alone test the truth of our explanations and predictions. For I see no method to model a theory of economic activity that does not oversimplify it in one way or another. Rational choice theory oversimplifies it with false assumptions about perfect knowledge and competition. Reflexivity theory would no doubt correct them. But it would then have to oversimplify its model of economic activity in some other way, if it wants to actually explain and predict events, for we cannot, on its own theory, know all that we need to know to do it. Such oversimplified models may be useful for some purposes and useless for others. And I am happy to take Soros' word for it if he says that the efficient market hypothesis is useless for investment. *But science is our attempt to rationally explain things we do not understand.* We may use it for other purposes. And we may fail in our attempt to explain things. But if we fail, then we are left with things we cannot understand.

The end of science

The philosophy of science, and its preoccupation with method, began when philosophers and scientists started to think that certain theories, such as Newton's, had an objectivity and certainty that other theories in what they then called natural and moral philosophy lacked. They ascribed this objectivity and certainty to 'The Scientific Method', which, they said, could justify our beliefs. But few philosophers and scientists, 100 and more years later, still believe this story about scientific method. Today we hear much more talk about scientific consensus and conviction than about verifiability and falsifiability. Today we believe that tests are never conclusive. Today we have string theory. And today the fact that 2000 or so scientists agree about something is cited as evidence that it is true.

Soros writes that 'If the cognitive function operated in isolation, without any interference from the manipulative function, it could produce knowledge'; where 'knowledge is represented by true statements' and 'a statement is true if it corresponds to the facts'. Such knowledge would still be fallible because humans are fallible. But Soros writes that 'if there is interference from the manipulative function, the facts no longer serve as an independent criterion because the statement may be the product of the manipulative function' (Soros, 2013, p. 312). He says that 'scientific method is supposed to be devoted to the pursuit of truth'. But he asks 'Why should social science confine itself to passively studying social phenomena when it can be used to actively change the state of affairs?' (Soros, 2013, p. 318). And he proposes that we protect both scientific method and the social sciences themselves by adopting a methodological convention that would recognize a fundamental difference between natural and social phenomena. He thinks that adopting such a convention would protect scientific method by preventing social science 'from parading with borrowed feathers' – and that it would protect the social sciences by liberating them 'from the slavish imitation of natural science' and 'from being judged by the wrong standards' (Soros, 2013, p. 320).

But what, exactly, are the *right* standards we should use to judge the social sciences?

Surely it is not the *certainty* of their theories. But should it be the accuracy and objectivity with which they describe what they describe? Should it be their ability to explain things we do not understand, and their ability to survive tests against observation and reason? Or should it be the role they play in helping social scientists, politicians, and policy-makers change our minds in directions that they – the social scientists, politicians, and policy-makers – prefer?

And if the latter, then should we regard social science as *science* in the same way that we regard the Holy Roman Empire as holy, Roman, and an empire? And what, in any event, would be the difference between social science and religion – or manipulation for that matter?

This, I confess, is one of my chief concerns about reflexivity in the social sciences. But it is also one of my chief concerns about science today – social and natural – with or without reflexivity. It is bad enough that we do not have a non-question begging criterion of truth. But it is far worse if scientists are actively trying to manipulate our beliefs.

We have all known about this possibility for a very long time. But today, my fear is that calling economics 'science' may itself be an attempt to manipulate our beliefs – that people today may use the idea that economic theories are 'scientific' to manipulate other people's understanding of the world so they accept public policies they might otherwise reject.

Here, I want to be clear that I agree with Soros that reflexivity exists; that it is an important phenomenon in economic, social, and political life; and that it introduces a new source of uncertainty into economics. But I also think that economics, and science in general, was already uncertain enough without it, and that their uncertainty has nothing to do with their methods. My sense is that the use of social science to manipulate our beliefs, as opposed to the question whether it needs a new method, is what should really concern us today.

The bottom line

Earlier I asked why Soros' project is important. My sense is that Soros thinks it is important because he believes that economics is neither certain, nor perfect, nor complete; that reflexivity has real effects in the real world; that any economic theory that ignores it must be mistaken; and that, being mistaken, it may leave us with false expectations that may eventually lead to economic disaster. He is, to that extent, following Popper's advice to kill our false theories before they kill us.

And I applaud him for it.

But Soros tells us that he makes conjectures about the market, derives predictions from those conjectures, acts upon them, and corrects his conjectures if and when his predictions come up false. And he is, to that extent, applying Popper's method of conjecture and refutation to finance – despite his insistence that social science needs a new non-Popperian method.

Soros also tells us that he would derive his 'human uncertainty principle' from his principles of fallibility and reflexivity. And I agree with him that reflexivity makes things 'less predictable and inherently more uncertain'. But I do not think we need to derive the principle – for economics, physics, or life in general – since fallibility, even on my more modest interpretation, takes us there straightaway.

Reflexivity did not introduce human uncertainty into science. The unreliability of our intellect and our sense organs did that – along with our recognition that empirical universal generalizations are underdetermined by empirical evidence, or, more simply, that inductive inferences are invalid. Soros knows this. He also knows that reflexivity involves actions as well as beliefs, for he describes it as the principle that our imperfect views can influence situations to which they relate through our *behavior*. And he knows that this can happen in natural science as well as social science, since he writes that an 'outside observer can obtain knowledge' and that 'based on that knowledge, nature can be successfully manipulated' (Soros, 2013, p. 317). But the beauty of reflexivity is enchanting – and he sometimes forgets it.

I have been critical of some of the details of Soros' theory about fallibility, reflexivity, and the human uncertainty principle in this paper. But you should not think that I am critical of his project. I have criticized some of its details because I agree with Popper that criticism is one of the greatest acts of friendship, even if some of your friends end up hating you for it, and because Soros is looking for criticism of his theory so that he can improve it. But, as I said at the outset, I agree with Soros that economics is an uncertain science, that fallibility and reflexivity are important phenomena in economic life, and that mainstream economic theory has largely ignored them. I do not agree with Soros that we need a special scientific method for the social sciences. But I do agree that economics could use a new paradigm. And I also agree with the substantive thrust of his theory, namely, that economics, and social science more generally, cannot know what it knows with the objectivity, certainty, and arrogance with which it once thought it could know it – and that we are now in very great danger of being manipulated by it.

This might be the place to remind you of Popper's old joke that 'Social science began with the idea that we need a new science so we can get rid of our social problems – and now our biggest social problem is how to get rid of the social scientists'. But my own sense is that physics, and natural science more generally, also cannot know what it knows with the objectivity and certainty with which we once thought it could. This, I think, should be wisdom enough for the ages. But if the theory of reflexivity proves too enchanting, if Soros tries to develop a mathematical model of it, as some people suggest he should, to make it more 'scientific' so economists in university departments of economics might take it seriously, then I fear he might find himself rowing upstream in the same epistemological boat as the rational choice theorists, though the rational choice theorists, being rational choice theorists, will no doubt eat most of the caviar – and Soros, being Soros, may very well end up paying for it.

References

Popper, K. (1957). *The poverty of historicism*. London: Routledge [Reprinted in 1991].
Popper, K. (1983). *Realism and the aim of science*. London: Routledge [Reprinted in 1992].
Popper, K. (1994). *The myth of the framework*. (M. A. Notturno Ed.), London: Routledge.
Soros, G. (2013). Fallibility, reflexivity and the human uncertainty principle. *Journal of Economic Methodology*, *20*, 309–329.

Reflexivity, uncertainty and the unity of science

Alex Rosenberg

Department of Philosophy, Duke University, Durham, NC, USA

The paper argues that substantial support for Soros' claims about uncertainty and reflexivity in economics and human affairs generally are provided by the operation of both factors in the biological domain to produce substantially the same processes which have been recognized by ecologists and evolutionary biologists. In particular predator prey relations have their sources in uncertainty – i.e. the random character of variations, and frequency dependent co-evolution – reflexivity. The paper argues that despite Soros' claims, intentionality is not required to produce these phenomena, and that where it does so, in the human case, it provides no basis to deny a reasonable thesis of the methodological or causal unity of science. The argument for this conclusion is developed by starting with a biological predator/prey relation and successively introducing intentional components without affecting the nature of the process. Accepting the conclusion of this argument provides substantial additional inductive support for Soros' theory in its economic application.

George Soros' insights about the economic processes and their explanation are at least as deep and as original as those of other important dissidents from the mainstream orthodoxy of mainstream economics, figures such as Hayek, Keynes, and Sen. More important, these insights are right, and need to be accommodated by any theory of market processes, especially those of financial markets. However, Soros unnecessarily and in my view wrongly holds two theses about his dissident theory.

First, he holds that the fact about economic processes he has identified result from differences between natural and social processes that undercut the methodological unity of the sciences. Second, Soros argues that though his insights are important factual claims about economic processes, they will not meet standards of scientific significance, in particular those that he draws from the work of Popper.

In this paper, I expound and defend what I hope are accurate versions of the insights Soros has advanced, and then I try to show that neither of the two broader philosophical claims he makes about them is correct.

Why should anyone care about whether Soros' metascientific observations about his scientific claims are correct or not? After all, he is an applied economist, not a philosopher of science. He cannot be much faulted for making mistakes in philosophy so long as his applied economics is vindicated in practice, no? As David Hume said, 'mistakes in philosophy are merely ridiculous.' There are several reasons why exposing Soros' putative errors about his own views is important for vindicating Soros' own economic theory, or at least for removing obstacles to their acceptance. One important reason derives from considerations of consilience in science generally. If a theory is really inconsistent with other claims that have substantial evidential support, then the theory must to that extent be subject to doubt. It is safe to say that evidence for the unity of science is strong. The scope for empirical methods drawn from the natural sciences in the social sciences has grown substantially, as have their results. Moreover, the explanatory reach of theories in natural science, especially biology, has extended into several areas of social science. These two developments bode ill for denials of the unity of science. If, as Soros holds, his economic theory implies or is implied by any such a doctrine, then it must be evidentially undermined. Second, and more important, Soros' views are actually strongly vindicated by considerations from natural science, indeed they reflect the reach of biology into human affairs. So, showing that there is no incompatibly between these views and the unity of science enables his theory to avail itself of consilience with a specific and well-established theory in natural science. In science generally, support by precise prediction across a range of circumstances is the most powerful evidence for a theory. Unarguably such support is lacking in the social sciences, and especially in economics. Whence the importance of improvements and advances in econometrics.

In this evidential vacuum occasioned by the absence of predictive success, the importance of alternative sources of empirical support increases. This is what makes otherwise very theoretical matters of consilience with other theories relevant to the evidential support of Soros' work. When these theories lie across the natural science/social science divide, the dismantling of any barrier between the two domains becomes of more than mere philosophical interest.

1. Uncertainty and reflexivity

In *The Alchemy of Finance* [2003], Soros makes two important claims:

The human uncertainty principle: humans are fallible, in fact usually mistaken in their expectations, including their probabilistic ones. They predict inaccurately and these predictions cannot be improved, for example by honoring the principles of probability theory more fully.

Reflexivity: agents' earlier expectations about future outcomes combine with their preferences in ways that change these very future outcomes, sometimes so greatly as to bear no resemblance to their earlier expectations and to fail to satisfy their preferences.

The first of these echoes important observations of Keynes (1936) and before him Knight (1921). The second claim is more original with Soros and has been a more useful insight in his own investment strategies. Reflexivity explains how several obvious facts absurdly denied by Rational Choice Theory-dominated economic theory in fact obtain – e.g. bubbles and busts.

The way in which uncertainty and reflexivity operate is best explained in an illustration. The illustration is Soros' own and I will employ it in order to advance my argument for consilience of Soros's claims with theories in natural science and their compatibility with the unity of science.

In the graph, the red curve of stock prices reflects the strategies of agents – mutual funds, hedge funds, individuals, etc. This curve is shaped by the aggregate of agents' uncertain, unforesighted expectations about companies' futures. The earnings/share line imperfectly reflects the business success of companies, i.e. the equally uncertain strategies and packages of strategies of CEOs, managers, sales reps, and the shop-floor workers, and consumers, who effect companies' actual earnings per share.

Following Keynes and Knight, Soros insists that the scope for probability is extremely limited: errors do not fall on a bell-shaped curve around the truth, and new evidence does not drive it in that direction either. For that reason mainstream economic theory's substitution of (von Neumann/Morgenstern) risk for the assumption perfect information is not a significant improvement the idealization of the original theory. Equally important, in Figure 1, the shapes of the two curves reflect the fact that earlier stock prices influence later earns per share, and vice versa. Initially, peoples' (fallible) expectations about future states of affairs have effects on how those future states turn out, and subsequently these future states effect people' later (and always fallible) expectations. The combination of reflexivity and uncertainty, when not held in check, produces swings in two (or more) factors locked in a reflexive relationship, and usually much wider swings on the expectations side of the relationship.

Note that expectations by themselves will not effect anything. They are, as Soros says, purely 'cognitive.' To have any effect, they need to be acted upon, applied to attain a purpose. Sometimes Soros calls this application of thought its 'manipulative' function, sometimes he calls it the 'participating' function. In the example above, the actions are individual or repeated security purchases. Let us describe these actions as the instantiation of strategies – one time purchase, repeated purchase, purchase on up-tick or down-tick, or when a double peak is breached or any other description of the rule the purposive action(s) realize. Of course the 'fundamental' share values that speculators form expectations about also reflect purposive behavior, on the shop floor, among the sales force, in the management offices and the union headquarters, etc. These two curves thus reflect strategies of behavior by individuals and organizations. To have an effect, reflexiveness must be a relationship between strategies. Soros holds that owing to ubiquitous uncertainty, strategies are driven by expectations that lack foresight. They are almost always individually wrong, very often also wrong on average, and when the expectations are right and drive successful strategies, they are right by accident! That, according to Soros, is why increasingly accurate prediction is impossible in financial markets.

Now, the combination of strategy–uncertainty and strategy–reflexiveness does not simply produce wild swings in financial markets – bubbles and bubble bursts. It operates everywhere in human affairs, because reflexivity is the rule and not the exception in these

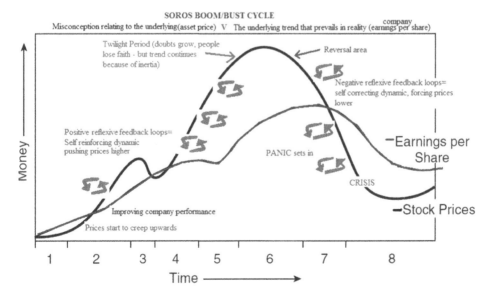

Figure 1. Stock prices track earnings and vice versa – i.e. reflexively.

affairs. Strategies that one set of agents and organizations employ to exploit other peoples' and other organization sets of strategies effect the second set of strategies, and these in turn effect the success and thus the spread and persistence of the first set of strategies. This makes human affairs unpredictable to participants owing to the ineliminable combination of uncertainty and reflexivity that drives the choice of strategies reflexively linked.

2. Soros meets Darwin

Why suppose Soros' theory is right? Because reflexivity and uncertainty reflect the operation of patterns well understood in evolutionary biology; indeed, they are instances of those patterns. The only obstacles to seeing how biology vindicates Soros are his independent and unwarranted argument that human intentionality is a distinctive source of uncertainty, and his view that it erects an epistemological and substantive barrier between the human and the natural sciences.

Figure 2 represents a typical predator–prey population cycle over time. In this case lynx and hare populations cycle between limits with a constant six-month lag between predator-population maxima and between prey-population minima.

The cause of this pattern is a combination of reflexivity and uncertainty. Lynx survive by employing hare-hunting strategies. Lynx-predatory strategies select for hare strategies that are good at avoiding lynx predation. Successful hare hunting strategies increase lynx populations, but this reduces later hare populations and so reflexively reduces lynx populations by reducing the pay-offs to their predation strategies.

The reflexiveness of the relationship between lynx and hare strategies is well understood in evolutionary biology: each set of strategies is subject to linked frequency-dependent selection with a lag. Each is maintained within a certain minimal and maximal range by stabilizing selection. Underneath this stable cycle, both lynx and hares are varying their behaviors randomly, without foresight. Whatever it is that drives predation strategies of lynx and predation-avoidance strategies of hares are blind to the reflexive cycles. Random genetic variation throws up new strategies continually, but they continue to be selected against as long as the local environmental circumstances producing the reflexive equilibrium remain in force.

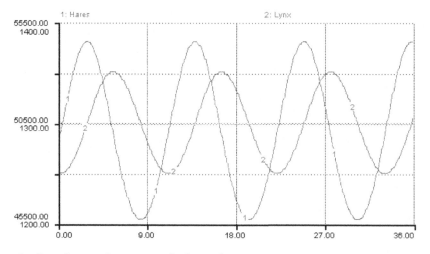

Figure 2.   Lynx/hare predator–prey reflexive cycle.

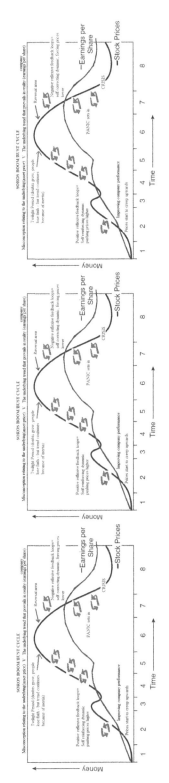

Figure 3. Linked stock price/earnings reflexivity.

Now, consider what several iterations of Soros' curve of boom/bust reflexivity would look like. It would be a cycle repeating itself in the relationships between financial asset markets and the underlying economic activity it is linked to, Figure 3.

Compare this iterated Soros boom/bust cycle curve to the predator/prey curve. It is the same curve of lagged reflexiveness of strategies which plays out among lynx and hare. Here, the strategies of stock purchase and business strategies that determine firm earnings are reflexively linked together. The difference is that the predator–prey graph covers four cycles, and Soros's original graph covers just one cycle. Of course Sorosian boom/bust reflexitivity does not repeat itself a second time, let along over and over again as in the biological case. We will return to this fact below.

More important is the recognition that the curves in each graph reflect the operation of a Darwinian selective process of reflexivity and uncertainty, the very sources Soros has identified at work in the economic domain. It is not just that the factors driving change that Darwin and Soros have identified are similar. They are the same factors. In biological contexts, *reflexiveness* is the linked frequency-dependent selection of strategies that compete, cooperate, are parasitical or symbiotic on one another.

In the biological case, behavioral strategies vary owing to the blindness of genetic variation (mutation, chromosomal duplication, recombination, etc.), and are selected by the reflexive processes of predation and predator avoidance. In human affairs, strategies vary because agents are blind about the future and when right only by accident. Their persistence depends on their reflexive success – positive feedback in Soros' terms, or failure – negative feedback, neither of which is the result of foresight in strategy choice. But whether the source of behavioral strategies is in radically unforesighted human intentionality or equally unforesighted genetic variation, the effect is the same!

But then, why do reflexive processes persist in unchanged cycles through periods in the biological realm, and almost never in human affairs? In Figure 3, the reflexivity of financial strategies and fundamental strategies is repeated three times to look like predator/prey cycles. But this kind of cyclical repetition is just what Soros rightly tells us does not occur. Seeing why not reveals why reflexivity really is the same in the biological and social domains.

Uncertainty and reflexivity operate in both domains. The difference between the biological and the cultural is a difference of degree – the tempo and mode of evolution. In the biological domain, reflexivity and uncertainty are usually kept in bounds that produce stable cycles, those that even vindicate some limited confidence in predictions among ecologists, agricultural scientists, even some epidemiologists. There are two reasons why biological cycles of reflexivity persist. Reflexivity is a matter of continual change in the environment of each strategy by its impact on the other strategy. Such a cyclical process rarely changes the environment within which one of the two strategies is played so much that it drives that strategy to extinction, or to complete dominance – fixation in the biologist's terminology. Extinctions are well understood. Fixations less so. The second constraint that keeps reflexive strategies in the biological domain cycling in balance is that the range of genetically driven random strategy variation is limited, the differences in reproductive pay-offs between the variants are small, and their rates of replication (the generation time of a lynx or a hare) are slow. All this means that some *local equilibria* in biology last long enough that it is worthwhile identifying them and trying to exploit them in for wildlife population management, for example. Of course there are other local equilbra in reflexively related biological strategies that we can identify, but not exploit, owing to the degree of uncertainty in variation and the shortness of generation time: the best examples are to be found in bacterial resistance, in which a local cyclical reflexive equilibrium between host and infectious agent is first broken by the introduction of an antibiotic and then re-established by antibiotic resistance through a new bacterial strategy whose random genetic sources prevent us from predicting and controlling, and so produce a new cycle of reflectivity among host's and bacteria's strategies.

In cultural processes, the forces move even faster, limiting a reflexive relationship to at most one round before driving one or both strategies to extinction. In human affairs, by contrast with biology, strategies vary at very high rates and replicate quickly (through imitation as well as instruction and enforcement). While recognizing this, it is crucial to bear in mind Soros' point that variant strategies are all lacking in foresight. That is just another way of saying that uncertainty rules. What is more, in human affairs, there has been very strong selection for strategies that track changes in other strategies and influence their pay-offs in positive and negative feedback loops, i.e. reflexivity. Finally, unlike biological environments, human environments change rapidly. Once cultural reflexivity crosses a threshold, environments never remain stable long enough to select repeatedly for the same pairs of reflexively linking strategies. Thus *repetition* of the same boom/bust cycles never happens.

In the biological domain, uncertainty and reflexivity are held in check by environments that change with geological slowness. This produces long-lived local equilibrium outcomes. In the human domain, the environment is cultural. It is composed of nested sets of strategies that are all affected by both reflexivity and uncertainty. The result of their operation is at most short-lived local equilibria, broken up by radical environmental change. The source of this radical environmental change in human cultural processes is obvious. It is the iterated unsynchronized combinations of reflexivity between strategies, and radical uncertainty in strategy variation. As the rate of change in the cultural environment increases, the lifetimes of local equilibria shorten until in most cases they disappear altogether. Human affairs appear chaotic because its reflexive processes are at the extreme end of the spectra of variations, of their rates of change, and of rates of strategy reproduction.

The problem reflexivity makes for all human agents is that almost all local reflexive equilibria of interest to us are too short lived to be exploited. Owing to reflexivity, many local equilibria last for an hour or a day or a week or a month. By the time people have figured out how to exploit them, they have evanesced, disappeared, been broken up by new variants that substitute new equally short-lived equilibria, or perhaps an arms race, rapidly searching though the 'space' of strategy variations for a new impermanent equilibrium. When some innovative strategy – deploying a new fashion, gadget, political slogan – does manage to exploit a local equilibrium, we can be confident that it arose without foresight, and that it will probably disturb the local equilibrium immediately, eventually breaking it up completely, and then itself falling victim to some newer strategy.

There are of course many very long-lasting local equilibria in human affairs. Most of them persist owing to benefits they accord people, some exist in spite of the net costs they impose on people. They can be exploited by policy design and implementation; some of them can even be unraveled by policy, for example consider the fate of tobacco smoking in Western society over the last half-century. Most long-lived widespread local equilibria are hard for small number of individuals to exploit or undermine. It is the short-lived local equilibria that are the targets of 'rent-seeking' especially in business. And they are too short lived for any simple recipe for securing such rents to succeed for long. This is one of Soros' morals for business.

3.   The real epistemic divide: unforesighted variation, not intentionality

Soros's resistance to this analysis will rest mainly on his claim that thought, and more generally intentionality – makes a difference to behavior; because it cannot be understood by the methods of the natural sciences, it makers social science into *Alchemy* at best. Whence Soros' denial of the unity of science.

There are several arguments against this view of intentionality, some abstract and philosophically tendentious, others more concrete and easier to accept. None of them offers any hope that the predictive and explanatory barriers that face social science and that Soros identifies can soon be breached. But all of them strengthen the consilience argument in favor of the importance of uncertainty and reflexivity to a real understanding of human affairs.

Here is the philosophically tendentious argument against intentionality, making a difference in kind between the natural and social sciences: intentional psychological events, states and processes just are brain processes. Unless intentionality, or perhaps consciousness, has some mysterious non-physical properties, there just seems no fundamental reason to suppose either one makes for a difference in kind, a metaphysical difference between the social and the natural realm. Nor any reason to think it makes an epistemic difference between the sciences that deal with them.

Assuming physicalism about the mind is right, let us turn to more concrete considerations. Enough evidence has been provided in Section 2 to show that Soros is mistaken to claim that reflexivity applies exclusively in situations that have thinking participants, and never in the domain of natural science. Every case of parasitism, symbiosis, mutualism, coevolution, from the level of virus particles up to caribou and wolf, is rife with Sorosian reflexivity. So, *pace* Soros reflexivity cannot be the source of unpredictability in general, nor can it provide the line of demarcation between natural and social science.

Soros will insist that the reflexivity he has uncovered differs from the biological variant: he writes that human

> reflexivity connects the universe of belief with the universe of fact, in the form of feed forward and feed back loops. The participant's views influence the course of events and the course of events influence the participant's views. The influence is continuous and circular.

But we can certainly accept that in the human case, thought plays a role while recognizing that the process is causally the same across the human/nonhuman divide. In fact for intentionality to have a role in the creation and persistence of reflexive processes, we must do so.

By themselves beliefs, expectations, desires – Soros' cognitive functions – can have no impact on the world unless they are linked to behavior, action, choices, etc. (Soros' manipulative function of thought). Unless they manifest themselves in behavior, thoughts and other intentional states cannot participate in any causal process that eventuates in reflexivity. On the other hand, it is because thoughts are hidden (sometimes even from their own thinkers), which *others* cannot identify the exact intentional content of the thoughts that drive the reflexive processes they participate in. That is why no one cannot exploit these processes persistently and efficiently. Each strategy in a reflexive relationship can only track the *behaviors* that manifest the other strategy, not its sources, whether intentional or genetic or conditioned learning or any other source.

There are several ways to see that reflexive relationships, whether biological or human, have the same causal structure regardless of whether intentionality plays a role in their emergence and persistence. One way to see this is to consider biologically reflexive processes in which intentionality is added one step at a time. Start with any version of mutualism among nonsapient creatures – even aphids and farmer wasps. Now make one party to the process human, choosing strategies intentionally. Consider slash and burn agriculture. Here, the human strategy is to burn a field and plant. The ground slashed, burned, and cultivated responds first with increased yields, then with decreasing yield, which leads humans to reduce intensity of cultivation, which allows the field to replenish, and eventually increases yield and so on in a cycle not unlike predator–prey dynamics. At some point, the reflexive relationship is broken up by a new strategy – fertilizing, kudzu, or an exogenous environmental change – colonization.

Let us move on to predator–prey relationships between megafauna and human hunter/gatherers. Or introduce domestication and consider the relationship between reflexive strategies of wolves and humans whose flocks they predate. Over time human thought-driven strategies of flock protection will reduce wolf predation and increase flock size, thus in turn making wolf predation more successful. Over time, variations in the size and spread of flocks will select for variation in strategies of risk taking by wolves, when flocks are smaller favoring wolves hard wired for risk aversion and then when they increase selecting for wolves hard wired for risk taking. Or perhaps risk-taking and risk-averse strategies are not hard wired but the result of wolves' cognitive processes.

Now consider a reflexive relationship between two persistently warring groups of humans, or between an ethnic group that persistently entraps and sells members of another group into slavery. Entrapment strategies and survival strategies will spread and shrink with a lag depending on their success and if neither slave-takers nor those they hunt communicate or recall successful and unsuccessful strategies, the pattern may persist for a long period.

Of course humans do think about strategies and their pay-offs, as well as how they interact with other strategies. They remember past records of success and failure, and they teach or otherwise communicate strategies to one another. These facts do not actually make for any difference in kind between human and biological reflexivity. All they do is accelerate the unraveling of any reflexive relationship and its replacement by a new one. The difference that thought makes is a matter of the rate of variation in strategies and the likelihood that a new strategy will destroy the environment of a particular reflexive relationship and break it up.

Our examples reflect the fact that the difference between the natural, or at least the biological, domain and the human domain is a matter of degree, not kind. The difference is not that thought creates a new domain where scientific methods cannot provide knowledge because predictive testing fails. In the biological domain, predictive testing fails long before we reach any limit on science's ability to provide knowledge. The reason prediction ceases to be feasible in biology is not just the number of causally relevant variables, but because of the role of shear randomness in the rate and nature of variation in traits, including of course behavioral strategies. As it increases, prediction becomes increasingly difficult. Once it crosses the threshold from genetic variation to behavioral variation, science must forswear the demand for increasingly reliable prediction as the mark of knowledge increase. But science crosses this threshold long before it becomes social science. That is why reflexivity, even when generated by thought, has no implications for the unity of science.

4. Conclusion

There are important morals here both for the thesis of the unity of science and for Soros' economic theory of reflexivity and uncertainty. What has been learned from the explanatory and confirmational methods in the biological sciences has had a major impact on the assessment of logical positivist, post-positivist, and Popperian views about the nature of science. In particular, it is now well understood that strict falsifiability of the sort Popper identified as a litmus test for empirical science is nowhere to be found in physics, chemistry, or biology. Nor for that matter is there any reason to embrace a strict explanation/prediction isomorphism. Views about the nature, extent, and role of scientific laws are now quite different from those that figured in Popper's prescriptions for what science should seek. These more nuanced views have greatly changed the terms of the debate about the unity or disunity of the social and natural sciences.

The implications for Soros's view are twofold: first, when it comes to the philosophical version of whether the methods of natural and social science can in principle be the same, there is no reason why Soros should not agree. Agreeing to the philosophical thesis leaves Soros the freedom rightly to emphasize that the differences of degree between human affairs and infra-human biological processes are so great that whatever the level of predictive knowledge we can acquire in the biological domain, the prospects are far poorer in the human domain.

The second and more important implication to be drawn is that the theoretical unity of Soros's theory and well-understood biological processes provides the best kind of evidence for his theory, evidence which would not be available were the role of thought in human affairs to erect a barrier to the unity of science.

References

Keynes, J. M. (1936). *The general theory of employment: Interest and money*. London: McMillan.
Knight, F. (1921). *Risk, uncertainty, and profit*. Boston: Houghton Mifflin.
Soros, G. (2003). *The Alchemy of finance* (3rd ed). New York: John Wiley.

On the role of reflexivity in economic analysis

Anwar Shaikh

Department of Economics, New School for Social Research, New York, NY, USA

Soros' theory of reflexivity is meant to apply to a variety of social processes. In economics, it implies that many processes will be subject to "boom-bust" patterns in which expected outcomes deviate for a considerable time from the actual path, and that the actual path in turn deviates from the underlying fundamentals. This is in sharp contrast to the reigning notions in orthodox economics. The hypothesis of Rational Expectations (RE) requires that the views of all participants will converge to a "single set correct of expectations" and the Efficient Market Hypothesis (EMH) posits that actual outcomes deviate from equilibrium in a random manner save for occasional exogenous shocks. In this paper I show that Soros' argument is similar to the classical and Keynesian notions of equilibration as a turbulent process in which actual and expected variables gravitate around some fundamental value. But Soros makes the important further contribution of emphasizing that the fundamental value itself will generally be affected, but not fully determined, by (diverse) expectations and actual outcomes. I demonstrate that Soros' theory of reflexivity can be formalized and that the resulting system is stable in in the sense that expected and actual variables will gravitate around a possibly moving fundamental value. The paper ends with a discussion of an alternate economic paradigm in which the principle of reflexivity would be central.

1. Introduction

Soros' theory of reflexivity is meant to apply to social systems. In these, the expectations and aspirations of thinking participants shape their actions, and by so doing, shape the system of which they are a part. At the opposite pole, there are natural systems in which the subjective aspect may lead to a change in outcome but will not alter the laws of nature. Biological systems lie in between. In the latter domain, Soros recognizes that a chimpanzee or a dolphin or even a sophisticated computer program may be similar to a thinking participant in some aspects. But in his view, humans are unique in terms of language, reasoning, and culture (Soros, 2013, pp. 318–319).

Human society is characterized by what Soros calls the *human uncertainty* principle. This involves two basic propositions. The *principle of fallibility* says that the multiple participants in any social act will generally have different views of the likely outcomes. Even the view of any one participant will be driven by a multiplicity of values which may not be self-consistent. So there is good reason to expect that the set of participants will have contradictory views whose net effect will be biased with respect to the actual outcomes. The *principle of reflexivity* says that the actions of participants based on their various views will generally change the reality to which they refer. In the natural world, actions change the state of nature but not the laws of nature, whereas in the social world, actions can change the laws of social life itself (Soros, 2013, pp. 310, 311, 319).

The human uncertainty principle implies that many economic processes will be subject to 'boom–bust' patterns in which expected outcomes deviate for a considerable time from the actual path and that the actual path in turn will deviate from the underlying fundamentals. This is a tri-partite affair: diverse and conflicting expectations about a variable (say a stock price) affect its actual path, which will in general deviate from the path justified by fundamentals (such as earnings per share). These divergences may not only persist for some time, but may also affect the fundamentals themselves, thereby initiating a self-reinforcing process that can lead to 'far-from-equilibrium' outcomes (Soros, 2013, pp. 322–324). Implicit in Soros' argument, to which I will return, is the notion that expectations cannot not simply create the fundamentals they suppose. Hence, as the process continues, actual outcomes get further away from the fundamentals. The growing gap in turn undermines expectations, until at some point there may be a sharp reversal in views: the boom engenders its own bust. Figure 4 in Soros' essay illustrates this general pattern. But he is careful to add that his argument also encompasses 'near equilibrium' processes in which the actual levels of variables fluctuate closely around the levels determined by fundamentals (Soros, 2013, pp. 323, 326).

This view stands in sharp contrast to the reigning notions in orthodox economics. The hypothesis of rational expectations (RE) requires that the views of all participants will converge to a 'single set correct of expectations', and the efficient market hypothesis (EMH) posits that actual outcomes deviate from equilibrium in a random manner save for occasional exogenous shocks (Soros, 2013, pp. 318, 320–322, 325–327). From Soros' point of view, these are very special cases involving particular types of near equilibrium outcomes. The general case is quite different.

2. Notions of equilibrium

I regret to say that I have little direct experience with economic equilibrium. Indeed, so far as I am aware, none at all. I sometimes see suggestions that we shall be moving toward equilibrium next year or perhaps the year after, but somehow this equilibrium remains firmly in the offing.[1] (Sir Gordon Richardson, Governor of the Bank of England, 1979)

Soros distinguishes reflexive processes from what he calls 'equilibrium', by which he means a state-of-rest. The latter is by far the most prevalent notion of equilibrium in both orthodox and heterodox economics (Blanchard, 2000, pp. 46–51). Yet, on Soros' own argument, even far-from-equilibrium booms eventually give way to busts. Implicit in his theory is a distinction between *equilibrium* as a state and *equilibration* as a turbulent gravitational process. In the former, expected and actual values coincide with fundamental values up to a random difference, as in RE and EMH; in the latter, the three can differ for extended periods of time in a characteristic boom–bust process.

I would argue that turbulent gravitation is also an essential concept in the classical tradition and in Keynes. According to Adam Smith, the 'actual price at which any commodity is commonly sold is called its market price. It may be either above, or below, or exactly the same with its natural price ... The natural price ... is, as it were, the central price to which the prices of all commodities are continually gravitating. Different accidents may sometimes keep them suspended a good deal above it, and sometimes force them down even somewhat below it, But whatever the obstacles which hinder them from settling in this center of repose and continuance, they are constantly tending toward it'

(Smith, 1973, pp. 158, 160, 161). The conventional reading of Smith is that each market price settles down at its long run equilibrium level at its 'center of repose and continuance'. Such a reading is abetted by the fact that much of Smith's analysis is focused on the properties of natural wages, profits, and prices. But what Smith actually says is that while various factors keep market prices above or below natural prices, competition forces the former back toward (and even beyond) the latter. Market prices are 'continually gravitating' around natural prices (Kurz & Salvadori, 1995, p. 5). David Ricardo appears to move closer to what Soros calls a near-equilibrium conception when he reduces gravitation to 'accidental and temporary deviations of the actual or market price of commodities from ... their ... natural price'. Yet, elsewhere he clarifies this saying that market prices will not be '*much* above, or much below, their natural price' for 'any *length* of time'. This is perfectly consistent with considerable deviations over shorter intervals (Ricardo, 1951, pp. 88, 91, emphasis added).

Keynes points out that there is no reason to believe that actual aggregate demand emanating from the expenditures of thousands and thousands of consumers and firms would just match the demand expected by tens of thousands of firms. The investment component of actual demand is ruled by expectations of the various estimates of the long term profitability of individual capital goods being put into place, and these particular expectations are notoriously volatile, subject to 'tides of irrational optimism and pessimism' that are dominant in the short run. On the other side, aggregate supply is ruled by the short term profit expected by thousands of individual firms from the anticipated sales of their finished products. The normal state of affairs would be an imbalance between the two sides, i.e. a positive or negative aggregate excess demand in the commodity market. Keynes goes even further to say that the business cycle is regulated by variations in expected rates of profit (Snowdon & Vane, 2005, p. 59).

Yet, when it came for formalizing his arguments in his 1933 lectures three years before the publication of the general theory (GT), and subsequently in the first draft of the book, Keynes himself used a static set of IS–LM equations to summarize his argument (Snowdon & Vane, 2005, p. 113). In 1937, one year after the GT, both Harrod and Hicks presented papers expressing Keynes's theory in terms of a static system of simultaneous equations. Keynes gave his cautious approval to Hicks' paper, although he did complain that Hicks had downplayed the importance of the volatility of expectations. Hicks' exposition was close to a Walrasian general equilibrium model, and his famous diagram dominated the exposition of Keynesian and orthodox economics thereafter (Nevile, 2000, p. 133; Snowdon & Vane, 2005, p. 169). There are Keynesian who rightly point out that the IS–LM representation in terms of stable functions has tended to sidestep Keynes' own emphasis on the volatility of both constituent relations (Asimakopulos, 1991, p. 95). One might say that a much more appropriate representation would be one in which both curves continually fluctuate in response to shifting expectations, and sometimes move in tandem in the face of changes in confidence. For instance, a rise in business confidence would shift the IS curve upward and raise output while at the same time it might reduce the demand for idle funds which would shift the LM curve outward and reduce the interest rate at any given level of output. Then a boom could be initially attended by rising output and stable or falling interest rates until various limits began to assert themselves. At some point, confidence might collapse, leading to a sharp fall in the IS curve as the expected rate of profit falls and a sharp inward shift in the LM curve as holding idle money becomes the more attractive alternative. The parallels with Soros' boom–bust arguments are evident.

3. Moving centers of gravity

Soros' second contribution is to point out that the fundamental value, the center of gravity of actual outcomes, is itself a moving target. This is why he refers to the path of the fundamental value as a 'trend' around which the actual value gravitates, as illustrated in Figure 4 of his essay. Once again, there are echoes of this point in classical and Keynesian traditions. It was obvious to the classicals that the natural prices around which market prices fluctuate are themselves continually changing in the face of ongoing technological change and the varying distribution of the social product (Smith, 1973, pp. 159, 165, 166). And of course in Keynes the expected and actual rates of return change not only over the cycle but also over time.

4. Stability of reflexive gravitation

Soros' third, and distinguishing contribution, is his argument that the fundamental value will generally be *affected*, but not fully determined, by (diverse) expectations and actual outcomes. This is a crucial point, because the responsiveness of the fundamentals is central to the generation of a boom while its partial autonomy is the basis for the eventual bust. Without the latter aspect, expectations would fully rule the roost and booms could only end for external reasons. What is at stake here is the stability of reflexive gravitation.

In his previous writings, Soros laid out the elements of his theory of reflexivity, which I will illustrate here with reference to financial markets. He advances three general theses: expectations affect actual values, actual values can affect fundamentals, and expectations in turn are influenced by the behavior of actuals and fundamentals. On the first proposition, a general expectation that a stock's price will rise will tend to raise its market price (Soros, 2009, pp. 3–5, 8, 10, 66–71, 73). The second proposition, which is 'the crux of the theory of reflexivity', is 'that market prices can influence the fundamentals' (Soros, 2009, p. 59). The first two propositions therefore imply that expectations affect both 'market prices ... [and] the fundamentals they are supposed to reflect' (Soros, 2009, pp. 66–71, footnote p. 73). The third proposition is that expectations are in turn influenced by both actual and fundamental prices. This proposition is stated less directly than the other two, but is nonetheless implicit in Soros' statements. For instance, he says that the 'change in fundamentals may then reinforce the biased expectations in an initially self-reinforcing *but eventually self-defeating process*' (Soros, 2009, p. 59, emphasis added). One may say that as actual values pull away from fundamentals, the growing distance between the two undermines the confidence that the boom will continue. Path dependence is a natural consequence of this theory, which means that social systems are non-ergodic. Market events 'are best interpreted as a form of history. The past is uniquely determined, the future is uncertain' (Soros, 2009, p. 106). Hence, 'financial markets cannot possibly discount the future correctly because they do not merely discount the future; they help to shape it' – even to the extent of affecting the fundamentals which they are supposed to reflect (Soros, 1994).

This argument can be formalized in a simple manner (Shaikh, 2010). Let p be the actual price, p^e be the average expected price, and p^* be the fundamental price (which of course depends on a particular specification of fundamentals). Then $(p^e - p)$ which is the excess of the average expected price over the market price is a measure of the *degree of bullishness* in the market, while $(p - p^*)$ which is the excess of the market price over the fundamental price is a measure of the *degree of overvaluation* in the market. We can now translate the preceding propositions into a set of formal relations between bullishness and overvaluation. The notion that actual prices are affected by expectations can be expressed as the proposition that the actual price will rise if the expected price is greater than the

Table 1. A formalization of reflexivity theory.

Thesis	
Market prices rise (fall) when sentiment is bullish (bearish)	$\dot{p} = f\left(\underset{+}{p^e - p}\right)$
Fundamental prices may rise (fall) when the asset is overvalued (undervalued)	$\dot{p}^* = h\left(\underset{+}{p - p^*}\right)$
Expectations are self-feeding but are undermined as a bubble grows	$\dot{p}^e = j\left(\underset{+}{p - p^e}, \underset{-}{p - p^*}\right)$

actual price, i.e. if the market is bullish. The notion that fundamentals can be affected by market prices can be expressed as the proposition that the fundamental price may rise if the actual price is above the fundamental price, i.e. if the asset is overvalued. Soros gives the example of debt and equity leveraging that permit companies to 'improve their earnings per-share at inflated prices – at least for a while' (Soros, 2013, pp. 319–320). Finally, the notion that expectations are self-reinforcing but will be undermined as the market price moves further away from fundamentals can be expressed as the proposition that the average expected price responds positively when the actual price is above the previous expected price (because actual outcomes have turned out to be even better than expected) but responds negatively to the gap between market and fundamental prices (i.e. negatively to the degree of overvaluation, which is the size of the bubble). Hence, a growing gap between market and fundamental prices progressively undermines the ebullience of the market. One can then see why a boom would be initially self-reinforcing but eventually self-defeating. Table 1 summarizes these possible mapping, with the notation $f()$, $h()$, and j () signifying functional relations, $\dot{p}$ signifying the change in p, etc., and the sign under particular terms indicating the direction of their linkage. Obviously all relations may be subject to shocks of various sorts.

In my previously cited paper, I proved the stability of the preceding system in the case of simple linear and nonlinear functional forms for the three relations. Here, I show that the reflexive process is stable – i.e. that its booms turn into corresponding busts – even in the case of general functional forms (Appendix A). I should add that everything said here in terms of asset prices could equally well apply to other variables such as rates of profit, so that the general system can also be the basis for a reflexive theory of business cycles, gravitation of market prices around classical 'natural' prices, etc. Finally, it is important to keep in mind that any posited functional forms would be valid only as long as the underlying social structure is maintained. There are times in which all roads lead to Tahrir Square and all bets are off. This too is inherent in Soros' general notion of social reflexivity.

5. Elements of a new paradigm

Soros expresses the hope that his notion of the human uncertainty principle will be embodied into a new paradigm of social interactions (Soros, 2013, pp. 327–328). This is certainly a hope I share. Following in the classical tradition, I had long emphasized the turbulent nature of market gravitation around the fundamental values of variables. But after encountering Soros' argument, I came to realize that I had failed to take into account the crucial effects of expectations and actual outcomes on the fundamentals themselves. In a forthcoming book *Modern Political Economy: Real Competition and Turbulent Dynamics*, I have tried to take the full set of effects into account.

This brings up two further points. First, a methodological break with standard economics is necessary but not sufficient. One must also have a consistent theoretical argument on a variety of more concrete principles. For instance, Ricardo and Keynes have similar notions of turbulent gravitation. Yet, they evidently disagree on the role of effective demand in the determination of output and employment. Ricardo adamantly affirms Say's Law, which is to say that 'demand is only limited by production' (Ricardo, 1951, p. 290). Keynes is equally adamant that production is generally limited by demand at least up to full employment. These are fundamental, one might say, paradigmatic differences in economic theory resting on a common methodological foundation.

The second point is undoubtedly more controversial. Neoclassical theory approaches the economic system as an idealized structure in which the hyperrationality of individual agents underpins the supreme optimality of the market. In this perfectly ordered form, the system equalizes all prices for comparable goods, all wage rates for comparable labors, and all profit rates for comparable degree of risk. Moreover, it fully utilizes all available resources, including available plant, equipment, and labor. All of this is accomplished without error, instability, or crisis. Soros suggests that the long success of this construction has something to with 'physic envy' (Soros, 2013, pp. 317–318). I would argue that it was (and continues to be) successful because it serves the convenient social function of idealizing the system, of justifying what he calls 'market fundamentalism' (Soros, 2013, pp. 318, 320).

Heterodox economics, most notably Post Keynesian theory, generally takes the opposite tack from neoclassical theory. It emphasizes the inefficiencies, inequalities, and imbalances generated by the system. In the place of perfect competition we get imperfect competition; in the place of automatic full employment we get persistent unemployment. Market outcomes now appear as conditional on history, culture, politics, chance, and most of all, on power: oligopoly power, class power, and of course, state power. Unemployment is more probable than full employment, while inflation and crises are always possible. From this point of view, there is an ever present need for social and economic intervention to fill in the spaces between the actual and the desired. What pure neoclassical economics promises through the workings of the invisible hand of the market, Post Keynesian theory promises though the visible hand of the state. Modern orthodox macroeconomics, New Keynesian and even New Behavioral economics, now tilts in the Post Keynesian direction in trying to incorporate a range of imperfections into the standard framework so as to make the pure theory more 'realistic' (Snowdon & Vane, 2005, pp. 29, 343, 360–365, 411–428).

The irony is that both sides end up viewing reality through an imperfectionist lens. Neoclassical economics begins from a perfectionist base and introduces imperfections as appropriate *local* modifications to the underlying theory. Heterodox economics generally accepts the perfectionist vision as adequate to some earlier stage of history but argues that imperfect competition is the rule rather than the exception. In either case, the perfectionist base lurks heavy in the background.

I would argue that if we are to truly make a break with the orthodoxy, we must start from an altogether different foundation. Theories of hyperrational behavior must be replaced by those of actual behavior, perfect competition replaced by real competition, and optimal micro- and macroeconomic processes replaced by turbulent reflexive processes. This, at any rate, has been my project for a long time.

Note

1. 'The Pursuit of Equilibrium', *Euromoney*, October 1979, cited in Davies (2002, p. 659).

References

Asimakopoulos, A. (1991). *Keynes' general theory and accumulation*. Cambridge: Cambridge University Press.

Blanchard, O. (2000). *Macroeconomics*. Prentice Hall: Upper Saddle River, NJ.

Davies, G. (2002). *A history of money from ancient times to the present day*. Cardiff: University of Wales Press.

Gandolfo, G. (1997). *Economic dynamics: Study edition*. Berlin: Springer.

Kurz, H. D., & Salvadori, N. (1995). *Theory of production: A long-period analysis*. Cambridge: Cambridge University Press.

Nevile, J. W. (2000). What Keynes would have thought of the development of IS–LM. In W. Young & B. Z. Zilberfarb (Eds.), *IS–LM and modern macroeconomics* (pp. 133–149). Boston, MA: Kluwer Academic Publishers.

Ricardo, D. (1951). *On the principles of political economy and taxation*. Cambridge: Cambridge University Press.

Shaikh, A. (2010). Reflexivity, path-dependence and disequilibrium dynamics. *Journal of Post Keynesian Economics, 33*(1), 3–16.

Smith, A. (1973). *The wealth of nations*. Harmondsworth, Middlesex: Penguin Books.

Snowdon, B., & Vane, H. R. (2005). *Modern macroeconomics: Its origins, development and current state*. Cheltenham, UK: Edward Elgar.

Soros, G. (1994, April). *The theory of reflexivity*. The MIT Department of Economics World Economy Laboratory Conference, Washington, DC. Retrieved from http://mertsahinoglu.com/research/the-theory-of-reflexivity-by-george-soros/

Soros, G. (2009). *The crash of 2008 and what it means*. New York, NY: Public Affairs.

Soros, G. (2013). Fallibility, reflexivity and the human uncertainty principle. *Journal of Economic Methodology, 20*, 309–329.

Appendix A

Defining $\pi^e \equiv (p^e - p)$ as the degree of bullishness and $\pi \equiv (p - p^*)$ as the degree of overvaluation, and noting that $(p - p^e) = -\pi^e$ appears with a positive sign in the expectations function, we can express the relations in Table 1 as a 2×2 nonlinear differential equation system.

$$\dot{\pi}^e \equiv (\dot{p}^e - \dot{p}) = j\left(\underset{-}{\pi^e}, \underset{-}{\pi}\right) - f\left(\underset{+}{\pi^e}\right) = k\left(\underset{-}{\pi^e}, \underset{-}{\pi}\right), \qquad (0.1)$$

$$\dot{\pi} \equiv (\dot{p} - \dot{p}^*) = f\left(\underset{+}{\pi^e}\right) - h\left(\underset{+}{\pi}\right). \qquad (0.2)$$

This system has an equilibrium point (not necessarily a state of rest) at $\dot{\pi}^e = 0$ and $\dot{\pi} = 0$ which means that expected, actual, and fundamental prices all gravitate around each other. Note that the equilibrium consists of two relations ($p^e = p, p = p^*$) among three variables, so that it is consistent with moving paths for the fundamental price (p^*). The Jacobian of this system is $\begin{pmatrix} \partial k/\partial \pi^e & \partial k/\partial \pi \\ \partial f/\partial \pi^e & \partial h/\partial \pi \end{pmatrix}$ with $\partial k/\partial \pi^e < 0$, $\partial k/\partial \pi < 0$, $\partial f/\partial \pi^e > 0$, $\partial h/\partial \pi < 0$ and trace $\mathrm{Tr} = \partial k/\partial \pi^e + \partial h/\partial \pi < 0$, determinant $\mathrm{Det} = (\partial k/\partial \pi^e)(\partial h/\partial \pi) - (\partial f/\partial \pi^e)(\partial k/\partial \pi) > 0$. In addition, $(\partial k/\partial \pi^e)(\partial h/\partial \pi) \neq 0$ so that by Olech's theorem the equilibrium of this system is asymptotically stable in the large (Gandolfo, 1997, pp. 354 and 355).

Broader scopes of the reflexivity principle in the economy

Yi-Cheng Zhang

Physics Department, Fribourg University, Fribourg, Switzerland

In this essay we show that the reflexivity principle can be extended to account for many economic phenomena; in fact it plays an essential role in a new theory that may rival mainstream economics.

The reflexivity principle of George Soros – that man's fallible understanding can have reflexivity impacts that shape reality – challenges mainstream economics in a fundamental way. This essay will outline a research program that corroborates the reflexivity principle and extends it to broader economic issues. We shall often use examples of consumer and finance markets, but the implications go beyond these examples. The following eight sections build up our main thesis that reflexivity plays an essential role in understanding the economy.

(1) Relative fallibility.
(2) Reflexivity impacts.
(3) Cognitive function.
(4) Manipulative function.
(5) Asymmetry between the two functions.
(6) Reflexive evolution.
(7) Reflexivity methodology.
(8) New paradigm.

1. Relative fallibility

Human cognitive fallibility is well recognized by scholars and practitioners alike. Soros places it center stage in his theory. Here we shall explore how fallible a man is and introduce the concept of relative fallibility.

In financial markets or consumer markets, agents seldom fully understand the reality they face, but rarely are they totally ignorant. We must therefore deal with a relative fallibility that is personal and contextual. People miss some and understand some; the glass is half empty or half full, depending on the point of view.

By 'half empty' we emphasize human failings, and by 'half full' we focus on limited cognitive capabilities. Therefore, we shall speak of fallibility and capabilities interchangeably.

In the reflexivity literature, the 'half empty' aspect is emphasized because many mainstream economists still downplay its importance (Soros, 2013, p. 310). Our aim in this essay is to emphasize that the 'half full' aspect deserves additional attention because agents' faulty understanding is still better than no understanding at all. Any means to make the glass a little bit 'fuller' will have further reflexivity consequences.

In market transactions, agents can be divided into two broad categories: *insiders* versus *outsiders*. The examples can be producers versus consumers, companies versus investors, employees versus employers (labor market), etc. Insiders can change reality by manipulating *substance* or *appearance* (Soros, 2013, p. 313); outsiders try to pierce the veil of appearance in order to understand substance. Insiders are on the *reality side* while outsiders are on the *cognitive side*.

Thanks to division of labor, people are outsiders most of the time, only on rare occasions are they insiders. Economic efficiency is achieved by matching outsiders' wants with insiders' offers.

Information is asymmetric between insiders and outsiders; sometimes the asymmetry is so severe that market failures can occur, as Akerlof (1970) showed. We extend Akerlof's work by postulating that information is relatively asymmetric everywhere and that most market transactions are neither successes nor failures. The new theory emphasizes that market transactions are limited by ubiquitous relative fallibility, with Akerlof's market failures being the extreme case.

The 'half full' aspect is ultimately responsible for enabling mutually beneficial transactions and thus powers economic growth. Greater economic efficiency can obtain if relative fallibility tilts more toward the 'half full' direction. We will focus on a gray scale of relative fallibility since there are many means to enhance or reduce it, and an important step will be to examine what happens if man's fallibility is shifted in either direction.

2. Reflexivity impacts

Human perception, whether poor or good, can shape reality; reflexive impacts have many pathways, and agents will react differently to different reflexive pressures.

Reflexivity impacts usually carry a negative connotation – benefiting one side and damaging the other (win-lose). We shall show that this need not be. Reflexivity impacts can yield lose-lose or win-win outcomes, and the latter is the most interesting.

Roughly speaking the agents capable of shaping reality have two types of strategies at their disposal: manipulating substance or manipulating appearance. Vendors and producers can improve their products when consumers are more informed and discerning; this we call substance manipulation. On the other hand, if consumers are less informed, insiders will be more tempted to manipulate appearance, to enhance the slippage between perception and reality. Appearance is less costly than substance – marketing gambits to embellish products are much easier than the production of a better variant. Since outsiders are always fallible to a degree, insiders must invest resources in both types of strategies and fine-tune the mix.

In general, the 'half full' aspect of relative fallibility impacts substance and the 'half empty' aspect impacts appearance. If vendors can deal with consumers of distinct cognitive capabilities, they may target them with separate strategies of different substance–appearance mixes. If they cannot tell them apart, they will target the average fallibility instead.

Who is responsible for reflexivity impacts? Outsiders' relative fallibility is the primary cause and insiders' reaction to it is the secondary one. In other words, outsiders perceive and react, and insiders manipulate substance and appearance according to outsiders' relative fallibility.

It is convenient to depict our theory on a cognitive chain, which is inspired from the cycle proposed by Beinhocker and Soros (contributions to this issue):

Reality (substance) $\rightarrow$ appearance $\rightarrow$ perception $\rightarrow$ reactions $\rightarrow$ reflexive impacts $\rightarrow$ new reality. Here we do not enjoin the links into a cycle to highlight the fact that the end point differs from the starting point. Each link is prone to relative fallibility and hence suffers slippage, and its complex mechanisms deserve careful analysis.

3.   Cognitive function

Cognitive capabilities depend on both sides of information transmission. If a message is misunderstood, both the receiver and sender are held responsible: the receiver for fallibility and the sender for distortion.

Insiders can use various gambits to distort appearance in order to mislead perception; the more fallible outsiders are, the more tempted insiders are to tamper with appearance. The distorted messages are not necessarily outright lies. For example, marketing campaigns often selectively highlight a product's good features while downplaying or ignoring the bad ones. Financial markets gurus promote stocks with biases to investors and companies game revenue records in the earnings report.

Not all appearance-tampering tactics are for fooling outsiders. More detailed analysis shows that there are conditions permitting producers and vendors to profit from genuinely helping cognitively challenged consumers (win-win outcomes). For example, vendors may choose to honestly educate consumers about the features of a new product by giving out free samples.

Relative fallibility is not homogeneous across the population: Soros mentioned that a slight edge was important for his trading career, it was like 'a one-eyed King reigning among the blind' (1987). In any market, some understand better than others, though no one has perfect knowledge. The difference in cognitive capabilities is due not only to skills and talent, but also to a variety of other factors.

One of these factors is how many tasks an agent must handle at a time. A consumer facing hundreds of offers for breakfast packages can get only a cursory look on each, a family choosing among many offers of seaside holidays may feel similarly overwhelmed, and an analyst covering 100 stocks will have less in-depth knowledge than her colleague covering only a single one. A large number of tasks can greatly increase relative fallibility, and our modern economy imposes an ever larger number of simultaneous tasks upon individuals.

Another factor is network information-sharing. The modern economy also provides the means to compensate our ever diluted cognitive capabilities (Personal communication, E. Beinhocker, 2013 also mentioned the concept of networked reflexivity). Information may flow from the more-informed to the less-informed consumers on social networks, and this can enhance the collective cognitive capabilities. Often social information sharing is not motivated by money, yet the economic consequences can be huge – the large scale improvement in cognitive capabilities will bring out economy-wide improvement.

Our modern economy not only overwhelms us with the ever larger number of tasks but also gives us potential tools to boost cognitive capabilities. Which factor will have the upper hand is not a sure bet, but it will crucially depend on the exploitation of the potential.

4.   Manipulative function

How do insiders manipulate reality? Manipulating appearance does not affect substance; it manipulates cognitive function. Manipulating substance can be regarded as truly changing reality. As we mentioned above, substance manipulation is generally costly, and insiders will only oblige when they are credibly pressed.

Substance manipulation can also be malicious. For example, food producers often add harmful additives to their products in order to look or taste better. Such substance manipulation is entwined with appearance manipulation.

Reflexive pressures can be directly caused by competition among insiders themselves. For example, competition obliges each competitor to offer better deals to the consumers. But it is outsiders' collective cognitive power that makes competition more effective in the first place. The opposite is also true: facing less-informed consumers, companies are more likely to allocate resources on appearance alone. For example, cognitive capabilities are notoriously low for medicines, and Big Pharma reportedly spends more on marketing (appearance) than on research and development (substance).

The reality side is seldom a single decision-maker. Reflexivity impacts not only trigger insiders to react, but the composition of the reality side can change as well. For example, if a company is misunderstood and its stock is persistently undervalued, its employees flee, clients shop elsewhere, and bankers stop lending. Hence, the so-called manipulative function must also include involuntary actions. On the reality side, there are often many decision-makers whose interests are only temporarily aligned. If reflexivity impacts become adverse enough, employees' personal interests may suddenly supplant those of their company, which may go bankrupt.

The results of the so-called manipulative function are sometimes eagerly pursued but sometimes they are resisted or grudgingly conceded. Hence, manipulative function may be more appropriately called as reality-changing function, but here we will stick to the traditional terminology.

We see substance manipulation represents a fertile ground of the reflexivity principle. Resources can be channeled into substance improvement, as compared to those wasted on appearance.

5. Asymmetry between cognitive and manipulative functions

Soros often deplores that while fallibility is well recognized, the manipulative function is consistently ignored by scholars. For example, behavioral economists generally agree with much of the fallibility principle and yet are completely silent about the ways that faulty cognition can shape reality. The deeper reason behind this is the asymmetry between cognitive and manipulative functions.

The asymmetry first manifests itself in reaction speed. Though outsiders are on the weaker side of information asymmetry, they typically react much faster than insiders. For instance, in financial markets, the minute after news about a stock is out, investors take new positions that instantly have an impact on prices. However, a mispriced stock will take considerable time to have repercussions on the substance of the company. Outsiders being faster than insiders is not due to their superior skills, but rather due to the asymmetry in complexities of operations. Substance shaping takes much longer time than perception forming.

Unlike the stock price movements that everyone can see, the manipulative actions are rarely posted for public scrutiny. Substance manipulation happens via myriad of pathways for which we have no statistics; it can be a slow process or a sudden event punctuating an otherwise dull period. Perceptive practitioners must dig deep in order to detect and make sense of the opaque details that seldom concern academics.

The asymmetry makes the views of practitioners and that of academics diverge. The former try hard to investigate all the idiosyncratic movements behind a stock ticker; the latter focus on well-documented statistics that rarely yield insights into the reflexivity impacts behind the scene.

The asymmetry hinders the mathematical formalization of reflexivity. Soros and other reflexivity thinkers face the dilemma: either drop a great many unquantifiable aspects of manipulative function in the pursuit mathematical formalism or develop the theory in full as a qualitative science akin to that of Darwin (instead of Newton).

6. Reflexive evolution

Reflexivity impacts, cumulated over long spans of time, give rise to spectacular economic evolution. The 'half full' aspect of relative fallibility is more likely to lead to better welfare for mankind. Therefore, the question naturally arises: can we reduce fallibility over time?

Fallibility does not stay constant in time, much less in history. Progress of all kinds happen in our economy and society; cognitively challenged agents may learn from their mistakes. Improvements must be addressed in any theory that is based on fallibility, and the next logic step for the reflexivity principle is to examine what happens if fallibility can be reduced.

The broad question is: if there is economy-wide improvement in people's cognitive capabilities, wouldn't fallibility gradually be reduced? Isn't it possible that one day it would become totally insignificant (as mainstream economists treat it already now)?

The short answer is no. We shall always live with fallibility, and it will continue to play an important, if not more important, role in the future. Though we are stuck with fallibility, our economy and welfare can improve without bounds. To understand this seeming paradox we need an evolution perspective.

In the big picture, our economy has a finite number of agents and each faces a finite number of tasks at any given point in time. Gradual improvement of cognitive capabilities on any particular task will tend to trigger two possible scenarios: (1) a current task will branch into multiple new directions and/or it will become more complex and (2) the current task will be better solved and the relevant agents will redirect part of their attention to new tasks.

Both scenarios will increase the total number of tasks and make them more complex. In other words, if agents can reduce fallibility on current tasks, they will take on new ones. Therefore, cognitive improvement can and will happen, and at the same time agents will expand their scope. They will neither be able to nor willing to push any particular problem-solving to perfection, but instead, the slight respite on their fallibility will encourage them to take on fresh challenges.

For producers, current products will gradually become less profitable since they represent diminishing returns and competition becomes more effective, they will be more likely to innovate in ways that cognitively improved consumers will appreciate. Evidence of such epic trends can be found in an ever increasing consumer product diversification and financial market sophistication.

Here we must add that insiders are also cognitively fallible; there is in fact a cognition chain that insiders in one context are outsiders in another. Producers are insiders with respect to their own products, but are outsiders facing suppliers, competitors, regulators, and others.

Fallibility is relative in a new sense: diminishing here but emerging there. Fallibility constantly diminishes on older problems and emerges on newer problems in the economy. Products in both consumer and financial markets do not just change from old to new, but also grow from few to many. The steady rise in our cognitive capabilities is met by the steady rise of the total number of complex tasks; in the economy as a whole there will always be enough fallibility to frustrate our wishes.

For example, the equity risk premium is a well-recognized puzzle within the contemporary finance literature. For more than a century, stocks outperformed bonds by a significant margin. Why were investors not capable of arbitraging away the differentials over such a long time? The reflexivity principle leads to a possible explanation to the puzzle. Over the long run, investors have been busy arbitraging away the differentials, but their action has had long-term reflexivity impacts on the reality side. More companies went public and offered more shares; the expanding economy constantly injects into financial markets new opportunities and attendant fallibility-prone tasks. This is evidenced by the continuously increasing capitalization of stock markets. The puzzle stems from the fact that finance theories failed to consider reflexivity impacts, which come from the economy outside of the stock markets. The evolutionary perspective recognizes that reflexivity impacts constantly draw new players into the game; we face a nonequilibrium phenomenon that does not fit into equilibrium theories.

The evolutionary perspective provides a nonequilibrium picture for both short-term movements as well as long-term epic trends. Fallibility acts as the main bottleneck preventing the economy from developing faster, and its gradual reduction can unleash economic agents' inexhaustible potential for both wants and productive skills. Indeed, economic evolution is based on the incessant fallibility renewal, and cumulated reflexivity impacts power economic growth in an endless evolution.

7. Methodology

Soros has emphasized that the tools designed for natural sciences are not appropriate for social sciences. In scientific investigations, scholars often record empirical observations and fit a curve in the hope to discern causality. This approach is proven successful for natural sciences but can be polemic for problems involving thinking agents.

Imagine that we plot a curve joining the dots for lung cancer rates versus cigarettes smoked (or similarly obesity rates versus calories consumed) and compare it with a curve of consumer product quality versus prices (or stock returns versus risks). These examples typify two distinct types of sciences. Though both involve human agents, in the former there is no reflexive feedback loops to worry about and we may keep collecting data to plot better curves until the underlying causal relationship is established. In the latter, agents' thinking will get in the way; if they believe the curve and take actions accordingly, it will become less true.

If all consumers believe the only way to get better quality products is to pay higher prices, nobody will check product details, and the quality to price ratio will degrade rapidly; if all investors believe that the only way to get better returns is to take on more risks, the much studied returns-to-risks curve will deteriorate as well. In both cases, it is the nonbelievers who try to beat the averages who in the end sustain the averages.

Determining quality of consumer products and stock returns requires skills and efforts beyond mathematics and statistics. Plotting a curve gives an illusion of a clean and easy causal relationship. Mainstream economics textbooks are full of such curves – they may be statistically accurate, but can still be misleading.

For example, Krugman (1998) in keeping with his mainstream faith in financial economics once wrote an essay titled 'There'll Always Be A Soros', suggesting that only by luck can an investor get above average returns. Mainstream finance theory does not accept that skills and efforts can make a difference in performance. If all students were convinced of the mainstream doctrine, they would focus only on the job of manipulating curves, and forego the work of digging into the underlying real causes. If investors are persuaded by mainstream theory, reflexive impacts would create a reality much worse than we have now – for example, stock markets would be flooded with Enrons, Pets.com, and the like.

Social sciences differ fundamentally from natural sciences in the following way. Objects like mountains, rockets, or elephants are amazingly complex. Upon dissecting them to the molecular, atomic, and subatomic depths, the physical world become much more understandable. With mankind, on the other hand, the more we know, the more will be revealed. In the ancient times, human wants and skills were for basic survival, and we might be tempted to envisage a future when mankind would be better understood. Humanity and the economy have coevolved; our capabilities and desires are gradually created and that makes the economy grow more complex. In fact the coevolution of man and the economy under reciprocal reflexivity impacts is ever more uncertain and open-ended.

The science that Darwin represents is fundamentally different from that of Newton. Darwin's general theory did not need much mathematics, but its logically sound structure opened up many fields of investigation that have kept scientists busy for centuries, and much of recent progress in genetics relies on advanced mathematics. Likewise the reflexivity principle at its top level provides a qualitative methodology to understand the economy, but its many particular applications may be precisely modeled.

8. New paradigm

Mainstream economics is rooted in the paradigm of resource allocation. Its methodology is optimization under fixed constraints. Optimal allocation would need infinitely capable agents; most mainstream economists would admit that the real life is full of imperfections, and agents at best will only approximately achieve the ideal target.

We propose a new paradigm that considers allocation and creation as equally important; it focuses on how the constraints shift under reflexivity impacts. One of the main constraints of optimal allocation is limited cognitive capabilities; any improvement will not only help the task of allocation but also create new opportunities and risks.

The new paradigm denies the very existence of an ideal target. Both the constraints and target shift under reflexivity impacts. Sometimes the shifts are intentional, often they are not, and any intentional effort will create inadvertent shifts. On the other hand, the target's shifting is beyond our control.

The old paradigm puts prices everywhere, even on information; it deals with priced parameters only on the surface. The new paradigm armed with the reflexivity methodology obliges us to consider a more extended challenge: dealing simultaneously with the surface and the underneath: allocation and creation.

Relative fallibility plays a pivotal role in the new theory. Outsiders will try to reduce fallibility wherever they can for their own benefits; the act of fallibility-reducing sends reflexive repercussions to insiders who will revise the reality, and some of the repercussions oblige insiders to innovate. New frontiers open up and this brings in new fallibility. But this is not a futile exercise – the economy is not stuck in equilibrium: the fallibility-beating-renewing process is accompanied by economic growth.

The working agenda is very different from that of the mainstream. The following general questions will be addressed: how can the observed constraints be shifted under reflexivity impacts, who may have the shifting incentives, and who may resist to the shifting? As there will be shifting in multiple directions, we need further ask ourselves which directions can improve on human welfare and how do we get there.

To lend credence to the above claims, detailed work lies ahead, as the initial steps are presented in a few dozen research papers, collected for open access (Zhang, 2013), but they just scratch the surface on the opportunities offered by the new paradigm. My forthcoming book (Zhang 2014/2015) will give a full account of the theory; this essay has only summarized the main points and emphasized its origins in reflexivity.

References

Akerlof, George A. (1970). The market for 'lemons': Quality uncertainty and the market mechanism. *Quarterly Journal of Economics, 84*, 488–500.

Krugman, Paul, *There'll always be a Soros, FORTUNE Magazine*.

Soros, George (1987). *The alchemy of finance: Reading the mind of the market*. Hoboken, NJ: Wiley.

Zhang, Y.-C. (2013). See the website www.nessbook.org for the collection of papers and sample chapters of the ongoing book cited below.

Zhang, Y.-C. (2014/2015). *The structure of information economy*. Oxford, UK: Oxford University Press. See the website www.nessbook.org for the collection of papers and sample chapters of this ongoing book.

Index

Printed in the United States
by Baker & Taylor Publisher Services